BUSINESS, TECHNOLOGY AND FINANCE

FINANCIAL CRISES AND PROGRAMS

DEVELOPMENTS, ANALYSES AND RESEARCH

BUSINESS, TECHNOLOGY AND FINANCE

Additional books and e-books in this series can be found on Nova's website under the Series tab.

BUSINESS, TECHNOLOGY AND FINANCE

FINANCIAL CRISES AND PROGRAMS

DEVELOPMENTS, ANALYSES AND RESEARCH

PATRICIA HALL

snova
New York

NOTICE TO THE READER

The Publisher has taken reasonable care in the preparation of this book, but makes no expressed or implied warranty of any kind and assumes no responsibility for any errors or omissions. No liability is assumed for incidental or consequential damages in connection with or arising out of information contained in this book. The Publisher shall not be liable for any special, consequential, or exemplary damages resulting, in whole or in part, from the readers' use of, or reliance upon, this material. Any parts of this book based on government reports are so indicated and copyright is claimed for those parts to the extent applicable to compilations of such works.

Independent verification should be sought for any data, advice or recommendations contained in this book. In addition, no responsibility is assumed by the publisher for any injury and/or damage to persons or property arising from any methods, products, instructions, ideas or otherwise contained in this publication.

This publication is designed to provide accurate and authoritative information with regard to the subject matter covered herein. It is sold with the clear understanding that the Publisher is not engaged in rendering legal or any other professional services. If legal or any other expert assistance is required, the services of a competent person should be sought. FROM A DECLARATION OF PARTICIPANTS JOINTLY ADOPTED BY A COMMITTEE OF THE AMERICAN BAR ASSOCIATION AND A COMMITTEE OF PUBLISHERS.

Additional color graphics may be available in the e-book version of this book.

Library of Congress Cataloging-in-Publication Data

ISBN: 978-1-53614-159-7

Published by Nova Science Publishers, Inc. † New York

CONTENTS

PREFACE

The first chapter of this book begins by explaining prior international tax rules and the revisions made in the new law. The second part of the report discusses the four major issues of concern under prior law – allocation of investment, profit shifting, repatriation and inversions – and how the new law addresses these concerns, or raises new ones. That section also discusses issues associated with international agreements. The final section summarizes commentary about problems and issues, including legal challenges and uncertainty, within the new international tax regime and options that have been suggested. The second chapter of this book examines the National Flood Insurance Program (NFIP), reinsurance and catastrophe bonds. The third chapter discusses regulatory reform 10 years after the financial crisis – Dodd-Frank and the securities law, as well as the systemic risk regulation of non-bank financial institutions. The last chapter looks at the politics and policies regulating the US Campaign environment. Campaign tactics aside, the campaign environment has been a steady source of concern in American politics.

In: Financial Crises and Programs
Editor: Patricia Hall
ISBN: 978-1-53614-159-7

Chapter 1

ISSUES IN INTERNATIONAL CORPORATE TAXATION: THE 2017 REVISION (P.L. 115-97)*

Jane G. Gravelle and Donald J. Marples

SUMMARY

One of the major motivations for the 2017 tax revision (P.L. 115-97) was concern about the international tax system. Issues associated with these rules involved the allocation of investment between the United States and other countries, the loss of revenue due to the artificial shifting of profit out of the United States by multinational firms (both U.S. and foreign), the penalties for repatriating income earned by foreign subsidiaries that led to the accumulation of deferred earnings abroad, and inversions (U.S. firms shifting their headquarters to other countries for tax reasons). In addition to lowering the corporate tax rate from 35% to 21% and providing some other benefits for domestic investment (such as temporary expensing of equipment), the 2017 tax bill also substantially changed the international tax regime.

The tax change moved the system from a nominal worldwide tax on all foreign-source income, with a credit against U.S. tax for foreign taxes

* This is an edited, reformatted and augmented version of a Congressional Research Service report, R45186, dated May 1, 2018.

due, to a nominal territorial system that does not tax foreign-source income. Nevertheless, both systems could be considered a hybrid of a worldwide and territorial system. Prior law reduced the tax on foreign-source income by allowing deferral (taxing income of foreign subsidiaries only if it was repatriated, or paid as a dividend to the U.S. parent) and cross-crediting of foreign taxes (so the credit for high taxes paid in one country could offset U.S. tax on income from a low-tax country). The new system exempts dividends, but also imposes a current worldwide tax on global intangible low-taxed income (GILTI), but at a lower rate. It also introduces a corresponding lower rate on intangible income derived from abroad from assets in the United States (foreign-derived intangible income, or FDII). The new law adds the base erosion and anti-abuse tax (BEAT) to existing anti-abuse measures aimed at artificial profit shifting. BEAT imposes a minimum tax on ordinary income plus certain payments to related foreign companies.

Despite the lower corporate tax rate, it is not clear that capital will be shifted into the United States from abroad; although a lower rate reduces the tax rate on equity-financed investments, it decreases the subsidy to debt-financed investments. Whether the capital stock increases or decreases depends on the magnitude of the tax changes (which appear largely offsetting) and the international mobility of debt versus equity. It is also not clear whether the capital stock will be allocated more efficiently or in a way more optimal for U.S. welfare, although economic theory suggests that reducing the tax subsidy for debt is a clear improvement.

Although a territorial tax may make profit shifting more attractive, overall, given other elements of the new system, it appears to make profit shifting less important. GILTI and FDII bring the tax treatment of income from intangibles in the United States and abroad closer together, and BEAT and stricter thin capitalization rules (rules limiting interest deductions) also limit profit shifting, including shifting through leveraging. The new system ends the penalties (except for portfolio investment in foreign firms) for repatriating earnings and thus eliminates the prior incentives to retain earnings abroad. A series of measures aimed at inversions appears to make inversions much less attractive.

Some of the measures may violate international agreements such as the World Trade Organization (WTO), bilateral tax treaties, and Organization for Economic Cooperation and Development (OECD) minimum standards to prevent harmful tax practices.

There have been a number of concerns about design features in the new regime, including the dividend deduction, GILTI, FDII, BEAT, and other features. A variety of options might be considered to address these issues.

This chapter begins by explaining prior international tax rules and the revisions made in the new law. The second part of the report discusses the four major issues of concern under prior law— allocation of investment, profit shifting, repatriation, and inversions—and how the new law addresses these concerns, or raises new ones. That section also discusses issues associated with international agreements. The final section summarizes commentary about problems and issues, including legal challenges and uncertainty, within the new international tax regime and options that have been suggested. That section discusses some of the more detailed rules.

INTERNATIONAL TAX TREATMENT UNDER PRIOR AND NEW LAW

The description of international tax law is divided into a section on basic rules, a section on allocation and anti-abuse rules, a section on tax treaties, a section on the new deemed repatriation rules, and a section on anti-inversion rules.[1]

Territorial or Worldwide: Basic Rules

Under a territorial or source-based tax, all income earned within a country is taxed only by that country, regardless of the nationality of the firms. Alternatively, under a worldwide or residence-based system, a tax would also be imposed on foreign-source income of domestic firms and a credit allowed for foreign taxes paid. For purposes of the corporate profits tax, most countries have a territorial system (although most have some type of anti-abuse rules, as discussed below in reference to the U.S. Subpart F rules).[2] With either regime, countries tax profits earned within their borders whether earned by a domestic or a foreign firm.

---

[1] A few minor international provisions of the new law are not discussed in this section. For a comparison of all the provisions of the new law with prior law, international and others, see CRS Report R45092, *The 2017 Tax Revision (P.L. 115-97): Comparison to 2017 Tax Law*, coordinated by Molly F. Sherlock and Donald J. Marples.

[2] Prior international tax rules are discussed in more detail in CRS Report RL34115, *Reform of U.S. International Taxation: Alternatives*, by Jane G. Gravelle; and CRS Report R42624, *Moving to a Territorial Income Tax: Options and Challenges*, by Jane G. Gravelle.

Prior Law: Deferral and the Foreign Tax Credit

The prior U.S. tax system was a hybrid. It had some elements of a residence-based or worldwide tax, in which income of a U.S. firm is taxed regardless of its location, and some elements of a source-based or territorial tax.

Glossary of Selected Terms

Base Erosion and Anti-Abuse Tax (BEAT): A minimum tax that applies a lower rate to an expanded base, including certain payments to foreign related firms.

Controlled Foreign Corporation (CFC): A foreign corporation with at least 50% of the shares owned by at least five U.S. shareholders owning 10% of more of the shares. Ownership is by value or voting power.

Expanded Affiliated Group (EAG): A group that includes a common parent with 50% ownership of the related firms. This group, which relates to inverted firms, is defined more broadly than affiliated group, where firms are linked by at least 80% ownership.

Earnings Before Interest and Taxes (EBIT): Earnings used as the permanent measure of income for restrictions on interest deductions under thin capitalization rules.

Earnings Before Interest, Taxes, Depreciation, and Amortization (EBITDA): Earnings used as the temporary measure of income for restrictions on interest deductions under thin capitalization rules.

Foreign Derived Intangible Income (FDII): A formulary measure of income earned by domestic firms from the use of intangible assets abroad and eligible for lower tax rates.

Global Intangible Low-Taxed Income (GILTI): A measure of income earned by controlled foreign corporations with exclusion for returns on tangible assets, and subject to current U.S. taxes, at a lower rate.

Subpart F: Also called CFC rules, provisions of the tax code that tax on a current basis certain easily shifted foreign-source income of controlled foreign corporations.

Surrogate Foreign Corporation: A term related to the movement of headquarters abroad in an inversion, and refers to the new foreign parent, where the former U.S. shareholders own at least 60% of the shares but not 80% or more. A surrogate foreign corporation is not subject to U.S. tax, whereas a firm where the former U.S. shareholders own 80% or more is treated as a U.S. corporation.

Income earned in the United States was taxed whether earned by a U.S. firm or a foreign firm. The provisions that introduced territorial features into a system that was nominally a worldwide system were deferral of income of foreign subsidiaries and cross-crediting of foreign taxes.

Deferral

Deferral allowed a firm to delay taxation of its earnings in foreign-incorporated subsidiaries until the income was paid as a dividend to the U.S. parent company. Some income, however, was taxed currently. Income that was not part of corporate profits, such as royalties and interest payments, and income earned by foreign branches of U.S. firms was taxed currently. In addition, certain easily shifted income, called Subpart F income, was included in income and taxed currently.

Foreign Tax Credits

The U.S. tax system allowed a credit against U.S. tax due on foreign-source income subject to tax for foreign income taxes paid. A foreign tax credit is designed to prevent double taxation of income earned by foreign subsidiaries of U.S. corporations. Thus, firms were not levied a combined U.S. and foreign tax in excess of the greater of the foreign tax or U.S. tax due if the income was earned in the United States. If the foreign tax credit had no limit, a worldwide system with current taxation and a foreign tax credit would produce the same result, for firms, as a residence-based tax. The tax effectively applicable would be the tax of the country of residence. Firms in countries with a higher rate than the U.S. rate would receive a refund for the excess tax, and firms in countries with a lower rate than the U.S. rate would pay the difference. However, to protect the nation's revenues from excessively high foreign taxes, the credit is limited to the U.S. tax due.

Cross-Crediting

Cross-crediting occurs when credits for taxes paid to one country that are in excess of the U.S. tax due on income from that country can be used to offset U.S. tax due on income earned in a second country that imposes little or no tax. If the limit were applied on a country-by-country basis, a firm would pay the maximum of the U.S. tax or the foreign tax in each country.

Cross-crediting allows income subject to a low tax to have its U.S. income tax offset by credits on highly taxed income. For this reason, foreign tax credit limits were applied to different categories of income, or baskets. The main baskets were passive and active baskets. Notably, however, royalties on active business operations were classified in the active basket, and because they were typically deducted in the country of source, they could benefit from excess credits against U.S. tax from foreign taxes on other active income. There were also restrictions on the use of excess credits generated from oil and gas extraction, which is often subject to relatively high foreign tax rates.

The combination of deferral, which allowed firms to choose the income to be subject to tax, and cross-crediting meant that multinational firms on average had relatively little U.S. tax; the effective U.S. residual tax was estimated at 3.3%.[3]

Sourcing Rules and the Foreign Tax Credit Limit

Because of the foreign tax credit limit, whether income is considered to be foreign-source income affects the tax liability of firms with excess credits: the greater the share of total income that is considered foreign-source income, the greater the ability to take foreign tax credits. Foreign-source income is also affected by deductions. Some deductions can be specifically attributed to foreign- or domestic-source income, but some general expenses incurred by the U.S. parent, such as interest and research and development costs, are allocated between U.S. and foreign income based on the relative size of foreign and domestic assets. After December 31, 2020, interest paid by foreign subsidiaries is to be allocated in the same way; that expansion to include worldwide rather than just U.S. interest would allocate some foreign interest deductions to the United States and

---

[3] See Melissa Costa and Jennifer Gravelle, "Taxing Multinational Corporations: Average Tax Rates," *Tax Law Review*, vol. 65, issue 3 (spring 2012), pp. 391-414. See also Melissa Costa and Jennifer Gravelle, "U.S. Multinationals Business Activity: Effective Tax Rates and Location Decisions," *Proceedings of the National Tax Association 103rd Conference*, 2010, at http://www.ntanet.org/images/stories/pdf/proceedings/10/13.pdf.

reduce foreign deductions, increasing the size of foreign-source income for the foreign tax credit limit.

Prior law allowed half of income from goods manufactured in the United States and sold abroad to be sourced to the country where the transfer takes place (the title passage rule). Since arranging a foreign transfer location for exports is relatively easy, this rule makes half of export income eligible for foreign tax credit offsets for firms with excess credits. In addition, as noted earlier, royalties paid in association with active business operations abroad were considered foreign-source income for purposes of the foreign tax credit limit, effectively shielding them from tax (since they are typically deductible as costs under foreign rules) for firms in excess credit positions.

New Law: Dividend Exemption, GILTI, and FDII

Perhaps the hallmark of the new law is that it virtually ends deferral. The system nevertheless remains a hybrid, albeit a different one, of worldwide and territorial approaches. The new law moves toward a territorial system with respect to its treatment of certain profits of tangible investments, such as plant and equipment. With respect to other income (primarily income from intangible assets) the system moves toward a current inclusion in income but at a lower rate, a minimum worldwide tax. It also maintains most of the existing treatment of included income (interest, royalties, rents, branch income, and Subpart F). Deferral of income and taxation at repatriation is retained only for portfolio investments (less than 10% U.S. ownership) in foreign firms. It also creates new foreign tax credit baskets.

Dividend Deduction

A 100% deduction for dividends is available for U.S. firms owning at least 10% of the foreign firm. No foreign tax credit is allowed, and the income is generally not subject to tax.

Global Intangible Low-Taxed Income (GILTI)

The new law, however, taxes, at a reduced rate, income of foreign subsidiaries (controlled foreign corporations, or CFCs) in excess of a deduction for 10% of intangible assets minus interest costs.[4] Subpart F income is excluded along with certain other income (foreign oil and gas income, related party dividends, and income effectively connected to the United States). GILTI income is included in currently taxed income, but a 50% deduction for this income is allowed for taxable years beginning after December 31, 2017, and through tax years beginning before January 1, 2025, resulting in a 10.5% rate at the new 21% corporate tax rate. For taxable years beginning after December 31, 2025, the deduction is to be reduced to 37.5%, resulting in a higher rate of 13.125%.

Foreign tax credits are allowed for 80% of foreign taxes paid. As a result, a residual U.S. tax is collected when foreign tax rates are below 13.125% in the initial years (0.105/0.80), and subsequently 16.406% (0.13125/0.80). GILTI income is in a separate foreign tax credit basket. The rules for allocating income for purposes of the foreign tax credit limit continue, and if those rules produce a foreign-source taxable income smaller than that measured for purposes of the foreign tax, GILTI applies at rates lower than 13.125% (or 16.406%). These rates correspond with the FDII rates (discussed below). The residual U.S. tax in the early years begins at 10.5% when foreign taxes are zero and decline to 0% when foreign taxes are 13.125% (in the later years 13.125% and 16.406%, respectively).

Foreign-Derived Intangible Income (FDII)

The new law also allows a deduction aimed at providing a lower tax rate on intangible income produced in the United States but derived from abroad. FDII is based on a formulary measure of domestic intangible income (deemed intangible income), which is then multiplied by the

[4] Tangible assets are measured at cost minus depreciation, with depreciation reflecting an alternative depreciation system with rules providing longer lives than that applied to domestic assets and determined at a straight line rate that is slower than depreciation of domestic assets.

estimated share of this income that is derived from foreign sales and use. Deemed intangible income is defined as deduction-eligible income in excess of 10% of tangible depreciable assets. Deduction-eligible income, in turn, is gross income minus excepted income minus deductions (including taxes) allocable to this income. Excepted income subtracted out is generally foreign-source income (Subpart F income, GILTI, dividends from CFCs, foreign branch income) as well as active financial services income, and domestic oil and gas extraction income. The purpose of all of these deductions is to estimate a reasonable measure of intangible domestic source income.

To determine the share of this deemed intangible income that is eligible for the deduction, it is multiplied by the ratio of foreign-derived deduction-eligible income over total deduction-eligible income. Foreign-derived deduction-eligible income is aimed at measuring income from the export of goods and services; it includes any deduction-eligible income that is from the sale of property for foreign use and the provision of services used abroad, including leases and licenses (and therefore royalties, both those in the active foreign tax credit basket and those from unrelated firms).

FDII is eligible for a deduction of 37.5% for taxable years beginning after December 31, 2017, and through taxable years beginning before January 1, 2025, resulting in a 13.125% rate (the 21% corporate tax rate multiplied by (1-0.375)). For taxable years beginning after December 31, 2025, the deduction declines to 21.875%, resulting in a rate of 16.406% (21% multiplied by (1- 0.21875)).

Taxable Income Limitation

The deduction for FDII and GILTI is limited if the sum of these amounts exceeds taxable income excluding GILTI. The excess is not allowed as a deduction and is apportioned between GILTI and FDII according to their shares of the total amount of GILTI and FDII.

Foreign Tax Credit Revisions

Several revisions are made in the foreign tax credit system. The taxes paid on dividends are no longer allowed as credits. In addition to a separate basket for GILTI income, there is also a separate foreign tax credit basket for branch income. As a result, foreign royalties associated with an active business is no longer sheltered by excess credits, although these royalties now benefit from the deduction for foreign-derived intangible income. The new law also eliminates the ability to shield exports with excess credits by repealing the title passage rule and sourcing exports where they are produced (which also increases the deduction for foreign-derived intangible income). The revision also requires assets to be valued on an adjusted tax basis (rather than a choice of fair market value or adjusted tax basis) for determining sourcing for the foreign tax credit limit.[5]

Allocation and Anti-Abuse Rules

In either type of system, territorial or worldwide with deferral, where taxes are paid and how much is determined by the allocation of income of multinational firms between different countries. The first right of taxation goes to the source country, regardless of whether the residence country has a territorial tax or a worldwide tax with a foreign tax credit.

Nexus is the first step in the process of determining whether a country has the right to tax any of a firm's profits. A U.S. firm that exports abroad, without taking part in an activity within the country it is exporting to, is not subject to profits taxes by that country. To establish the right to tax, a firm has to have nexus, or connection, with the country, which requires a permanent establishment. A permanent establishment is generally viewed as having a physical presence, which means that some assets are in the country (and a profits tax is a tax on the return to assets). A firm that manufactures abroad or has retail stores abroad has a physical presence, but other circumstances with a minimal presence are less clear. If nexus is

---

[5] The adjusted tax basis is original cost reduced by depreciation deductions and increased by capital additions.

established, then the amount of income sourced in that country must be determined. In the U.S. tax law, this establishment of a presence is termed *effectively connected income* and generally must require a physical presence or be derived from assets that are used in the United States. Tax treaties (discussed below) also contain provisions on permanent establishment.

Once the right to tax has been established, the allocation of income in each country must be determined. Although income can be allocated in a straightforward way for transactions between unrelated firms, related firms can potentially manipulate the location of profits by shifting the location of passive income, by setting the price of transactions between them to shift earnings (transfer prices), and to locate deductions, such as interest, in high-tax countries. The more income a firm can assign, for tax purposes, to a foreign subsidiary in a low-tax country, the lower its overall tax burden, since taxes in the residence country can be deferred on income or shielded by cross-crediting. The overall allocation of foreign-source income also affects the limit on the foreign tax credit.

Prior Law: Subpart F; Transfer Pricing; Interest Deductions and Thin Capitalization Rules

Subpart F

Like many other countries, the United States has anti-abuse rules to tax income that is relatively easily shifted on a current basis. The primary anti-abuse rule deals with CFCs. CFC rules are also commonly referred to as Subpart F rules, after the section of the tax code containing the rules. The rules applied to foreign firms in which U.S. shareholders that each own 10% of the voting power together own at least 50% of the voting power or value. Many CFCs are wholly owned by a single U.S. parent.

There are other anti-deferral rules, most importantly rules relating to passive foreign investment companies (PFICs) that are not CFCs and whose income is primarily passive.

The principal category of income taxed under Subpart F is called foreign base company income, and includes passive income (such as dividends, interest, rents, and royalties) received by a subsidiary and certain income from business operations. Income from business operations includes foreign base company income of sales and services subsidiaries in foreign countries where the production and consumption of those goods and services take place in other countries, and foreign oil-related income (income derived from processing, transporting, or selling oil and gas). In addition to foreign base company income, Subpart F includes income from insurance of risks outside the country (or within the country if receiving the same premiums).

Income invested in U.S. property (including lending to the parent) was taxed currently (to prevent a way to repatriate without paying dividends). There are de minimis exclusions (for small amounts or shares or tax rates more than 90% of the U.S. rates) and full inclusion rules (when Subpart F income is more than 70% of total income). A firm is not classified as a CFC unless stock has been held for 30 days.

Since the late 1990s, the scope of Subpart F has been reduced by the adoption of check-the-box rules. Check-the-box was a regulatory provision, but it has been codified and extended through the temporary look-through rules, set to expire after 2019. The provision allows a foreign subsidiary of a U.S. parent to elect to disregard its own (second-tier) subsidiary, incorporated in a different country, as a separate entity. If the second-tier subsidiary borrows from the first-tier subsidiary, it can deduct the interest in the country of incorporation; normally, the payment of interest would be considered Subpart F income and taxed currently. Under check-the-box, the payment is not recognized because there is no separate second-tier entity. If the first-tier subsidiary is in a no-tax jurisdiction, the interest is deducted, but not taxed currently. This type of arrangement creates what is referred to as a hybrid entity, one characterized differently in different jurisdictions.

Transfer Pricing

The current system generally requires firms to set hypothetical *transfer prices*, which are required to approximate the prices two firms would agree on if they conducted their transactions with unrelated parties (arm's length). These prices can be difficult to determine. When there are comparable transactions between unrelated parties that can be observed, establishing an arm'slength price is relatively straightforward. For many transactions, especially those associated with intangible assets or licenses for the right to use intangible assets (such as inventions, formulas, and trademarks), the intangible asset may be unique, and transfer prices are more difficult to establish.

Interest Deductions and Thin Capitalization Rules

One method of shifting profits is to claim interest deductions in the high-tax country. Although there was an allocation to foreign sources of interest for purposes of the limit on the foreign tax credit, there is not one to allocate interest between U.S. firms and related firms incorporated in other countries, whether subsidiaries to a U.S. parent or a subsidiary of a foreign parent.

There was a rule that limited the total amount of interest a firm can deduct, applying to all firms, sometimes referred to as Section 163(j) rules, or thin capitalization rules. The deduction for net interest was limited to 50% of adjusted taxable income (income before taxes, interest deductions, and depreciation, amortization or depletion deductions) for firms with a debt-to-equity ratio above 1.5. (This measure of income is referred to as EBITDA, for earnings before interest, taxes, depreciation, and amortization.) Interest paid above the limitation may be carried forward indefinitely. Most firms would not be constrained by a restriction, especially in light of the safe-harbor debt equity ratio (which would lead to a debt share of 60%). In addition, by allowing a fairly high limit to interest deductions and making it a percentage of income before deductions for depreciation, most firms with significant amounts of tangible property would be unlikely to be affected by this restriction even if the safe harbor did not apply.

New Law: BEAT, Modifications to Subpart F, Transfer Pricing Changes, Stricter Thin Capitalization Rules

Base Erosion and Anti-Abuse Tax (BEAT)

The new law introduces a general anti-abuse provision whose focus is primarily on U.S. subsidiaries of foreign parents, although it applies in general to related parties (although as noted below, it may also affect U.S. multinationals with foreign-source income from higher-tax locations). Unlike Subpart F or the new GILTI provision, BEAT is not aimed at including income but at taxing deductions. BEAT imposes a minimum tax equal to 10% of the sum of taxable income and base erosion payments on corporations with average annual gross receipts of at least $500 million over the past three tax years and with deductions attributable to outbound payments exceeding 3% of overall deductions. The rate is 5% in 2018 and 12.5% for taxable years beginning after December 31, 2025. (Applicable taxpayers that are members of an affiliated group that includes a bank or registered securities dealer under Section 15(a) of the Securities Exchange Act of 1934 are subject to an additional increase of one percentage point in the tax rates, and the tax applies when base erosion payments exceed 2% of deductions.)

Base erosion payments include payments to related foreign parties, including those that would result in a deduction under Chapter 1 of the *Internal Revenue Code* (such as interest, rents, royalties, and services), the purchase of depreciable or amortizable property, certain reinsurance payments, and payments to inverted firms or foreign persons that are a member of an affiliated firm that includes the inverted firm that became inverted after November 9, 2017 (but not firms that continue to be treated as U.S. firms). Cost of goods sold would not be included, and cost of services would not be included if determined under the services cost method under the transfer pricing rules in Section 482.[6] Disallowed interest under the thin capitalization rules, which are tightened (as discussed below), would be first

[6] There is some uncertainty about whether services with a markup or that cannot use the services cost method would include the whole payment for services or just the markup. See discussion in the final section summarizing commentary on the new rules.

allocated to unrelated parties. Base erosion payments are reduced to the extent that withholding taxes are applied.[7]

A related person is a person who owns 25% of the taxpayer or another entity controlled by the same interests. The constructive ownership rules treat a taxpayer owning 10% of a firm as controlling 100% of the firm. (In other provisions of the code a taxpayer must have a 50% ownership to be considered as controlling 100% of the firm.)

Because BEAT is effectively a lower tax rate on a broader base, it will not apply to all taxpayers who have related party payments. Only taxpayers with base erosion payments that are large relative to their taxable income will be affected.

BEAT can increase the cost of certain transactions between U.S. subsidiaries and their foreign parents by including interest payments and royalty payments to the foreign parent in their BEAT base. These payments are targeted because they are also used to shift profits out of the United States.

Although BEAT appears to be aimed at profit shifting out of the United States through royalty payments and interest payments, presumably to a foreign parent, BEAT is calculated in a way that allows the tax to be reduced by the research credit and 80% of the sum of three credits (the low-income housing credit, the renewable electricity production credit in Section 45(a) of the code, and credits for renewable energy, such as wind), but not other credits. A taxpayer falling under the BEAT minimum tax will not be eligible for foreign tax credits on foreign-source income. Thus a firm could have a higher tax liability under BEAT because it had large amounts of foreign tax credits relative to tax liability before credits.

Modifications to Subpart F

Subpart F is retained with only minor modifications. Foreign oil-related income is no longer included as Subpart F income, and a provision

---

[7] Withholding taxes are applied to dividends, some interest, and royalties, but are often reduced to very low rates by tax treaties.

for recapturing certain prior shipping income is eliminated.[8] The 30-day holding period is eliminated. The determination of 10% ownership is based on shares of stock by value or voting power rather than just by voting power.[9] Check-the-box is not altered.

Transfer Pricing

The new law modifies, and attempts to clarify, rules determining the valuation of intangible property. It adds goodwill, going concern value, or the value of workforce in place to the list of intangible property (which currently includes items such as patents, inventions, formula, processes design, pattern, know-how, copyrights, compositions, and other specified items). It also includes any other item with a value not attributable to tangible property or services of any individual. It specifies that the Secretary of the Treasury has the authority to require aggregation of intangible assets for valuation purposes (since value as a group may be different from the sum of individual values) and to use realistic alternative principles (a taxpayer may enter into the transaction if there is no realistic economically preferable outcome). For example, the taxpayer's earnings from licensing of an intangible asset to produce a product (such as a drug formula) could be compared to the income if the taxpayer instead manufactured the product (e.g., the drug).

---

[8] Foreign base company shipping income (income associated with international transport by aircraft or vessel) has undergone several treatments under Subpart F. It is currently excluded, but between 1975 and 1986 it was excluded but reduced by the extent the income was reinvested in the business, and in 1986 it was excluded without a reinvestment requirement. If those reinvested funds are repatriated, that income is Subpart F income. The revision eliminates that coverage under Subpart F.

[9] The legislation also modifies the definition of a CFC. In determining whether a foreign corporation is a CFC (50% owned by U.S. persons who each own 10%), direct, indirect, and constructive ownership rules apply for determining CFC status (although only direct and indirect ownership applies for determining the share of Subpart F income). If a person owns 50% of the voting power, she is considered to own 100% of the stock under the constructive attribution rules. Constructive attribution rules also take into account related parties. Current law, however, does not allow these constructive attribution rules to apply so that a U.S. person is attributed stock owned by a foreign person even though they are related. The new allow allows attribution of stock owned by a related foreign person. This provision was primarily aimed at inverted firms and is discussed in that section.

Thin Capitalization Rules

Three revisions to the thin capitalization rules cause them to apply to more firms. First, the safe-harbor debt-to-equity-ratio rule (i.e., the provision that requires debt to be 1.5 times equity value for the limit on the deduction for interest to apply) is eliminated. Second, deductible interest is reduced from 50% to 30% of adjusted taxable income for businesses with gross receipts greater than $25 million. Finally, for years beginning after December 31, 2021, adjusted taxable income does not allow a deduction for depreciation, amortization, and depletion (this base is called EBIT). The provision also has an exception for floor plan financing for motor vehicles (including boats and farm equipment as well as cars and trucks). Real estate can elect a longer depreciation period instead of limits on interest deductions which would be attractive for heavily mortgaged properties. In any case, real estate is not the normal target of concerns about earning stripping (concerns are generally directed at inverted firms and multinationals).

Hybrid Entities and Instruments

Hybrid entities and instruments can confer tax advantages on related parties if they are treated differently in different jurisdictions. An example of a "hybrid instrument" is one where a royalty or interest payment (which is deductible in the United States) is not included in income in the jurisdiction where the interest or royalty is received. A "hybrid entity" is one that is recognized as a separate entity in one jurisdiction but not the other, which affects whether they include payments in income. The tax revision disallows a deduction by a related party for an interest or royalty payment to a recipient in a foreign country if that payment is not taxed (or is included in income and then deducted) in the foreign country.

Tax Treaties

The United States and other countries have tax treaties designed to avoid double taxation. A significant area of coverage in treaties is the agreements regarding withholding taxes, but treaties cover other issues as well, such as the recognition of a permanent establishment or other grounds to impose source-based taxes, such as corporate profits taxes. For U.S. firms' subsidiaries incorporated abroad, the treaties of those countries of incorporation and other countries are also relevant.

A change in domestic law, as in P.L. 115-97, in the United States would override treaty provisions, and certain provisions in the new law may be in conflict with treaties, as discussed subsequently (basically the most recently enacted provision is treated as primary).[10]

Repatriation Rules

Prior Law: Voluntary Repatriation

U.S. firms with overseas operations could indefinitely postpone paying U.S. tax on foreign income by operating through a foreign subsidiary and reinvesting the earnings abroad. U.S. taxes were due when the earnings were repatriated to the United States as an intra-firm dividend or other payment. These earnings were taxed at the then corporate tax rate of 35%.

The U.S. firm paid taxes on its overseas earnings only when they were paid to the U.S. parent corporation as intra-firm dividends or other income.

With respect to repatriated dividends, U.S. firms can claim foreign tax credits for foreign taxes paid by their subsidiaries on the earnings used to pay the repatriated dividends. The ability to defer U.S. tax thus poses an incentive for U.S. firms to invest abroad in countries with low tax rates. Proposals to cut taxes on repatriations are based largely on the premise that even this deferred tax on intra-firm dividends discourages repatriations and encourages firms to reinvest foreign earnings abroad and that a cut in the tax would stimulate repatriations.

---

[10] See CRS Legal Sidebar LSB10047, *What Happens if H.R. 1 Conflicts with U.S. Tax Treaties?*, by Erika K. Lunder.

New Law: Deemed Repatriation

A deemed repatriation is imposed on accumulated post-1986 foreign earnings determined as of a certain measurement date, without requiring an actual distribution, upon the transition to the new participation exemption system. The transition rule requires mandatory inclusion of such deferred foreign income as Subpart F income by U.S. shareholders of deferred foreign income corporations.[11] The included amount is taxed at a reduced rate that depends on whether the deferred earnings are held in cash (which are taxed at 15.5%) or other assets (which are taxed at 8%) with applicable foreign tax credits similarly reduced. (These rates are technically accomplished via a deduction that results in the stated rate.) The resulting tax may be paid in installments over eight years.[12]

S corporations are subject to a special rule. Shareholders of an S corporation are allowed to elect to maintain deferral on such foreign income until the S corporation changes its status, sells substantially all its assets, ceases to conduct business, or the electing shareholder transfers its S corporation stock.

Anti-Inversion Rules

Prior Law: Section 7874

In the American Jobs Creation Act of 2004 (P.L. 108-357), Congress responded to an increase in the prevalence of corporate inversions by enacting Section 7874 of the Internal Revenue Code (IRC). Section 7874 imposes negative tax consequences on an inverted company, by reducing or, in some cases, eliminating the tax benefits of an inversion. Section 7874 creates two different taxing regimes for the inverted corporation

---

[11] In particular, for the last tax year beginning before January 1, 2018, the Subpart F income of a deferred foreign income corporation (as otherwise determined for that tax year under Code §952) is increased by the greater of (1) the accumulated post-1986 deferred foreign income of the corporation determined as of November 2, 2017, or (2) the accumulated post-1986 deferred foreign income of the corporation determined as of December 31, 2017.

[12] If installment payments are elected, the payments for each of the first five years equal 8% of the net tax liability. The amount of the sixth installment is 15% of the net tax liability, increasing to 20% for the seventh installment and 25% for the eighth installment.

depending on whether 60% or 80% of the inverted company is owned by shareholders of the U.S. company. If at least 60% of the foreign parent's stock is held by former shareholders of the U.S. company, then the U.S. subsidiary (and related persons) is limited in its ability to claim credits and deductions against certain income when calculating its U.S. income taxes. If the 80% threshold is met, then the foreign parent is treated as a domestic corporation for U.S. tax purposes and subject to tax on its worldwide income. The section generally applies to companies that inverted after March 4, 2003, and is not applicable if the substantial activities test is met. Inverted firms not taxed as U.S. firms are referred to as surrogate firms.

Since 2004, additional regulatory steps have been taken to reduce the incentives for inversion transactions and their benefits. In 2012, Treasury Regulations (T.D. 9592, June 12, 2012) increased the safe harbor for the substantial business activities test from 10% to 25%. In 2014 and 2015, Treasury Notices 2014-52 and 2015-79 limited access to earnings of U.S. foreign subsidiaries and addressed several techniques that could be used to artificially reduce the calculated share of U.S. shareholders. In 2016, Treasury regulations regarding these notices put in place several anti-inversion rules that target groups that have engaged in a series of inversion or acquisition transactions as well as a rule that restricts postinversion asset dilution and restricts the ability of foreign-parent groups to shift earnings out of the United States through dividends or other economically similar transactions (under Section 385).[13]

New Law: Additional Restrictions on Inversions

The new law contains several measures that affect inverted firms that are not treated as U.S. firms.

Recapture of Deemed Repatriation Rate Reduction

A special recapture rule applies on deemed repatriations of newly inverted firms. This recapture rule applies if a firm first becomes an

[13] For a more detailed discussion of prior rules and inversion activity, see CRS Report R43568, *Corporate Expatriation, Inversions, and Mergers: Tax Issues*, by Donald J. Marples and Jane G. Gravelle.

expatriated entity at any time during the 10-year period beginning on December 22, 2017, with respect to a surrogate foreign corporation that first becomes a surrogate foreign corporation during that period (i.e., post-enactment). In this case, the tax will be increased from 8% and 15.5% to 35% tax for the entire deemed repatriation, with no foreign tax credit allowed for the increase in tax rate. The additional tax is due on the full amount of the deemed repatriation in the first tax year in which the taxpayer becomes an expatriated entity.

Excise Tax on Stock Compensation

The excise tax rate on stock compensation received by insiders in an expatriated corporation is increased from 15% to 20%, effective on the date of enactment for corporations that first become expatriated after that date.

Individual Tax on Dividends from Inverted Companies

Dividends (like capital gains) are allowed lower tax rates than the rates applied to ordinary income. The rates are 0%, 15%, and 20% depending on the rate bracket that ordinary income falls into. Certain dividends received from foreign firms (those that do not have tax treaties and PFICs[14]) are not eligible for these lower rates. Dividends paid by firms that inverted after the date of enactment of P.L. 115-97 are added to the list of those not eligible for the lower rates.

Base Erosion Payments to Expatriated Entities

Base erosion payments generally do not include any amount that constitutes reductions in gross receipts, including payments for costs of goods sold (COGS). However, an exception applies for certain payments to expatriated entities, described below.

Base erosion payments include any amount that results in a reduction of gross receipts of the taxpayer that is paid or accrued by the taxpayer

---

[14] A PFIC is a passive foreign investment company, a foreign corporation that primarily holds passive assets. It does not fall under CFC rules, but has a separate set of anti-avoidance rules that generally were not changed by the new law.

with respect to (1) a surrogate foreign corporation that is a related party of the taxpayer, but only if such corporation first became a surrogate foreign corporation after November 9, 2017; or (2) a foreign person who is a member of the surrogate foreign corporation's expanded affiliated group (EAG).

A surrogate foreign corporation is a foreign corporation that meets the following criteria:

- It acquires (after March 4, 2003) substantially all of the properties held by a U.S. corporation, or substantially all of the properties constituting a trade or business of a domestic partnership,
- After the acquisition, the U.S. corporation's former share-holders, or the domestic partnership's former partners, own at least 60% of the stock (by vote or value) of the foreign acquiring corporation.
- The surrogate foreign corporation's EAG does not have substantial business activities in the country where that corporation is organized or created compared to the total business activities of the EAG.

A surrogate foreign corporation does not include a foreign corporation where the former shareholders of the U.S. corporation or the former partners of the domestic partnership hold 80% or more (by vote or value) of the stock of the foreign acquiring corporation after the transaction. The EAG includes the foreign acquiring corporation and all companies connected to it by a chain of greater than 50% ownership.

Modification of Attribution Rules

The constructive ownership rules for purposes of determining 10% U.S. shareholders, whether a corporation is a CFC and whether parties satisfy certain relatedness tests, were expanded in the 2017 tax revision. Specifically, the new law treats stock owned by a foreign person as attributable to a U.S. entity owned by the foreign person (so-called "downward attribution"). As a result, stock owned by a foreign person may generally be attributed to (1) a U.S. corporation, 10% of the value of the stock of which is owned, directly or indirectly, by the foreign person; (2) a U.S. partnership in which the foreign person is a partner; and (3) certain U.S. trusts if the foreign person is a beneficiary or, in certain circumstances, a grantor or a substantial owner.

The downward attribution rule was originally conceived to deal with inversions. In an inversion, without downward attribution, a subsidiary of the original U.S. parent could lose CFC status if it sold enough stock to the new foreign parent so the U.S. parent no longer had majority ownership. With downward attribution, the ownership of stock by the new foreign parent in the CFC is attributed to the U.S. parent, so that the subsidiary continues its CFC status, making it subject to any tax rules that apply to CFCs (such as Subpart F and repatriation taxes under the old law, and Subpart F and GILTI under the new law).

Issues in Prior Law and Implications for New Law

The Location of Investment in the United States and Other Countries

A long-standing concern about the international tax system involved the effects of taxes on the location of investment in the United States rather than in other countries. One target of concern was the higher tax rate in the United States, and lowering that rate (of 35%) was an objective of the drive for tax revision.

Two questions can be raised about the prior law. One is the question of the potential effects of the tax changes on the allocation of investment. A related issue is whether the tax change makes the allocation of investment more efficient (increasing worldwide output) or better for the United States (increasing aggregate welfare in the United States by moving closer to an optimal treatment).

To address these issues, the first section begins with the comparison of U.S. tax rates with those of other countries before the tax change, and addresses the importance of considering effective tax rates. The next section examines the effect of the new generally applicable tax revisions (the rate changes and changes in depreciation on U.S. domestic investment). The final section examines the effects of the new international rules, or related rules, including the thin capitalization rules, GILTI, FDII, and BEAT. The section concludes with a discussion of what these findings imply for the allocation of investment and the efficiency or optimality of that allocation.

U.S. Tax Rates Compared to Other Countries Before the Revision

The U.S. corporate tax rate (combining federal and average state and local taxes, and accounting for the deductibility of state and local taxes) of 39% was higher than the statutory rate in any other major country, including the countries in the Organization for Economic Cooperation and Development (OECD) and the G-20. Using an average weighted by GDP, the statutory tax rate in the OECD countries outside of the United States was 27%. The rate for the G-20 was 28%.[15]

The statutory corporate tax rate, however, is more relevant for the profit-shifting issue to be discussed subsequently. Investment location is determined by the effective tax rate. Two measures of effective tax rates are the average effective tax rate and the marginal effective tax rate.

The average effective tax rate divides tax liability by some measures of profit, and thus captures to some degree special deductions and credits in the system as well as the statutory tax rate. The average effective tax rate captures many smaller provisions, but it does not capture the significant

---

[15] Data for tax rates of the OECD countries are from the OECD data. See http://www.oecd-ilibrary.org/economics/oecd-economic-surveys-norway-2018/norway-s-corporate-tax-rate-has-been-lowered_eco_surveys-nor-2018-graph33- en. Data for other countries in the G-20 are from Congressional Budget Office, *International Comparisons of Corporate Tax Income Tax Rates*, March 8, 2017, at https://www.cbo.gov/publication/52419. Data on GDP are from the Central Intelligence Agency *World Factbook*, estimated for 2017, at https://www.cia.gov/library/publications/theworld-factbook/rankorder/rawdata_2001.txt. The unweighted (simple) average of the OECD is about a percentage point lower. Typically larger countries have higher tax rates. Tax rates are based on weighted pre-tax returns, that is, a weighted average of 1/(1-t) rather than of t.

timing issues associated with accelerated depreciation and expensing.[16] To capture timing, a tax rate needs to be based on looking forward to the expected tax payments for a representative investment and take into account the time value of money.

A marginal effective tax rate measures the difference between the return on the investment before taxes are considered to the return after taxes. This amount is the share of the return collected in taxes on a present value basis, and that amount is divided by the pre-tax return to obtain a marginal effective tax rate. The term *marginal* is used because it applies to marginal investments that break even (i.e., an investment that earns just enough to be worth undertaking). This measure is, in theory, the best measure to determine how the corporate income tax affects investment, but it requires a lot of information about depreciation practices. Because of the data demands, for example, studies often use a representative equipment investment, although there is a wide variation in the tax treatment and durability of equipment. Thus, these marginal effective tax rates should be considered as rough measures of relative tax burdens. In addition, the effective tax rates depend on the assets included in the measure and whether the measure includes the effect of debt finance.

A variety of different estimates in recent years have been made examining these two effective tax rates. In general, most studies of average effective tax rates found these tax rates (federal, state, and local combined) to be relatively close, whereas the U.S. marginal effective tax rate tended to be about 6 percentage points above the weighted average of the OECD.[17] These estimates were for equity investment (buildings,

---

[16] Depreciation allows the cost of the asset to be deducted from earnings over a period of years. Depreciation is accelerated when it is allowed more quickly than the decline in the value of an asset, or economic depreciation. Expensing, the most extreme form of accelerated depreciation, allows cost to be recovered immediately, when the asset is acquired.

[17] See CRS Report R41743, *International Corporate Tax Rate Comparisons and Policy Implications*, by Jane G. Gravelle. This report explains the different concepts of tax rate and also illustrates the importance of using tax rates where each country is weighted by GDP to make comparisons. A variety of estimates are presented in this report, although some of these estimates reflect tax rates that do not fall into the category of a standard marginal tax rate, or do not confine themselves to income tax rate comparisons. For example, a measure called an effective average tax rate (EATR) is a blend of statutory and marginal tax rates, and a measure by Mintz and Chen of the University of Calgary (Jack Mintz and Duanjie Chen, "U.S. Corporate Taxation: Prime for Reform," *Tax Foundation, Special Report No.*

equipment, intangibles, and inventory), with the marginal effective U.S. tax rate estimated at about 22%.[18] These estimates assume the tax base for purposes of state and local taxes is the same as for federal taxes. The marginal effective tax rate for OECD countries outside of the United States, weighted by GDP, is 16.4%.

Considering equipment and buildings separately, equipment earnings were subject to a 22.5% marginal effective tax rate, compared to an 18.9% marginal effective tax rate in other OECD countries (a difference of 3.6 percentage points), whereas buildings were subject to a 28.4% marginal effective tax rate in the United States and a 23.6% marginal effective tax rate in the rest of the world (a difference of 4.8 percentage points).

In 2016, the Treasury estimated a marginal effective tax rate in the United States (federal and subnational) of 18.1%, which compares to a 19.4% marginal effective tax rate in the rest of the G7. The U.S. rate allowed for bonus depreciation.[19]

228, February 4, 2015, available at https://taxfoundation.org/us-corporate-taxation-prime-reform; and Jack Mintz, "Corporation Tax: A Survey," *Fiscal Studies*, vol. 16, issue 4 (1995), pp. 23-68) includes the state and local sales tax (which sometimes falls on business capital assets) in the U.S. marginal tax rate. A study prepared for the Alliance for Competitive Taxation (*International Comparison of Effective Corporate Tax Rates Prepared for Alliance for Competitive Taxation by Price Waterhouse*, 2016, at http://www.actontaxreform.com/wp-content/uploads/2016/09/ International-Comparison-of-Effective-Corporate-Tax-Rates_FINAL_20160926.pdf) reports these two measures. They also report a marginal effective tax rate (termed EMTR) estimated in an EU study that includes property and wealth taxes. The EU study does not provide a mean, and the reported comparison in the Alliance for Progress Study uses a simple average rather than a weighted average. See *Effective Tax Levels Using the Devereux/Griffith Methodology – Update 2015*, at http://www.zew.de/en/publikationen/effective-tax-levels-using-the-devereuxgriffith-methodologyupdate-2015/?cHash=b54a84e000c7e4e1ad65cdd59c575c10. Two measures of average effective tax rates are included in the Alliance for Competitive Taxation summary, one of which was included in the CRS report, but the other, by the World Bank, was for a hypothetical firm and not based on actual data.

[18] Separate rates were reported for investments not eligible and eligible for the domestic production activity deduction; weighting these by estimated shares of earnings eligible and not eligible (73% and 27%) for the deduction produces an overall rate of 21.7%.

[19] The *President's Framework for Business Tax Reform: An Update, A Joint Report by the White House and the Department of the Treasury*, April 2016, https://www.treasury.gov/resource-center/tax-policy/Documents/ThePresidents-Framework-for-Business-Tax-Reform-An-Update-04-04-2016.pdf.

In 2017, the Congressional Budget Office (CBO) released a study of statutory, average effective, and marginal effective tax rates for the G-20.[20] The G-20 includes some of the larger economies of the world that are excluded from the OECD, especially the BRIC countries (Brazil, Russia, India, and China). Although the CBO data were from 2012, the study provided some updates for the changes in statutory rates through 2015 in the text. Making some further proportional changes for the minor tax rate reductions since that time (and excluding Saudi Arabia, where full data were not available), the estimates are a weighted statutory tax rate outside of the United States of 27.9%, compared to a 39.1% U.S. statutory rate. The average tax rate was 29% in the United States and 22.2% in the rest of the G-20 outside of Saudi Arabia.

The marginal effective rate, which accounted for debt finance as well as equity finance, was 18.6% in the United States, compared to a marginal effective tax rate of 10.9% in the rest of the G-20. Since the corporate tax subsidizes debt, including it in marginal effective tax rates would lower those rates.

The CBO report also provided data for marginal effective tax rates of tangible assets (buildings and equipment). Its estimate for equipment in the United States was 10.5%, compared to a 17.3% rate for the rest of the G-20; its estimate for buildings was 20.1%, compared to an estimated rate of 11.1% for the rest of the G-20.

These comparisons in the CBO study suggest that the rates of tax in the United States were several percentage points above the rest of the G-20 for all four categories of assets and for buildings, but lower for equipment.

Changes in Marginal Effective Tax Rates

This section provides estimates of federal marginal effective tax rates from the basic changes in the treatment of domestic investment: the reduction in the statutory tax rate from 35% to 21%, the repeal of the production activities deduction, the temporary expensing of equipment (allowed at 100% for the first five years and then phased out over the next

[20] Congressional Budget Office, *International Comparisons of Corporate Income Tax Rates*, March 8, 2017, at https://www.cbo.gov/publication/52419.

five years), and the provision requiring the amortization over five years, that is, deducting the costs in equal amounts over five years (rather than expensing) for research and experimentation, to begin in 2022.

Table 1. Marginal Effective Tax Rates for Equity-Financed Investment

Asset	2017 Law With Bonus Depreciation (%)	2017 Law Without Bonus Depreciation (%)	New Law: Temporary Provisions (%)	New Law: Permanent Provisions (%)
Equipment	13.4	23.6	0.0	13.7
Public Utility	14.2	24.9	0.0	14.5
Structures				
Nonresidential	30.8	30.8	18.5	18.5
Residential	28.1	28.2	16.7	16.7
Intangibles				
Research	-63.3	-63.3	-63.3	-30.2
Advertising	0.0	0.0	0.0	0.0
Other	0.0	0.0	0.0	0.0
Total	15.6	19.7	3.2	10.9

Source: Congressional Research Service (CRS). See CRS Report R44638, *Corporate Tax Integration and Tax Reform*, by Jane G. Gravelle; and CRS Report R44242, *The Effect of Base-Broadening Measures on Labor Supply and Investment: Considerations for Tax Reform*, by Jane G. Gravelle and Donald J. Marples, for method of computation and assumptions.

Notes: The corporate statutory rate used for 2017 law is 34.14% to reflect the production activities deduction. The other assumptions and underlying data include a corporate after-tax real discount rate of 7% and an inflation rate of 2%, used in all simulations. The research credit is 11.3% (see CRS Report R44522, *A Patent/Innovation Box as a Tax Incentive for Domestic Research and Development*, by Jane G. Gravelle). Note that these tables do not include land, which is not reproducible, and inventories, whose short lives make them likely relatively insensitive to the rates of return. Both are taxed at rates above the rates for other nonresidential structures (land at the statutory rate and inventories above the statutory rate). Other intangibles primarily reflect human capital investment.

In 2017, investments in equipment were allowed bonus depreciation, with half of the cost expensed and half depreciated. That bonus depreciation was, under prior law, to be phased out and be eliminated entirely after 2019, so the tables also report effective tax rates without bonus depreciation. Which comparisons are appropriate depend on what might have been expected to happen to bonus depreciation, which has been in place as a temporary provision since 2008 and has been continuously extended, as well as expectations as to whether the permanent provisions for depreciation of equipment and amortization of research investments will occur.

Table 1 reports the effective tax rates on equity-financed investments by asset group for 2017 law with and without bonus depreciation, and then for the temporary provisions in the new law (providing expensing of equipment and retaining it for research costs) and the permanent provisions (depreciation of equipment and five-year amortization for research). For purposes of bonus depreciation and expensing, public utility structures are considered equipment and are eligible.

Calculating from the tax rates as shown in this table, under 2017 law, investment in tangible assets is subject to positive effective tax rates ranging from 38% (0.134/0.35) to 88% (0.308/0.35) of the statutory rate with bonus depreciation and from 67% to 88% without bonus depreciation.[21] These differences reflect the degree of acceleration of the present value of depreciation deductions as compared with economic depreciation (the rate of decline in the value of an asset). Depreciation is more accelerated for equipment than for structures. Intangible investments are taxed at zero or negative rates. Intangible assets are eligible for expensing (the maximum amount of acceleration in depreciation), which produces a zero effective tax rate. The addition of a research credit results in a negative tax rate for investment in research. (Note that the magnitude of negative tax rates may appear to be more powerful subsidies than are actually the case because of the method of calculating effective tax rates.[22])

[21] These categories are aggregates of in some cases very heterogeneous assets. Effective tax rates under 2017 permanent law without bonus depreciation range from 17% to 32% for equipment. Nonresidential structures include oil and gas investments with an effective tax rate of 11% and various types of buildings taxed at rates ranging from 26% to 35%.

[22] In calculating the effective tax rate, the required after-tax return is held constant: positive taxes increase the pre-tax required return, and negative tax rates reduce that pre-tax return. As the pre-tax return falls to a very low rate, the share received as a subsidy can become large when expressed as a percent of that rate. An alternate way to present the tax rate is as a tax wedge, t/(1-t), which indicates how much higher or lower the pre-tax return would have to

Overall, investment returns are taxed at an effective rate of 15.6% with bonus depreciation, or 45% of the statutory rate, and at 19.7% without bonus depreciation, or 57% of the statutory tax rate. The tax on tangible investment is much larger than the tax on intangible investment.

The temporary provisions (allowing expensing of equipment and public utility structures and retaining the expensing of research) would cut the effective tax rate on equity-financed investment to 3%, whereas the permanent provisions would reduce the rate to 11%. If the assumption is made that temporary benefits become permanent, the appropriate comparison is the 2017 rate with bonus depreciation to the temporary provisions of the new law, showing an overall decline in the tax rate from 15.6% to 3%, a reduction of almost 13 percentage points. Comparing the permanent provisions, the rate falls from 19.7% to 10.9%, a slightly smaller reduction of 8 percentage points.

Table 2 provides estimates with assets financed by debt. Corporate investment financed by debt is subsidized rather than taxed. In a world without inflation and with tax depreciation equal to economic depreciation, the effective tax rate on debt-financed investments would be zero: the deduction for interest exactly offsets the tax on the earnings from the investment. The presence of inflation and accelerated depreciation causes debt-financed investments to be subsidized, because the deduction for interest is allowed a full rate on nominal income (including the inflation portion of the interest rate) and at the statutory rate, whereas only the real return is taxed and at a lower effective rate.

The effective tax rates for debt-financed assets are negative, but the rates rise (or subsidies decrease) under the new provisions, as the value of deducting interest at 21% is smaller than the value at 35%. The overall tax rates under the new temporary provisions change little from 2017 law without bonus depreciation, as the benefits for equity (expensing for equipment) offset the reduced debt subsidy due to the lower rate. The tax

---

rise or fall to break even. Tax wedges are larger than tax rates for positive tax rates and smaller for negative ones. For example, the 30.8% tax rate is a wedge of 44.4%, whereas a minus 63.3% tax rate is a wedge of -38.8%.

rates under the permanent provisions lead to a reduced subsidy with tax rates becoming a smaller negative.

Table 2. Marginal Effective Tax Rates for Debt-Financed Investment

Asset	2017 Law With Bonus Depreciation (%)	2017 Law Without Bonus Depreciation (%)	New Law: Temporary Provisions (%)	New Law: Permanent Provisions (%)
Equipment	-59.4	-38.8	-40.1	-20.0
Public Utility	-63.0	-44.4	-40.1	-21.4
Structures				
Nonresidential	-27.5	-27.5	-13.8	-13.8
Residential	-38.9	-38.9	-18.5	-18.5
Intangibles				
Research	-701.4	-701.4	-252.0	-147.3
Advertising	-87.1	-87.1	-40.1	-40.1
Other	-87.1	-87.1	-40.1	-40.1
Total	-64.0	-53.5	-48.4	-27.4

Source: Congressional Research Service (CRS). See CRS Report R44638, *Corporate Tax Integration and Tax Reform*, by Jane G. Gravelle; and CRS Report R44242, *The Effect of Base-Broadening Measures on Labor Supply and Investment: Considerations for Tax Reform*, by Jane G. Gravelle and Donald J. Marples, for method of computation and assumptions.

Notes: The corporate statutory rate used for 2017 law is 34.14% to reflect the production activities deduction. The other assumptions and underlying data include a nominal interest rate of 7.5% and an inflation rate of 2%, used in all simulations. The research credit is 11.3% (see CRS Report R44522, *A Patent/Innovation Box as a Tax Incentive for Domestic Research and Development*, by Jane G. Gravelle). Note that these tables do not include land, which is not reproducible, and inventories, whose short lives make them likely relatively insensitive to the rates of return. Both are taxed at rates above the rates for other nonresidential structures (land at the statutory rate and inventories above the statutory rate).

Table 3 and *Table 4* combine the debt and equity investment using two different leveraging rates, one estimated by CRS (36%) and one used in CBO effective tax rate estimates (32%). Rates in either case are small under current law, ranging from -0.3% to 5.7% and 7.8%.[23] Under the

[23] The 7.8% rate is higher than the rates in the CBO international study discussed above. It seems likely that the higher rate is due to inclusion of R&D, but not other intangibles (only R&D intangibles are in the National Income Accounts) and the inclusion of inventories, which are taxed at higher rates. The CBO report with the 32% debt share is *Taxing Capital Income:*

temporary provisions of the new law they receive an overall subsidy, whereas under the permanent provisions they receive a small effective tax rate of 2% to 3%. The provisions for the assets that are probably of most concern with shifting of investment (i.e., equipment and nonresidential structures) would have taxes fall more significantly.

Table 3. Marginal Effective Tax Rates for Debt- and Equity-Financed Investment, 36% Debt Share

Asset	2017 Law With Bonus Depreciation (%)	2017 Law Without Bonus Depreciation (%)	New Law: Temporary Provisions (%)	New Law: Permanent Provisions (%)
Equipment	-0.9	11.1	-9.6	5.4
Public Utility				
Structures	-0.8	11.3	-9.6	5.8
Nonresidential				
Structures	19.2	19.2	10.7	10.7
Residential				
Structures	15.2	15.2	8.2	8.2
Intangibles				
Research	-116.3	-116.3	-95.4	-52.2
Advertising	-16.7	-16.7	-9.6	-9.6
Other	-16.7	-16.7	-9.6	-9.6
Total	-0.3	5.7	-6.6	1.8

Source: Congressional Research Service. See CRS Report R44638, Corporate Tax Integration and Tax Reform, by Jane G. Gravelle; and CRS Report R44242, *The Effect of Base-Broadening Measures on Labor Supply and Investment: Considerations for Tax Reform*, by Jane G. Gravelle and Donald J. Marples, for method of computation and assumptions.

Notes: The corporate statutory rate used for 2017 law is 34.14% to reflect the production activities deduction. The other assumptions and underlying data include a real discount rate for equity of 7%, a nominal interest rate of 7.5%, and an inflation rate of 2%, used in all simulations. The research credit is 11.3% (see CRS Report R44522, *A Patent/Innovation Box as a Tax Incentive for Domestic Research and Development*, by Jane G. Gravelle). Note that these tables do not include land, which is not reproducible, and inventories, whose short lives make them likely relatively insensitive to the rates of return. Both are taxed at rates above the rates for other nonresidential structures (land at the statutory rate and inventories above the statutory rate)

Effective Marginal Tax Rates Under 2014 Law and Selected Policy Options, December 18, 2014, at https://www.cbo.gov/publication/49817.

Table 4. Marginal Effective Tax Rates for Debt- and Equity-Financed Investment, 32% Debt Share

Asset	2017 Law With Bonus Depreciation (%)	2017 Law Without Bonus Depreciation (%)	New Law: Temporary Provisions (%)	New Law: Permanent Provisions (%)
Equipment	1.0	12.8	-8.4	6.5
Public Utility	1.3	13.2	-8.4	6.9
Structures				
Nonresidential	20.8	20.8	11.7	11.7
Structures				
Residential	17.1	17.1	9.3	9.3
Structures				
Intangibles				
Research	-107.6	-107.6	-90.9	-49.2
Advertising	-14.9	-14.9	-8.4	-8.4
Other	-14.9	-14.9	-8.4	-8.4
Total	1.7	7.8	-5.4	3.0

Source: Congressional Research Service. See CRS Report R44638, *Corporate Tax Integration and Tax Reform*, by Jane G. Gravelle; and CRS Report R44242, *The Effect of Base-Broadening Measures on Labor Supply and Investment: Considerations for Tax Reform*, by Jane G. Gravelle and Donald J. Marples, for method of computation and assumptions. The debt share is from Congressional Budget Office estimates. See CBO, *Taxing Capital Income: Effective Marginal Tax Rates Under 2014 Law and Selected Policy Options*, December 2014, at https://www.cbo.gov/publication/49817.

Notes: The corporate statutory rate used for 2017 law is 34.14% to reflect the production activities deduction. The other assumptions and underlying data include a real discount rate for equity of 7%, a nominal interest rate of 7.5%, and an inflation rate of 2%, used in all simulations. The research credit is 11.3% (see CRS Report R44522, *A Patent/Innovation Box as a Tax Incentive for Domestic Research and Development*, by Jane G. Gravelle). Note that these tables do not include land, which is not reproducible, and inventories, whose short lives make them likely relatively insensitive to the rates of return. Both are taxed at rates above the rates for other nonresidential structures (land at the statutory rate and inventories above the statutory rate).

Other Provisions Affecting Location of Investment

In addition to the basic domestic changes affecting investment, and captured in the preceding tables, other elements may affect the tax burdens on domestic relative to foreign investment.

Restrictions on Interest Deductions

One element is the tighter limit on the deductibility of interest. In order to explore how important this issue is, consider the revenue estimate in the first full year of $17.7 billion, which, assuming a 21% tax rate, accounts for 14% of net interest paid, according to the National Income Accounts (calculation excludes financial corporations).[24] The estimate increases about 54% after the income base no longer allows depreciation deductions, and would then be about 20% of interest. This provision thus appears to be significant. If interest is not deductible at the margin, the overall effective tax rates would be similar to the equity rates in *Table 1*. For these firms, the overall effective tax rate of 7.8% would rise to around 11% under the permanent provisions and fall to 3% for the temporary ones.

As a conservative illustration of the possible aggregate effect, *Table 5* shows overall tax rates at a 32% debt share, with 20% of the interest disallowed, which causes the overall tax rate under the new law to rise by about two percentage points relative to the tax rates computed in *Table 4*. The effects would likely be larger because more of the disallowed interest would have marginal effects.

Effects of the International Provisions: Dividend Relief, GILTI, FDII, and BEAT

The international changes will likely affect the choice of investment location, although in a way that is difficult to quantify. The exemption of dividends combined with the deduction for a return on tangible assets under the GILTI will make investing in plants and equipment abroad largely exempt from U.S. tax on foreign-source income through foreign subsidiaries. Most evidence suggests that returns to investment abroad were subject to a relatively small residual rate of around 3%. Thus, moving to a zero rate would not likely create a significant change in tax treatment of foreign earnings, which in prior law are reduced by deferral and cross-crediting.

---

[24] See Table 7.1 of the National Income and Product Accounts, at https://www.bea.gov/iTable/iTable.cfm?reqid=19&step=2#reqid=19&step=3&isuri=1&1921=survey&1903=288.

Table 5. Marginal Effective Tax Rates for Debt- and Equity-Financed Investment, 32% Debt Share, 20% of Interest Disallowed Under New Law

Asset	2017 Law With Bonus Depreciation (%)	2017 Law Without Bonus Depreciation (%)	New Law: Temporary Provisions (%)	New Law: Permanent Provisions (%)
Equipment	1.0	12.8	-6.6	8.0
Public Utility	1.3	13.2	-6.6	8.5
Structures				
Nonresidential	20.8	20.8	11.7	12.3
Residential	17.1	17.1	9.3	10.9
Intangibles				
Research	-107.6	-107.6	-86.3	-45.9
Advertising	-14.9	-14.9	-8.4	-6.6
Other	-14.9	-14.9	-8.4	-6.6
Total	1.7	7.8	-3.6	4.7

Source: Congressional Research Service. See CRS Report R44638, *Corporate Tax Integration and Tax Reform*, by Jane G. Gravelle; and CRS Report R44242, *The Effect of Base-Broadening Measures on Labor Supply and Investment: Considerations for Tax Reform*, by Jane G. Gravelle and Donald J. Marples, for method of computation and assumptions. The debt share is from Congressional Budget Office estimates. See CBO, *Taxing Capital Income: Effective Marginal Tax Rates Under 2014 Law and Selected Policy Options*, December 2014, at https://www.cbo.gov/ publication/49817.

Notes: The corporate statutory rate used for 2017 law is 34.14% to reflect the production activities deduction. The other assumptions and underlying data include a real discount rate for equity of 7%, a nominal interest rate of 7.5%, and an inflation rate of 2%, used in all simulations. The research credit is 11.3% (see CRS Report R44522, *A Patent/Innovation Box as a Tax Incentive for Domestic Research and Development*, by Jane G. Gravelle). Note that these tables do not include land, which is not reproducible, and inventories, whose short lives make them likely relatively insensitive to the rates of return. Both are taxed at rates above the rates for other nonresidential structures (land at the statutory rate and inventories above the statutory rate).

Because of the formula approach to exempting the returns to tangible investments, tangible investments in assets with a lower return than the 10% rate specified will also reduce the scope of GILTI coverage, whereas those with a higher return will subject some of the income from the intangible asset to GILTI. The opposite effect occurs with FDII, where low-yield tangible investments will increase the FDII deduction (by increasing gross income by less than the deemed return), whereas high-yield tangible investments will reduce the FDII deduction.

The international provisions in general are aimed at making the location of intangibles in the United States more attractive than in past law. The returns are subject to the GILTI tax rate on a current basis, a subsidy is allowed for intangibles located in the United States but licensed abroad, and intangible returns earned abroad may also face a current tax without a foreign tax credit under BEAT. However, for economic activity, the concern is where intangibles are created. In this case, intangibles, to the extent they are subject to a lower statutory rate in the United States due to FDII, would experience even higher overall tax burdens through the loss of the benefits from debt finance, given expensing. That is, equity investment is not affected by the lower tax rate with expensing (which is always zero), but the lower tax rate reduces the subsidy for debt, making the overall subsidy smaller (which means a higher burden). With five-year amortization in the case of research and development, the benefit of the lower rate on equity finance would roughly offset the burden of the lower rate on debt.

Although a separate basket for GILTI would have reduced opportunities under the title passage rule to increase the foreign tax credit limit, that rule has been repealed in any case. The loss of tax benefits for exports may also encourage more production abroad.

Effects on the Location of Investment

Overall, it is unlikely that the location of investment will be significantly affected by the tax change. Equity investment in tangible assets, especially the temporary investments for equipment, could increase. These effects are much smaller when debt is included. Moreover, adding intangible assets leads to an even smaller differential. These differences narrow further when restrictions on the deductibility of interest are in effect. (Other international provisions are probably not important to the location of investment.)

The importance of capital flows to the economy would also be limited. First, the corporate capital stock, where the principal effects of the reductions in equity capital would matter, is only a share of the business capital stock, and an even smaller share of the total capital stock in the country (even aside from land). Corporations account for about 55% of tangible business assets and 60% of tangible and intangible assets. Multinational corporations are a subset of that corporate share. Economic forces limit the amount of capital that can be absorbed (which is constrained by labor resources available to combine with production), and in general, capital investments in different locations in the world are imperfect substitutes.[25]

Moreover, it is not clear that the capital stock in the United States would increase. First, debt-finance costs would also rise for the noncorporate sector. Moreover, if debt is more mobile than equity, the corporate-sector capital stock could contract, since lower tax rates, although making equity finance more attractive, make debt finance more costly.[26]

Finally, although the size is likely to be small even though the direction is uncertain, the effects are also likely to be offset by the lowering of corporate rates elsewhere in the world. Such a fall in rates occurred the last time the United States lowered its corporate rate.[27] Moreover, there have been indications of lowered corporate tax rates after the momentum toward a lower corporate tax rate began in the United States. In July 2017, Belgium announced a rate reduction from 33.99% to 25% by 2020. In September, France announced its rate, already planned to fall from 33.33% to 28% by 2020, would be reduced further to 25%.[28] China has adopted a tax holiday for foreign companies investing in certain sectors, Australia is considering a reduction from 30%, and Israel has recently reduced its tax

---

[25] See CRS Report R41743, *International Corporate Tax Rate Comparisons and Policy Implications*, by Jane G. Gravelle, which suggests a small (0.2%) increase in GDP when a change of a similar size is made, without allowing for the possibility of debt finance.

[26] The possibility of lowering the corporate tax rate leading to a reduction in the U.S. capital stock was made by Harry Grubert and John Mutti, "International Aspects of Corporate Tax Integration: The Role of Debt and Equity Flows," *National Tax Journal*, vol. 47, no. 1 (1994), pp. 111-133.

[27] See CRS Report R41743, *International Corporate Tax Rate Comparisons and Policy Implications*, by Jane G. Gravelle.

[28] Amanda Athanasiou, "Big Banks Detail Costs and Benefits of Tax Reform," *Tax Notes International*, February 19, 2019, pp. 741-744.

rate from 24% to 23% and possibly more in the future.[29] Germany has agreed to phase out a 5.5% surtax on corporate and individual income.[30]

Effects on Efficiency and Optimality

Will the tax change lead to a more efficient or optimal system? Generally, efficiency refers to rules that will maximize worldwide welfare, which requires allocating capital to its best uses. That objective, in turn, requires that investments face the same tax rate so that they equalize their pre-tax returns. Optimality would require the same rules if maximizing world welfare, but different rules would apply in maximizing U.S. welfare. The method that produces efficiency is called *capital export neutrality*, whereas the method that produces optimal treatment for outbound investment is called *national neutrality*.[31]

Referencing the CBO study cited earlier, investment in equipment was already favored in the United States relative to the rest of the world, and the tax changes increase that favoritism, particularly in the case of expensing, where the overall marginal tax rate is negative. In the case of buildings, however, the United States had higher tax rates than other countries, and lowering the rates moved toward more efficiency. Note that the international comparisons use a representative asset, and the nonresidential structures category in the previous tables is a composite. Considering industrial and commercial buildings that tax rate is approximately the statutory rate, so that buildings tax rates on equity would fall from around 35% to 21% (plus about 4 percentage points for state and local taxes), which would bring them to a 25% rate, which is very close to the remaining G-20 average for equity-financed buildings of 23.8%.

Optimal rules differ for outbound and inbound capital. For outbound capital (investments of U.S. firms abroad), taxes should be imposed by allowing a deduction for foreign taxes paid so that the return received by

---

[29] Mindy Herzfeld, "Competition or Coordination: Responses to the Tax Cuts and Jobs Act," *Tax Notes International*, January 15, 2018, pp. 209-212.

[30] Stephanie Soong Johnston, "German Leader Vows No Tax Hikes, Wins Backing for Coalition Deal," *Worldwide Tax Daily*, February 27, 2018.

[31] See CRS Report RL34115, *Reform of U.S. International Taxation: Alternatives*, by Jane G. Gravelle, for a detailed discussion of the efficiency and optimality issues.

the United States (whether in the form of profits or taxes on profits) from domestic versus foreign investments is equalized. Moving to a largely territorial tax for investments in tangible assets would move further from that optimal goal. For inbound investment (investments by foreigners in the United States), the optimal tax is 1/E, where E is the elasticity of capital inflow with respect to the after-tax rate of return. That rate maximizes the benefit for the United States from foreign investors. Setting a lower tax rate might induce more equity capital, but it would also reduce the amount of tax collected in the United States (the earnings from the investment accrue to foreigners). For equity, the elasticity is probably less, around two, so the optimal tax is around 50%.[32] Since the effective tax was already below this optimal rate, lowering it further will likely lead to a less optimal system. In the case of debt, however, the system moves toward a more optimal one. The optimal tax rate on inbound investment is never less than zero, and by reducing the subsidy for debt, the system moves closer to an optimal one, even if the elasticity of debt inflows is infinitely large.

There are also welfare gains for the United States aside from international considerations that arise largely from the corporate rate reduction, due to the reduction of subsidies for debt, which also brings overall tax rates across asset types closer together.

In sum, therefore, as in the case of investment, the effects on efficiency and optimality are mixed, with gains in some cases and losses in others.

---

[32] An elasticity is a percentage change in quantity divided by a percentage change in price. For a substitution elasticity it is the percentage change in relative quantities divided by the percentage changes in relative prices. For a review of the empirical evidence on the elasticity of substitution between domestic and foreign capital with respect to the after-tax rate of return, indicating that the value is around 3, see Jennifer C. Gravelle, *Corporate Tax Incidence, Review of General Equilibrium Estimates and Analysis: Working Paper 2010-03*, Congressional Budget Office, May 20, 2010, at https://www.cbo.gov/publication/21486. To transform a substitution elasticity that considers the relative quantities (dKd/Kd –dKf/Kf) where the first term is the percentage change in domestic capital and the second the percentage change in foreign capital stock, into an elasticity for the percentage change in the domestic capital stock, multiply by the foreign share of the worldwide capital stock, estimated to be approximately 70%, leading to an elasticity of 2.

A Note on Cash Flow, Employee Bonuses, Investment, and Stock Buybacks

There were news reports at the end of 2017 and early in 2018 that companies were using the tax cut to increase employees' pay, primarily in bonuses.[33]

Economic theory suggests that the availability of cash, whether from the tax cut or from access to funds held abroad, should not lead to increased pay directly.[34] Since employee compensation is deductible, it is not affected by the change in the tax rate or cash flow, and a firm that is maximizing profits should pay its workers the same amount regardless of the tax rate or cash on hand. There is, however, an advantage in making planned pay raises while the 35% rate is still in effect (the lower rate applies for tax years beginning after December 31, 2017, and not all firms have tax years that match the calendar year, so some bonuses paid in 2018 would also be deductible at the higher rate). Other explanations that have been made for the announced pay increases are that pay raises were already planned due to a tightening labor market (and new minimum-wage increases going into effect in 2018) and that tying them to the tax cut was a public relations measure (especially as many of the firms are in industries that are heavily regulated by the government).[35]

Employee wages could increase if investment increases the capital stock. Cash should not directly affect investment unless the firms were previously liquidity constrained, and U.S. firms in general already had large cash reserves as well as access to low-cost debt. Any effects on wages should come from the incentives to invest in the United States, an effect that happens slowly and, as indicated earlier, may be relatively small.

---

[33] See, for example, Adam Shell, "List of Companies That Paid Bonuses or Boosted Pay," *USA Today*, January 11, 2018. This article identifies about $870 million in one-time bonuses. See also data posted on the Americans for Fair Taxation, which is tracking bonuses, stock buybacks, and other spending, at https://americansfortaxfairness.org/ trumptaxcuttruths/.

[34] See Alan D. Viard, "Economic Effects of the Corporate Rate Reduction," *Tax Notes*, March 5, 2015, pp. 1393-1406.

[35] Martha White, "Companies Are Announcing Raises and Bonuses, But is Trump's Tax Plan the Reason?" *NBC News*, January 23, 2018, at https://www.nbcnews.com/business/business-news/companies-are-announcing-raisesbonuses-trump-s-tax-plan-reason-n839871.

There is some evidence that much of the tax cut and cash flow is being used to repurchase shares, an action equivalent to paying dividends. Statistical studies following the 2004 repatriation holiday found that most of the repatriation was used for this purpose.[36] According to one source, firms have repurchased $290 billion in stock (compared to $6.7 billion in bonuses),[37] and financial analysts have estimated buybacks in 2018 of $650 billion and $800 billion.[38] Paying dividends or repurchasing shares is consistent with what economic theory suggests in the short term, that a tax cut would benefit shareholders. To the extent the cut induces investment, it would occur over time.

Profit Shifting

Two methods used to recognize more profit in low-tax jurisdictions than economic reality suggests are increased leveraging in high-tax countries and use of transfer pricing, primarily of intangible assets such as drug formulas, technological advances, and trademarks.

To shift profits through leveraging, firms locate their debt in high-tax countries, including the United States. This technique involves both U.S.

---

[36] See CRS Report R40178, *Tax Cuts on Repatriation Earnings as Economic Stimulus: An Economic Analysis*, by Donald J. Marples and Jane G. Gravelle.

[37] As of mid-February 2018, $170 billion in buybacks were announced. See Patti Domm, Market Insider, CNBC, February 15, 2018, at https://www.cnbc.com/2018/02/15/companies-buying-back-stock-at-record-pace-since-trumptax-bill-may-aid-markets-comeback.html. For the $290 billion figure and a list, see "More Than $290 Billion in Share Buybacks," Senate Democrats, at https://www.democrats.senate.gov/goptaxscam (site visited May 1, 2018). See also *Americans for Tax Fairness, Trump Tax Cut Truths*, https://americansfortaxfairness.org/trumptaxcuttruths/; Matt Egan, "Goldman Sachs Warns Against Falling in Love with Stock Buybacks," *CNN Money*, April 26, 2018, http://money.cnn.com/2018/04/26/investing/stock-buybacks-goldman-sachs/index.html.

[38] These estimates are from Goldman Sachs and J. P. Morgan. See Jeff Cox, "Companies Projected to Use Tax Cut Windfall for Record Share Buybacks, JP Morgan Says," *CNBC*, March 2, 2018, at https://www.cnbc.com/2018/03/02/ companies-projected-to-use-tax-cut-for-record-share-buybacks-jp-morgan.html. A survey of Morgan Stanley analysts predicted that firms would use 43% of the tax cut for buybacks and dividends, 19% for mergers and acquisitions, 17% for investment, and 13% for bonuses. See Editorial Board, "Well-Heeled Investors Reap the Republican Tax Cut Bonanza," *New York Times*, February 25, 2018, at https://www.nytimes.com/2018/02/25/opinion/investors-republican-tax-cut.html.

multinational firms locating their debt in the United States rather than abroad and foreign parents of U.S. subsidiaries locating debt in their U.S. subsidiaries.

The second method of profit shifting is through transfer pricing methods that determine the price associated with a transfer of goods and assets. The standard for transfer pricing is that goods and assets bought and sold between related firms should reflect arm's length pricing, that is, the price that would be paid by two unrelated firms. If a U.S. firm sells a good or asset to its foreign subsidiary for a price that is too low, profit in the United States is reduced and profit abroad is increased. Most of the transfer pricing issues arise due to intangible assets that are often unique, so there is not a market to observe arm's length prices. A variety of different methods are used to determine transfer prices. When an intangible asset is transferred abroad (such as the right to sell a mobile phone or to sell advertising for a search engine), there is sometimes a buy-in payment by the foreign subsidiary, followed by cost-sharing payments. The subsidiary pays for a share of the research costs in the United States in return for a share of the rights (to future technological advances).

Estimates have suggested that leveraging is responsible for about 25% of profit shifting, and pricing of intangibles is responsible for the remaining 75%.[39]

Profit shifting would likely be reduced with a lower tax rate. As noted earlier, the U.S. statutory tax rate was higher than the average rate weighted by GDP in the OECD countries, 27%, and the G20 countries, 28%. Lowering the U.S. rate to 21% and adding about five percentage points for state and local taxes (the additional state tax rate slightly higher than the 4% in prior law because of the lower saving from the federal deduction with the lower federal rate) places the U.S. statutory rate close to the middle of other countries, at least at current foreign tax rates. Most profit shifting is estimated to be associated with low-tax or no-tax

[39] Jost H. Heckemeyer and Michael Overesch, *Multinationals' Profit Response to Tax Differentials: Effect Size and Shifting Channels*, Center for European Economic Research, Discussion Paper 13-045, July 2013, at http://ftp.zew.de/ pub/zew-docs/dp/dp13045.pdf.

countries where profits of multinationals are out of line with the size of the country.[40] In that case, rate reduction alone might not affect profit shifting.

Based on estimates of elasticities of profit location based on tax rate, the rate reduction alone restores between 0.5% and 5% of profits in the United States.[41] Since the revenue lost directly from the rate cut (given the corporate alternative minimum tax was repealed) was about 35% of profits, if the primary objective of the rate cut was to address profit shifting, the rate cut costs more than the potential revenue gain, by some estimates much more.

Other provisions would also affect profit shifting, although some are more difficult to quantify. They include the thin capitalization rules and BEAT for leveraging, and GILTI, FDII, and BEAT for transfer pricing. If the rate reduction may be termed a "carrot" (a tax cut to induce less profit shifting), FDII would also be a carrot, whereas the remaining provisions could be termed "sticks" (tax increases to reduce profit shifting).

FDII therefore can be seen as the same as a rate cut but applicable only to domestic income and in proportion to exports. As an additional rate reduction it appears to be only around a percentage point (based on the size of revenue effects), although it would be more significant for exporters and for firms that have a lot of intangibles, as is its objective (to provide a similar tax rate on the return to intangibles in foreign and domestic locations).

GILTI is the other half of the base erosion provisions designed to encourage intangibles to remain in the United States and might be more effective per dollar of gain, because it has a very direct effect of raising taxes for firms that operate largely in tax havens (although the effect would be

---

[40] See CRS Report R40623, *Tax Havens: International Tax Avoidance and Evasion*, by Jane G. Gravelle, for a discussion.

[41] An elasticity is the percentage change in quantity divided by the percentage change in price, although the elasticities used here are semi-elasticities measuring the percentage change in quantity divided by the absolute change in the tax rate. These estimates represent a range of effects from studies: an elasticity of 1.848 with current profit shifting accounting for 19% of profits, an elasticity of 1.41 with a share of profits at 15%, and an elasticity of 0.8 with a share of profits at 5%. The formula for measuring the effects is EdtS, where E is the elasticity, dt is the tax change (set at 0.14), and S is the current share of U.S. profits being shifted, consistent with the elasticities. See Jane Gravelle, "Policy Options to Address Profit Shifting: Carrots or Sticks?" *Tax Notes*, July 4, 2016, pp. 121-134.

more targeted with a per-country foreign tax credit limit). Although there is still a gap between the tax rate under FDII and under GILTI (if a firm operated solely in a no-tax jurisdiction, its rate abroad would be 10.5% on an additional amount of profit shifted, whereas it would be 13.125% in the United States, with these rates rising to 13.125% and 16.406% after 2025) assuming both investments were to serve foreign markets.

If firms were investing abroad to manufacture and export to the United States as compared to manufacturing and selling in the United States, the GILTI rate would be considerably below the standard corporate tax rate of 21% (as the FDII would not come into play, and BEAT does not cover cost of goods sold).

The movement of intangibles and their associated profits might take some time, as moving existing intangibles back to the United States would incur a tax (a provision allowing those assets tax-free status was in the Senate bill but was eliminated in conference).[42]

Both the tightening in the thin capitalization rules and the inclusion of interest payments in the BEAT would limit the amount of profit shifting that might be achieved through interest deductions. A more effective method (although perhaps one with certain administrative challenges) may be to allocate interest within firms in a multinational group in proportion to the firm's share of earnings or assets. This provision was included in both the House and Senate bills but dropped in conference.

Overall, it appears the new provisions have taken significant steps to reduce the incentives for profit shifting.

Repatriation

The prior law's application of the deferral principle allowed a firm to delay taxation of its earnings in foreign-incorporated subsidiaries until the income was paid as a dividend to the U.S. parent company. This tax contributed to U.S. companies holding an estimated $2.6 trillion in

---

[42] For further discussion, see Isabel Gottlieb, "Will Tax Reform Bring Back Patents?" Bloomberg BNA *Daily Tax Report*, January 19, 2018.

unrepatriated earnings that could not be directly used for U.S. operations.[43] Concerns were raised that the inability to use these funds could reduce U.S. economic growth and job creation. As noted earlier in the discussion of investment location, however, the holding of funds abroad was unlikely to affect domestic investment.

After the assessment of the deemed repatriation tax in the 2017 tax revision, U.S. companies will have unrestricted access to previously unrepatriated funds. In addition, future overseas earnings will generally not be taxed when repatriated to the United States as a result of the dividend exemption.[44]

Inversions

Corporate inversions occur when U.S. firms reorganize their structure so that the "parent" element of the group is a foreign corporation rather than a corporation chartered in the United States. A main objective of these transactions is U.S. tax savings, and they involved little to no shift in actual economic activity. These tax benefits included earnings stripping in the U.S. operation (in part by leveraging), future operation under a territorial system, and finding ways to effectively repatriate earnings of foreign subsidiaries. Since 2004, U.S. policy (both enacted law and regulations) has attempted to limit the benefits of inversion transactions.

The anti-inversion provisions in the 2017 tax revision significantly reduce the tax incentives available for newly inverted firms, especially in the next 10 years, when inversion triggers a retroactive taxation of deemed repatriations at a 35% rate, rather than rates of 8% and 15.5%. After that time, the base erosion tax on cost of goods sold, the downward attribution rules, and the taxation of dividends to individual shareholders at ordinary rates make inversions less attractive. The restrictions on interest deductions

---

[43] Institute on Taxation and Economic Policy (ITEP), "Fortune 500 Companies Hold a Record $2.6 Trillion Offshore," March 28, 2017, https://itep.org/fortune-500-companies-hold-a-record-26-trillion-offshore/.

[44] Portfolio investment will remain subject to U.S. tax when repatriated.

under the tightened thin capitalization rules make loading the U.S. firm with debt less feasible, although there are currently regulations aimed at inverted companies that treat some related party debt as equity. These regulations are, however, scheduled for review and could be changed, potentially making the thin capitalization rules more important as an anti-inversion measure.

Other provisions in the new law would also make U.S. headquarters more attractive, including the lower corporate rate, the move to a territorial tax to the extent of the dividend exclusion, and FDII, although GILTI and BEAT would make a U.S. location less attractive.

Issues with International Agreements: Tax Treaties, WTO, and OECD Minimum Standards

Several legal scholars and practitioners have pointed out conflicts between the new law and current international agreements.[45] This section summarizes the current agreements and that debate.

Current Agreements Bilateral Tax Treaties

The United States has bilateral tax treaties with approximately 65 countries that are intended to reduce the incidence of double taxation and

---

[45] See David Kamin et al., *The Games They Will Play: Tax Games, Roadblocks, and Glitches Under the New Legislation*, December 7, 2017, at https://papers.ssrn.com/sol3/papers.cfm?abstract_id=3084187 and *The Games They Will Play: An Update on the Conference Committee Tax Bill*, at https://papers.ssrn.com/sol3/papers.cfm?abstract_id=3089423; Reuven Avi-Yonah, *Beat It: Tax Reform and Tax Treaties*, University of Michigan Public Law and Legal Theory Research Paper No. 587, January 2018, at https://papers.ssrn.com/sol3/papers.cfm?abstract_id=3096879, and *The Elephant Always Forgets, Tax Reform and the WTO*, University of Michigan, Public Law and Legal Theory Research Paper No. 585, January 18, 2018, at https://papers.ssrn.com/sol3/papers.cfm?abstract_id=3095349; Alison Bennett, "Legislation Raises Tax Treaty Concerns for U.S. Multinationals," Bloomberg BNA, *Daily Tax Report*, December 14, 2017; Joe Kirwin, "EU Contemplates WTO Challenge to U.S. Tax Reform," Bloomberg BNA, *Daily Tax Report*, December 22, 2017; Stephanie Soong Johnston, "EU Commission Mulls 'All Options" in Wake of Final U.S. Tax Bill," *Worldwide Tax Daily*, December 26, 2017; Bret Wells, "Get With The Beat," *Tax Notes*, February 19, 2018, pp. 1023-1032; J. P. Finet, "WTO Challenges to Tax Reform's International Provisions Likely," *Tax Notes International*, December 11, 2017.

prevent tax evasion.[46] Under these treaties, residents (not necessarily citizens) of foreign countries are taxed at a reduced rate, or are exempt from U.S. taxes on certain items of income they receive from sources within the United States. These reduced rates and exemptions vary among countries and specific items of income. Under these same treaties, residents or citizens of the United States are taxed at a reduced rate, or are exempt from foreign taxes, on certain items of income they receive from sources within foreign countries. Treaties contain a number of provisions affecting the sourcing and taxation of profits.

World Trade Organization (WTO)

The WTO, established in 1995, succeeded the General Agreement on Tariffs and Trade (GATT, established in 1947), which was created to foster an open international framework. The WTO provides a mechanism to settle disputes on practices that affect trade.

The United States had, in the past, a dispute over a series of tax provisions that were struck by GATT and then the WTO as prohibited export subsidies. The first provision was found to be a prohibited provision and was replaced by a second that was in turn found to be prohibited, then replaced by a third, also found illegal (the Domestic International Sales Corporation, or DISC, enacted in 1971; the Foreign Sales Corporation, or FSC, enacted in 1984; and the Extraterritorial Income regime, or ETI, enacted in 2000). Following the last finding, where countries could have levied countervailing tariffs, the ETI provisions were repealed (in 2004).

Organization for Economic Cooperation and Development (OECD)

Although the OECD (with a membership of 34 countries) has no special authority, the United States is a party to the organization, which provides many standards for tax practices, such as transfer pricing. Recently, the OECD has engaged in a project to reduce base erosion and

[46] For a list of countries with which the United States has income tax treaties, see https://www.irs.gov/businesses/international-businesses/united-states-income-tax-treaties-a-to-z.

profit shifting (BEPS).[47] One hundred and two countries including the United States have agreed to four minimum standards, one of which is countering harmful tax practices, a standard primarily aimed at patent boxes (regimes that provide lower tax rates on income from intellectual property).

The New Law: Issues with Tax Treaties, WTO, and the OECD BEPS Agreement

Tax Treaties and BEAT

There is some disagreement over whether BEAT violates tax treaties. The primary reason such a violation might occur involves nondiscrimination rules, which require the same deductions be allowed to residents and nonresidents, and might apply because BEAT taxes payments to foreign related partners but not domestic ones. However, BEAT does not disallow deductions but rather includes them in a minimum tax base, leaving this issue uncertain. In addition, it is unclear what sort of action could be taken, at least by EU member states, whose tax laws are constrained by EU agreements.

WTO, FDII, and BEAT

There is considerably more agreement that FDII is also a prohibited export subsidy under the WTO. There are also some technical reasons to see parts of BEAT as inconsistent with the WTO as a tax on imports. BEAT excludes cost of goods sold, but includes imports of depreciable property and costs of goods sold for firms that invert. These latter instances may be so rare or so unlikely (i.e., if the law virtually ends inversions) that the practical consequence could be limited.

OECD Standards and FDII

One of the minimum standards agreed to by the United States was countering harmful tax practices, including patent boxes located in

[47] See CRS Report R44900, *Base Erosion and Profit Shifting (BEPS): OECD Tax Proposals*, by Jane G. Gravelle.

countries where the activities to create intangibles were not performed. The regime created by FDII could be viewed as in conflict with that agreement, since there is no connection to the economic activity creating the income being located in the United States. According to Douglas Poms, Treasury's international tax counsel, the OECD's Forum on Harmful Tax Practices will soon assess whether FDII violates the minimum standard for preferential regimes.[48]

CONCERNS AND OPTIONS IN THE NEW TAX FRAMEWORK

During consideration of the tax legislation and after its enactment, numerous issues have been raised about the general system and about specific aspects of the new law, including GILTI, FDII, BEAT, and other provisions. This section discusses some of the more technical issues within the framework of the new law, but some lawmakers have proposed more basic changes. Representative Doggett and Senator Whitehouse each introduced a bill entitled the "No Tax Break for Outsourcing Act" on February 27, 2018 (H.R. 5108, S. 2459), which would increase the GILTI rate to 21%, eliminate the deduction for the return on tangible assets, treat foreign corporations that are managed and controlled in the United States as domestic corporations, treat inverted firms as U.S. firms when the shareholders of the former U.S. company own more than 50% of the shares, and limit interest deductions in the United States to the proportionate share of the firm's assets.[49] The last proposal (to allocate worldwide interest) was in both the House and Senate versions of H.R. 1 (in somewhat different form) but was not retained in the final legislation.

[48] Ryan Finley, "Online Platform Users Shouldn't Create a PE, US Official Says," *Worldwide Tax Daily*, March 28, 2018.

[49] See https://doggett.house.gov/media-center/press-releases/rep-doggett-sen-whitehouse-introduce-bill-end-tax-breaksexporting-jobs. The allocation of interest in H.R. 5108 and S. 2459 is based on the U.S. domestic corporation's share of worldwide earnings before interest, taxes, depreciation, and amortization (EBITDA).

Many of the issues discussed in this section have been raised by many individuals discussing different aspects of the bill, both in conferences and in individual articles.[50]

General Issues in the Move to a Territorial Tax and the Dividend Deduction

Some critics have expressed general concerns about the overall system and the move to a territorial tax that treats operations and owners differently.[51] The dividend deduction applies only to income of businesses organized as foreign corporations and not to branches. At the same time, elements of the new law make it costlier to incorporate a new business. The elimination of the active trade or business exception in Section 367(a)(3) of the tax code taxes transfers of assets used in a foreign branch (and increases recognition of gain when incorporating branches with losses). The additions of goodwill, going concern value, and workforce in

---

[50] Although some specific issues have particular references (including a number of articles from various publications by *Tax Analysts* reporting on tax conferences), the following are general sources for many of the points discussed in this section. Two reports coauthored by 13 law professors appeared during the course of the debate and after the conference report: David Kamin et al., *The Games They Will Play: Tax Games, Roadblocks, and Glitches Under the New Legislation*, December 7, 2017, at https://papers.ssrn.com/sol3/papers.cfm?abstract_id=3084187, and *The Games They Will Play: An Update on the Conference Committee Tax Bill*, at https://papers.ssrn.com/sol3/papers.cfm?abstract_id= 3089423; Reuven Avi-Yonah, *Beat It: Tax Reform and Treaties*, University of Michigan Public Law Research Paper No. 587, March 22, 2018, at https://papers.ssrn.com/sol3/papers.cfm? abstract_id=3096879. A conference held by the International Tax Policy Forum and Institute and Georgetown Laws Institute for International Economic Law, "Can an Internationally Competitive Tax Protect Its Tax Base?" on February 2, 2018, featured many experts in international tax law who commented on the new tax regime. Some of the slides are posted at https://www.itpf.org/conferences.

[51] This discussion summarizes comments made in Mindy Herzfeld, "How Some Taxpayers Got Cut Out of The Tax Cuts and Jobs Act," *Tax Notes International*, January 22, 2018, pp. 277-281. It does not cover some of the narrower and technical points made, especially with respect to the tax treatment of foreign investors. The treatment of individuals under GILTI is also discussed in Martin Sullivan, "More GILTI than You Thought," *Tax Notes*, February 12, 2018, pp. 587-592.

place to the definition of intangibles and the increased IRS authority over transfer pricing will increase the value of assets being transferred.[52]

In addition, the system treats individual owners of foreign corporations and portfolio investors differently from corporations with 10% ownership. There is no deduction for dividends because the provision was enacted as an expansion of the intercorporate dividend deduction, although the repatriation tax applies to corporate and individual shareholders that have at least one U.S. corporate shareholder owning 10% of the firm. Thus individuals pay the repatriation tax, which can be viewed as a transition tax to move to a system with the deduction, although they do not benefit from dividend deduction.

GILTI is treated as Subpart F income so it will be imposed on individual shareholders, without the indirect foreign tax credits; in addition, they do not get the GILTI deduction, and income is taxed at ordinary rates (although in some cases they would be eligible for lower rates on qualified dividends). They are also not eligible for a FDII deduction.[53]

The sale of stock will not be eligible for a dividend deduction, so firms may be encouraged to sell the underlying assets abroad to be eligible for the lower GILTI rate.[54]

At the same time, at least with respect to the dividend deduction, the individual shareholder is the final taxpayer, whereas a corporation's earnings from abroad would be taxed again to shareholders if distributed as a dividend.

One technical point relating to the dividend relief proposal is that the legislation did not change the rules treating as a deemed distribution when CFC stock is pledged as security on a loan of the U.S. firm, or when the

[52] See Alexander Lewis, "U.S. Tax Reform Bill's International Provisions Require Quick Action, Practitioners Say," *Tax Notes Today*, December 19, 2017.

[53] As with Subpart F, individuals are required to include GILTI but can't get the foreign tax credit. There are some restructuring possibilities or elections that may provide individuals with tax reductions. See Sandra P. McGill et al., "GILTI Rules Particularly Onerous for Non-C Corporation CFC Shareholders," McDermott, *Will & Emery*, January 30, 2018, at https://www.mwe.com/en/thought-leadership/publications/2018/01/gilti-rules-particularly-onerous-noncorporation.

[54] Alexander Lewis, "Taxpayers Should Prepare Now for GILTI and FDII," *Worldwide Tax Daily*, January 29, 2018.

CFC directly guarantees the loan. In that case, such income would be subject to tax, although an actual dividend would be deductible. This provision was included in the House and Senate bill but not in the final legislation.[55]

GILTI

GILTI has been criticized by some for being too harsh and by some as not capturing enough income.

Perhaps the major concern that GILTI is too harsh involves the foreign tax credit. The law retains the existing rules for the allocation of deductions for purposes of the foreign tax credit limit. These rules allocate interest, R&D spending, and overhead to a narrowed GILTI foreign tax credit basket (which excludes a variety of foreign-source income, including royalties that may be associated with domestic research and development). Allocating too many deductions to foreign-source income can cause GILTI to apply at a higher rate than 13.125%. In addition, there is no foreign tax credit carryback or carryforward, so that unused foreign tax credits are lost, and no credits are allowed for loss CFCs.[56] CFCs with losses also lose the tangible asset return exclusion, as well as foreign tax credits, and foreign tax credits of other CFCs are reduced to the extent that the loss offsets another CFC's income.[57]

Another criticism is that interest is offset first against deemed tangible income, so if a firm borrows to buy an intangible asset and has some net

---

[55] Winston and Strawn LLP, "Tax Reform: Impact on Lending," January 16, 2018, at https://www.winston.com/en/thought-leadership/tax-reform-impact-on-lending.html.

[56] In addition to being discussed in the general sources mentioned earlier, many of these points about GILTI are made by Martin Sullivan, "More GILTI than You Thought," *Tax Notes*, February 12, 2018, pp. 587-592. Sullivan also notes that the GILTI deduction is reduced when GILTI and FDII exceed taxable income. Sullivan's objective in the article appeared to be explaining these features of GILTI rather than necessarily suggesting revisions. Others have made the point that the taxable income limit is to prevent GILTI and FDII deductions from sheltering other taxable income. See Lee Sheppard, "News Analysis: International Clawbacks and Minimum Taxes in Tax Reform," *Tax Notes*, January 1, 2018.

[57] Alexander Lewis, "Taxpayers Should Prepare Now for GILTI and FDII," *Worldwide Tax Daily*, January 29, 2018.

tangible income, the expense reduces the exemption and is, in effect, not deductible. An alternative would be to allocate interest in proportion to the shares of tangible deemed income and overall income before interest deductions.

Many critics note that GILTI income is not focused on intangible income but on any residual income not associated with tangible property, and thus captures excess profits, along with income from finance or insurance.

Another issue is the basing of tangible property on cost less depreciation rather than fair market value. The depreciation rules in that case provide for slower recovery than those used for domestic equipment (although they are similar for structures), but basis is not adjusted for inflation, so it seems more likely that tangible property will be undervalued, making the tangible exemption too small. Using cost minus depreciation does, however, avoid disputes over fair market value.

Others argue that GILTI could be made stronger. Unlike some earlier proposals for a minimum tax to limit profit shifting under a territorial tax, which were to be imposed on a per country basis, GILTI allows cross-crediting over all countries, which can help shield income from the U.S. tax. Cross-crediting creates incentives to blend operations in high-tax and low-tax countries. Under cross-crediting, if a firm is paying tax, there is an incentive to shift operations from the United States to a country with a similar tax rate to generate foreign tax credits to shield income potentially taxable under GILTI.[58] That is, under these circumstances, investment in intangible assets abroad is subsidized.

Another criticism of GILTI is that the 10.5% tax rate would still apply to operations in a zero-taxrate country, and to match the FDII rate, the tax rate should be set at 13.125% as a method to protect the U.S. tax base. (These rates apply initially, but subsequently the rate should be set at 16.406%.)

---

[58] This incentive was pointed out early in the tax debate. Gene B. Sperling, "How Trump's Corporate-Tax Plan Could Send American Jobs Overseas," *The Atlantic*, November 1, 2017, at https://www.theatlantic.com/business/archive/2017/12/tax-jobs-overseas/547916/?wpmm=1&wpisrc=nl_daily202.

Others have argued that the deemed return on tangible income may be too high and is fixed rather than variable. Thus, it cannot reflect inflation or variations in real interest rates. An alternative is to set the rate at a riskless return plus a fixed risk premium. Another concern about the tangible investment exemption is that it will encourage low-margin tangible investments to move abroad to generate additional GILTI deductions, which might support setting the deemed return rate lower.

Finally, given the criticisms of FDII (with respect to violating the WTO), incentives to locate abroad could also be offset by eliminating both the GILTI and FDII deduction, while allowing a 100% foreign tax credit. Or, alternatively, FDII could be eliminated, and the foreign tax credits allowed for GILTI could be in proportion to the share of income taxed (i.e., 50% of foreign taxes allowed with a 50% deduction, and 62.5% allowed when the exclusion is 37.5%), so a residual tax would apply whenever the foreign tax rate was less than the U.S. corporate rate.

Some other, more technical issues have also been raised about GILTI.[59] One issue is that there is not a clear allocation method for attributing foreign taxes to GILTI income.[60]

Options for Revision

Most of the revisions that might respond to criticisms are relatively straightforward, such as allowing foreign tax credit carryforwards (including for loss CFCs), allowing the same level of exemptions for GILTI as for FDII, apportioning interest deductions based on the share of tangible earnings, imputing income for tangible assets with a riskless return plus a risk premium, or disallowing GILTI and FDII deductions altogether or disallowing FDII and reducing foreign tax credits under

---

[59] Elizabeth J. Stevens and H. David Rosen, "GILTI Pleasures," *Worldwide Tax Daily*, February 28, 2018, express concern that the statute does not appear to assign the gross-up of taxes (taxes added back to after-tax income to produce after-tax income) to the GILTI basket. Andrew Velarde, "Is Treasury Reconsidering Interest Limitation Role on GILTI?" *Tax Notes International*, February 12, 2018, p. 663 suggests that the law is unclear about interaction between the interest limitation and whether it applies to CFCs for determining GILTI.

[60] See Lee Sheppard, "News Analysis: International Clawbacks and Minimum Taxes in Tax Reform," *Tax Notes*, January 1, 2018.

GILTI. Others, such as apportioning deduction allocations across the relevant foreign tax credit baskets, using a per country limit, or valuing tangible assets at market value, may represent administrative and policy challenges.

FDII

FDII has attracted considerable criticism because it appears likely to violate WTO rules, to the point that some have recommended it be eliminated altogether. As noted above, the same relative tax treatment at home and abroad can be obtained by eliminating both the GILTI and FDII deductions.

Commentary has pointed to mechanisms for a firm to increase the benefits of FDII, such as round tripping (selling abroad to an independent firm and then reimporting products), selling unfinished goods to foreign manufacturers, or buying goods from a foreign supplier for resale abroad. It might also be possible to sell to an unrelated foreign firm with advertising and marketing requirements and price restrictions to accomplish round tripping. A firm could also buy from a foreign supplier for resale abroad.

FDII also encourages more high-margin tangible investment in the United States to increase the base for FDII (just as GILTI encourages low-margin manufacturing abroad). At the same time, FDII would be available to firms with no manufacturing or employees in the United States.

As indicated above, one of the major concerns about FDII is that it would probably violate the WTO rules against export subsidies. FDII might also be viewed abroad as a harmful tax regime (similar to some patent boxes), although it might be noted that its objective is to remove tax as a factor in locating intellectual property, as is the case of the OECD BEPS-compliant patent boxes. However, FDII has a mechanical rule rather than being based on transfer pricing and no nexus requirement (i.e., no direct connection against the cost of developing the intangible and revenue, and thus may be noncompliant).[61] Germany also has a provision for a royalty barrier that disallows a deduction for royalties paid to related firms that benefit from noncompliant patent box regimes.[62] Loss of a deduction for royalties would more than offset the benefit of FDII in that case.

Options for Revision

As noted under the discussion of GILTI, the potential for FDII violating WTO as an export subsidy had already led some observers to argue that FDII should never have been enacted. Bringing together tax rates for U.S. and foreign locations could also be reached by eliminating both the FDII and GILTI deductions, as noted in the section on GILTI. If GILTI were also imposed on a per-country basis, the incentive for locating intangibles abroad rather than in the United States would largely be eliminated, especially now that the United States has tax rates at or below those of most developed countries. Revenues might be used for other purposes (for example, allowing intangibles to be brought back to the United States without paying tax, a provision originally contained in the Senate version of H.R. 1). A related option would be to restrict both GILTI and FDII treatment to tax havens or low-tax countries.

Another option is to make FDII elective so that if U.S. firms face retaliation from countries denying royalty deductions, they could have an option to forgo the deduction (an election that is country-by-country would provide more flexibility).

Proposals introduced in the past to move to a territorial system would have provided reduced rates on royalties, which may or may not violate the BEPS agreement, but probably would not have been viewed as an export subsidy. They were proposed for a different purpose, to provide relief from firms that had formerly shielded active royalties from the U.S. tax through excess foreign tax credits, based on the expectation that foreign tax credits

---

[61] "Taxpayers Should Prepare Now for GILTI and FDII," *Worldwide Tax Daily*, January 29, 2018. For a discussion of the OECD BEPS initiative, see CRS Report R44900, *Base Erosion and Profit Shifting (BEPS): OECD Tax Proposals*, by Jane G. Gravelle. Note that the United States agreed to four minimum BEPS standards, among them harmful tax practices, which would include patent boxes.

[62] Robert Goulder, "Achtung! U.S. Tax Reform Stumbles Over German Royalty Barrier," *Tax Notes International*, January 22, 2018, pp. 375-378.

would largely disappear. Since the United States retains significant taxation abroad with foreign tax credits, one option would be to add active royalties back to the foreign tax credit basket that contains GILTI income.

Finally, FDII relies, as does GILTI and BEAT, on a formulaic treatment. Formulas simplify the tax law and reduce disputes with the tax authorities, but a move away from a formulaic treatment might allow FDII to be redesigned to be BEPS compliant by establishing nexus. And if it were limited to royalties it might also avoid violating both BEPS and WTO.

BEAT

BEAT was aimed at profit shifting out of the United States via outbound payments and may be seen as particularly targeted to U.S. subsidiaries of foreign parents (although it applies to any related firm payments). For example, a U.S. subsidiary of a foreign parent might pay excessively large royalties for rights to use intangible assets as well as higher than arm's length prices for goods and services, while also having more of the debt and interest deductions, all with the objective of minimizing income subject to U.S. tax (which was perhaps a greater issue when the United States had a 35% tax rate).[63]

Many comments have been made about the lack of a credit for foreign taxes under BEAT. BEAT might therefore be triggered for companies that have a lot of foreign-source income from high tax countries along with relatively modest base erosion payments (enough to trigger BEAT). In that case, BEAT acts primarily as a tax on foreign-source income rather than achieving the objective of limiting profit shifting through outbound payments.

---

[63] A number of uncertainties, including measuring gross receipts and defining the related group, are discussed in Jasper L. Cummings, "Selective Analysis: The BEAT," *Tax Notes*, March 26, 2018.

BEAT also excluded cost of goods sold from its base (except for surrogate firms[64] that inverted after November 9, 2017), along with the exclusion for services if valued at cost. Both treatments have led to some criticism. By completely excluding cost of goods sold, it is possible to effectively avoid including royalties in the base by embedding them in inventory. That is, when a U.S. firm is paying a foreign related firm from tangible property to sell and also paying a royalty for distribution rights or rights to use a logo, the royalty could be eliminated and the price of the goods increased. Thus, royalties will be taxed only if separated, or for firms that do not keep inventory. Other planning possibilities may be associated with the exclusion of costs of goods sold, including supply chain restructuring.[65]

An issue of extensive debate is whether the cost component of services with a markup can be excluded.[66] The statute states that services using the

---

[64] These are firms that inverted and are not taxed as U.S. firms; these would be firms with between 60% and 80% of ownership.

[65] Planning possibilities arising through the exclusion of cost of goods sold have been discussed in the general comments referenced earlier, and also by Bret Wells, who first proposed the general idea of taxing payments to related parties. See "Get With the Beat," *Tax Notes*, February 19, 2018, pp. 1023-1032.

[66] See Lowell D. Yoder et al., "The New Base Erosion Minimum Tax," McDermott, Will and Emery, January 17, 2018, at https://www.mwe.com/en/thought-leadership/publications/2018/01/the-new-base-erosion-minimum-tax; Andrew Velarde, "Failing BEAT's Services Cost Method Exception Could Cost Big," *Tax Notes International*, January 29, 2018, pp. 419-421 reports on a District of Columbia Bar Community of Taxation event hosted by Jones Day in Washington, DC. The Velarde article notes that tax counsel for the House Ways and Means Committee Loren Ponds indicated that the whole payment is included, as did Jennifer Acuna, counsel for the Senate Finance Committee. David Noren of McDermott, Swill & Emery said some legislative history supports only the markup being included. Marty Sullivan, "Economic Analysis: Can Marked-Up Services Skip the BEAT," *Tax Notes*, February 5, 2018, pp. 705-709 argues that services with a markup will be taxed in full, but Manal Corwin et al., "A Response to an Off-Beat Analysis," *Tax Notes*, February 12, 2018, pp. 933-936 said that services cost will be excluded even if a markup used. Ryan Finley, "BEAT Clear on Markup Question, Former Treasury Official Says," *Worldwide Tax Daily*, February 16, 2018, reports that Mike McDonald of Ernst and Young and formerly of the Treasury Department indicates the cost component can be excluded even if the component eligible for services is required to be marked up. Alexander Lewis, "Officials Differ on Importance of BEAT Legislative History," *Tax Notes Today*, February 16, 2018, reporting on the same conference discusses a dispute about whether a colloquy between Sens. Hatch and Portman on the Senate floor on December 1, 2017, might justify a deduction for the cost component and should be considered part of the legislative history. Mark Prater, staff member of the Senate Finance Committee, said that the Conference Report makes it clear that the exclusion applies only to services with no markup. Barbara Angus, staff member of the Ways and Means Committee, said the colloquy should be

service cost method with no mark-up can be excluded as a base erosion payment. Some see that and other relevant information from the legislative history as indicating that any service with a markup, whether eligible for the cost method or not, would be included in BEAT in its entirety. Others argue that only the markup would be included.

Issues have been raised about whether individual payments will be aggregated, an issue important to financial institutions (i.e., whether interest payments will be assessed on a net or gross basis), applying to other payments as well (for example, where a services hub pays for foreign related party services but also receives a payment for services provided to foreign related parties).[67] There are related issues about the extent to which BEAT applies to ordinary transactions. Some have noted that BEAT includes nonabusive commercial transactions such as repos (short-term repurchase agreements for securities) and securities lending but not derivatives. Some have expressed concerns that routine lending between groups thus may be penalized. BEAT can have important effects on intragroup interest payments made by banks, securities dealers, and other

---

considered, but the article does not indicate that she took a position. Martin Sullivan, "Marked-Up Services and the BEAT Part II," *Tax Notes*, February 26, 2018, pp. 1171-1175, responding to the previous critique of his earlier article by Manal Corwin et al., argues the entire payment is taxed if it contains a markup. In a related discussion at the earlier conference, Andrew Velarde, "Failing BEAT's Services Cost Method Exception Could Cost Big," *Tax Notes International*, January 29, 2018, pp. 419-421 also reports on a discussion about whether tax accounting could be changed to treat services the same as inventory (as a reduction in gross receipts) allowing services to be excluded under BEAT. This issue was raised by Viva Hammer, staff member of the Joint Committee on Taxation, but David Noren indicated that a subcontractor service fee was in the scope of BEAT. Joseph Calianno of BDO USP LLP argued that economically similar transactions should be treated the same, but Kevin Nichols, from the Treasury Office of International Tax Counsel, indicated that the tax code's existing rules on inventory should be referenced and do not include services in cost of goods sold.

[67] According to some experts, it appears that interest will be included on a gross basis, which could produce significantly tax liability under BEAT for banks. See Lowell D. Yoder et al., "The New Base Erosion Minimum Tax," *McDermott, Will and Emery*, January 17, 2018, at https://www.mwe.com/en/thought-leadership/publications/2018/01/the-new-base-erosion-minimum-tax; Yalman Onaran, "How Trump's Tax Overhaul Could Hit Big Foreign Banks," *Bloomberg*, December 29, 2017, at https://www.bloomberg.com/news/articles/2017-12-29/trump-s-tax-overhaul-maypunish-foreign-banks-with-u-s-units.

regulated financial intermediaries. Firms may also try to replace intragroup debt with leases, convertible debt, or short-term debt.[68]

There are also no look-through rules to the final suppliers. For example, if a services payment is made to a related party that in turn subcontracts with an unrelated party for part of the services, the entire payment to the related party would be included in the base (that is, there is no recognition that part of the services were supplied by an unrelated party). Lack of a look-through rule would encourage the domestic corporation to make separate contracts with the unrelated party to minimize the amount of payment included in BEAT.[69]

Another criticism of BEAT is that it has too high a threshold ($500 million in revenue) for applicability, an amount that is 10 times the size of the threshold for the Treasury regulations aimed at earnings stripping.[70]

A general criticism of BEAT is that it is not targeted to abuse but simply captures all payments of a certain type (which may be a reason it is incompatible with international agreements).[71]

Moreover, because it is a minimum tax, it is most likely to apply to firms with thin margins, that is, with a lot of costs relative to profits, since a large amount of deductible base erosion payments compared to taxable income leads to effects of BEAT.[72]

---

68 See Lowell D. Yoder et al., "The New Base Erosion Minimum Tax," McDermott, Will and Emery, January 17, 2018, at https://www.mwe.com/en/thought-leadership/publications/2018/01/the-new-base-erosion-minimum-tax; Lee A. Sheppard, "Corporate Borrowing After Tax Reform," *Tax Notes*, January 29, 2018, pp. 565-69, reporting on a conference on BEAT and interest restrictions. See also Lee A. Sheppard, "News Analysis: Can a DISC Beat BEAT?" *Tax Notes*, March 5, 2018, pp. 1312-1319. The last article also discusses the possibilities of avoiding BEAT by setting up an IC-DISC (an interest charge domestic international sales corporation) to receive payments.

69 Lowell D. Yoder et al., "The New Base Erosion Minimum Tax," *McDermott, Will and Emery*, January 17, 2018, at https://www.mwe.com/en/thought-leadership/publications/2018/01/the-new-base-erosion-minimum-tax.

70 Bret Wells, "Get With The Beat," *Tax Notes*, February 19, 2018, pp. 1023-1032. The Treasury press release from April 4, 2016, regarding the new regulations is at https://www.treasury.gov/press-center/press-releases/Pages/jl0405.aspx. Wells also indicates that BEAT plus the interest deduction limits make these regulations unnecessary, although they would apply to smaller firms that are not affected by BEAT.

71 See Stephanie Soong Johnston, "EU Commission Mulls 'All Options' in Wake of Final U.S. Tax Bill," *Tax Notes*, December 26, 2017, p. 60.

72 This point is made by James P. Fuller and Larissa Neumann, "U.S. Tax Review," *Tax Notes International*, February 5, 2018, pp. 533-547.

Options for Revision

There are a number of revisions to BEAT that might be considered, some that lose revenue and some that raise revenue. Most follow from the various issues that have been raised. These might include allowing a foreign tax credit, and including payments for goods but allowing a deduction for the cost component (which would address the embedding of royalties). A parallel treatment for services could be adopted (in any case, the treatment of services with a mark-up could be clarified).

Interest payments might be removed from the BEAT coverage, substituting a worldwide allocation of interest (that is, allowing a U.S. firm to deduct only the share of interest in the United States consistent with its share of worldwide income or assets). Such a provision was originally in both the House and Senate versions of H.R. 1 and was dropped in conference.

A more general proposal for BEAT is to restrict the tax to payments to tax havens or low-tax countries. Another approach is to substitute stricter transfer pricing rules for BEAT.

Thin Capitalization

A number of comments have been made about ways to avoid the proposed interest restrictions. One possibility is that financial institutions that tend to have positive net interest can lease assets, and the rental payments on those leases would be deductible. Other possibilities are to substitute floating-rate debt that has lower interest rates for fixed-rate debt along with a hedge.[73] Firms affected can also make the choice to borrow outside of the United States or to issue preferred equity.

Although thin capitalization rules are applied generally, an important target is multinational firms where the incentive to locate interest deductions in higher-tax countries has been an issue. A provision more specifically targeted to international profit shifting that was in addition to

[73] Lee A. Sheppard, "Corporate Borrowing After Tax Reform," *Tax Notes*, January 29, 2018, pp. 565-69.

the general thin capitalization rules, providing a restriction on the U.S. firm's share of debt (based on either a measure of income or assets), was contained in both the House and Senate bills but not included in the final version.[74]

As noted earlier, the thin capitalization rules are coordinated with BEAT by treating disallowed interest as associated first with unrelated party and net operating losses (NOLs), a provision that strengthens the effect of BEAT.

One uncertainty is whether GILTI will be included in the earnings base, which includes items attributable to the taxpayer's business, since GILTI is not associated with the domestic business.[75]

Options for Revision

A major option that may be considered is to restore the worldwide interest allocation measure, probably in the form of an allocation based on income.

Deemed Repatriation Tax

A number of comments have been made concerning the deemed repatriation, which imposes a tax of 15.5% on cash equivalents held abroad and 8% on other unrepatriated earnings. One concern is that the proposed definition of cash equivalent is overly broad.[76] Under Treasury Notice 2018- 07,[77] the IRS stated that it intends to treat as cash a number of financial instruments—such as options contracts, futures contracts, and

[74] Arguments have been made that the asset basis used in the Senate version would be difficult to implement because of lack of data. See Robert Goulder, "Tax Reform And The Desirability Of Interest Barriers," *Forbes*, December 16, 2017, at https://www.forbes.com/sites/taxanalysts/2017/12/16/tax-reform-and-the-desirability-of-interest-barriers/#4c93cc914e1c.

[75] Raymond Wynman and Andrew Wai, "Interest Expense Limitation and the New I.R.C. § 163(j): Not Just a Foreign Concept Anymore," February 13, 2018, https://gtmtax.com/knowledge/interest-expense-limitation-new-i-r-c%C2%A7-163j/.

[76] Alison Bennett, "Repatriation Tax on Derivatives: Hard on Financial Companies," *Daily Tax Report*, January 10, 2018.

[77] The full notice can be viewed at https://www.irs.gov/pub/irs-drop/n-18-07.pdf.

non-bona fide hedging transactions—held overseas and tax them at 15.5%. Commentators have questioned whether this treatment is overly harsh, as some of these financial instruments may not be liquid or may serve a nonspeculative business purpose.

A second concern is that the downward attribution rules may unintentionally result in the inclusion of income in the deemed repatriation tax.[78] A reading of the 2017 tax revision legislative language along with the changes in the downward attribution could increase the number of taxpayers being defined as a U.S. shareholder of a CFC (and subject to the deemed repatriation tax) above the level intended by Congress, according to the American Institute of Certified Public Accountants (AICPA).

Another concern that has been raised is the dates used to calculate the base for the deemed repatriation tax.[79] Specifically, setting the base as the higher measured base on two testing dates,

(November 2, 2017, and December 31, 2017) could result in an overstatement of cash positions (subject to the higher 15.5% tax rate) if tax expenses incurred during the year were not booked prior to the earlier testing date or if cash was transferred abroad (via a loan from a U.S. parent) for a pending acquisition. This issue, however, was recently addressed in IRS guidance providing that foreign taxes would be allocated between the two portions of the tax year (through November 2, 2017, and to the period following ending on December 31, 2017).[80]

Another issue related to the testing dates is the effect on taxpayers that use a different tax year than the calendar year (such as Microsoft, with a year ending on June 30, or Apple, with a year ending on September 30). The measuring point for determining the aggregate cash position is greater than the average of the end of the two taxable years ending before November 2, 2017, or the end of the last tax year beginning before January 1. Since the dividend exclusion takes effect on January 1, 2018, these firms

---

[78] Andrew Velarde, "AICPA Lobbying for Downward Attribution Transition Tax Relief," *Tax Note International*, March 19, 2018.

[79] Letter from Pamela Olson, Price Waterhouse Coopers, to Dana Trier, Esq., Treasury Deputy Assistant Secretary-Tax Policy, February 5, 2018; and Ryan Finley, "Treasury Has Limited Authority on Transition Tax, Officials Say," *Worldwide Tax Daily*, February 27, 2018.

[80] IRS Notice 2018-26, April 2, 2018, https://www.irs.gov/pub/irs-drop/n-18-26.pdf.

can avoid additional cash accumulations by paying out any increase as dividends.[81]

Some individuals will likely be subject to the deemed repatriation tax, as a result of owning 10% or more of a foreign corporation, though they do not appear eligible to claim foreign tax credits.[82] Finally, the constitutionality of the deemed repatriation has been questioned by a set of researchers.[83]

Options for Revision

The legislation provides the Secretary with the authority to define cash equivalents. The basic idea was to distinguish liquid (cash and its equivalents) and illiquid (e.g., plant and equipment) assets. Drawing the line with respect to financial assets is complex. For example, the Treasury guidance excluded bona fide hedging transactions (which have the purpose of reducing risk). The regulatory process is ongoing, and although Congress could define specific assets by legislation, a regulatory approach is more flexible.

Limiting the downward attribution rules to only corporations may be an appropriate way to address the scope of the rules if they were primarily introduced to limit corporate inversions.

Another option is to generally revisit the treatment of individual shareholders under the deemed repatriation tax as well as under other rules (such as GILTI), especially when foreign tax credits are not allowed.

---

[81] See Stephen E. Shay, "Treasury Can Close a Potential Loophole in the Treatment of Deferred Foreign Income in the Tax Cuts and Jobs Act—Will It Act?," December 26, 2017, at https://dash.harvard.edu/bitstream/handle/1/34596007/ Shay_12_26_17.pdf? sequence=1; Lynnley Browning, "Tax Law Quirk Could Help Apple and Microsoft Lower Their Bills," *Bloomberg*, April 3, 2018.

[82] Lee A. Sheppard, "News Analysis: Individuals and the Repatriation Tax," *Tax Notes Today*, March 12, 2018; Letter from Meyer H. Fedida and Daniel I. Hanna to Editor, *Tax Notes Today*, March 5, 2018; and Charles M. Bruce, *Tax Reform Bill (*H.R. 1*) and Americans Abroad: What Happened? What's Next?* American Citizens Abroad, December 22, 2017, at https://www.americansabroad.org/tax-reform-bill-hr1-and-americans-abroad-what-happened-whats-next/.

[83] Mark E. Berg and Fred Feingold, "The Deemed Repatriation Tax-A Bridge Too Far?" *Tax Notes*, March 8, 2018.

The issue of two testing dates might be addressed with a facts and circumstances consideration of any cash movements and investments (in assets or acquisitions).

Anti-Inversion Rules

The 2017 tax revision changes in attribution rules are likely to result in more CFCs than under prior law.[84] Specifically, with downward attribution of the shares of the foreign subsidiary to the U.S. subsidiary, the foreign subsidiary becomes a CFC, and the U.S. shareholder could be subject to the deemed repatriation tax. Although it is thought that the change in the attribution rules was intended to block decontrolling transactions made after an inversion, commentators expect a broader reach to other corporate structures unrelated to inversion transactions.[85] In addition, certain CFC income will also likely be included as income for the deemed repatriation tax due to the downward attribution rule.

Although the new law included some anti-inversion measures proposed in the past (such as the thin capitalization rules) as well as other measures to restrict inversions, the new law did not include other measures proposed in the past (and currently in H.R. 5108 and S. 2459), such as treating firms that merge with 50% ownership and/or firms with 25% of business income in the United States, or firms managed and controlled in the United States as U.S. firms.

Options for Revision

As noted above, Congress might consider whether to revisit the scope of the downward attribution rules. Additional measures to discourage inversions might be considered, including proposals described above and codifying the regulations treating certain related party interest as equity.

---

[84] Lee A. Sheppard, "News Analysis: Corporate Borrowing After Tax Reform," *Tax Notes Today*, January 29, 2018.

[85] Jasper L. Cummings, "Selective Tax Act Analysis: Subpart F and Foreign Tax Credits," *Tax Notes*, January 29, 2018. See also Jeffrey L. Rubinger and Summer Ayers LePree, "The (Unintended?) Consequences of Tax Reform on Inbound Financing," *Tax Notes*, March 12, 2018, pp. 1511-1516.

In: Financial Crises and Programs
Editor: Patricia Hall
ISBN: 978-1-53614-159-7

Chapter 2

THE NATIONAL FLOOD INSURANCE PROGRAM (NFIP), REINSURANCE, AND CATASTROPHE BONDS*

Diane P. Horn and Baird Webel

SUMMARY

Insurance generally serves to transfer risk from one entity who does not want to bear that risk to another entity that does. An initial insurance purchase, such as homeowners buying a policy to cover damage to their home, however, is often only the first transfer of that risk. The initial (or *primary*) insurer may then transfer (or *cede*) some or all of this risk to another company or investor, such as a *reinsurer*. Such risk transfers are, on the whole, a net cost for primary insurers, just as purchasing insurance is a net cost for homeowners.

The Homeowner Flood Insurance Affordability Act of 2014 (P.L. 113-89) revised the authority of the National Flood Insurance Program (NFIP) to secure reinsurance from "private reinsurance and capital markets." Risk transfer from the private market could reduce the

---

* This is an edited, reformatted and augmented version of a CRS Insight report, IN10887, dated April 17, 2018.

likelihood of the Federal Emergency Management Agency (FEMA) needing to borrow from the Treasury to pay claims. In addition, this could allow the NFIP to recognize some of its flood risk up front through the premiums it pays for risk transfers rather than after the fact borrowing from Treasury. Using reinsurance to cover losses that occur in the more extreme years could help the NFIP to reduce the volatility of its losses over time. However, because reinsurers understandably charge the NFIP premiums to compensate for the assumed risk as well as the reinsurers' costs and profit margins, the primary benefit of reinsurance is to manage risk, not to reduce the NFIP's long-term fiscal exposure.

Reinsurance

The most common form of risk transfer is for a primary insurer to purchase a policy covering its risks from another (re)insurer. The primary insurer would typically continue to service the policy, while the reinsurer operates in the background. Reinsurance is particularly important to smaller insurers, who may not be large enough to spread local risks that are geographically correlated, such as a storm hitting a particular area. Reinsurers, however, often have the scope to diversify their risks on a global scale. It is also not uncommon for reinsurers to transfer (or *retrocede*) risks to other reinsurers.

National Flood Insurance Program (NFIP) Purchase of Reinsurance

Begun in September 2016 with a small amount to test the market, larger reinsurance purchases began in January 2017, as FEMA purchased $1.042 billion of reinsurance for an annual premium of $150 million. The reinsurance covered 26% of losses between $4 billion and $8 billion arising from a single flooding event. FEMA has so far paid over $8.6 billion in claims for Hurricane Harvey, triggering a full claim on the 2017 reinsurance.

FEMA purchased $1.46 billion of reinsurance in January 2018, for a premium of $235 million. The agreement is structured to cover losses in 2018 above $4 billion for a single flooding event, covering 18.6% of losses between $4 billion and $6 billion, and 54.3% of losses between $6 billion and $8 billion.

CATASTROPHE BONDS

In addition to reinsurance, new forms of "alternative" risk transfer have also been developed. One category of alternative risk transfer instruments are known as insurance linked securities (ILS)—financial instruments whose values are driven by insurance loss events. The most common form of ILS are catastrophe bonds (or cat bonds), which are structured somewhat like other bonds, but whose payout is dependent on the occurrence of a particular catastrophe, like a hurricane or earthquake of a particular strength.

Catastrophe bonds were first used in the private sector in the mid-1990s following Hurricane Andrew and the Northridge earthquake. Catastrophe bonds transfer major natural disaster risks to capital market investors. Such bonds are tradable and access global capital markets more directly than reinsurance, where a reinsurer acts as an intermediary. Catastrophe bonds are structured so that payment depends on the occurrence of an event of a defined magnitude or that causes an aggregate insurance loss in excess of a stipulated amount. Only when these specific triggering conditions are met do investors begin to lose their investment. There are three main types of triggers:

- *Indemnity*—bonds triggered by the actual losses experienced by the sponsoring insurer following the occurrence of a specified event; e.g., a bond triggered if an insurer's residential property losses from a hurricane in Florida exceeded $25 million in 2018;
- *Industry Loss*—bonds triggered by a predetermined threshold of industry-wide losses following the occurrence of a specified event;

e.g., a bond triggered if a total of all insurers' residential property losses from floods in 2018 exceeded $20 billion; or

- *Parametric*—bonds triggered by the actual physical conditions occurring during a disaster such as wind speed or earthquake size; e.g., a bond triggered by an eight-meter storm surge hitting New Orleans in 2018.

The public sector has become increasingly interested in the use of bonds. In 2009, Mexico became the first sovereign to issue cat bonds and the World Bank is now one of the largest participants in the catastrophe bond market. The New York City Metropolitan Transit Authority issued catastrophe bonds to protect against storm surge. According to the insurer Swiss Re, more than $10.5 billion in catastrophe bonds were issued in 2017, with the overall amount outstanding at $278.0 billion.

NFIP and Catastrophe Bonds

In April 2018, FEMA announced that it would seek to transfer NFIP risk to private markets through an ILS transaction. According to the notice of procurement, this would happen through a reinsurance procurement in which the reinsurer acts as a transformer to transfer NFIP-insured flood risk through the issuance of a catastrophe bond, to be effective for a term of "likely" three years. The notice also indicates that proceeds from the issuance of the catastrophe bond would be transferred into a reinsurance trust account, with FEMA as the sole beneficiary, for satisfying claims under the reinsurance agreement between FEMA and the transforming reinsurer. Thus, apparently, the catastrophe bonds would not be issued by the United States as a sovereign entity, but instead would be issued by the private reinsurer. The amount of the cat bond and the precise design are not yet known.

In: Financial Crises and Programs
Editor: Patricia Hall

ISBN: 978-1-53614-159-7

Chapter 3

REGULATORY REFORM 10 YEARS AFTER THE FINANCIAL CRISIS: DODD-FRANK AND SECURITIES LAW*

Nicole Vanatko

SUMMARY

From 2007-2009, the United States experienced what many commentators believe was the worst economic crisis since the Great Depression. In the wake of the crisis, Congress passed the Dodd-Frank Wall Street Reform and Consumer Protection Act (Dodd-Frank) in 2010. Title IX of Dodd-Frank, entitled "Investor Protections and Improvements to the Regulation of Securities," focuses on the powers and authorities of the Securities and Exchange Commission (SEC) and authorizes the SEC to promulgate certain rules intended to enhance corporate accountability and corporate governance. This chapter discusses recent developments with respect to two aspects of Title IX, including legislative proposals such as the Financial CHOICE Act of 2017 (H.R. 10, 115th Cong.) that would change or repeal aspects of Title IX.

---

* This is an edited, reformatted and augmented version of a Congressional Research Service report, R45163, dated April 13, 2018.

First, in February 2018, the Supreme Court issued a potentially significant decision in *Digital Realty, Inc. v. Somers*. The case involved the new SEC whistleblower program instituted by Section 922 of Dodd-Frank and resolved a dispute that had arisen among the lower courts as to the scope of individuals who could avail themselves of anti-retaliation protections provided by the Act. In *Digital Realty*, the Court held that Dodd-Frank's whistleblower protections do not apply to internal whistleblowers—that is, those who report violations within their organizations but *not* to the SEC. The dispute between the parties (and the lower courts) resulted from the tension between Dodd-Frank's definition of the term "whistleblower" and its incorporation of a reference to the Sarbanes-Oxley Act of 2002 in Section 922's anti-retaliation provision. As this chapter discusses, the Supreme Court's decision has potentially important implications for the enforcement of securities law, especially as Congress considers further changes to Dodd-Frank's whistleblower program.

Second, in early 2018, reporting companies began to formally comply with the SEC's "pay ratio rule." That rule was promulgated pursuant to Section 953(b) of Dodd-Frank, which requires public disclosure of the ratio between the annual total compensation of a company's median employee to the annual total compensation of its Chief Executive Officer (i.e., the company's median worker to CEO pay ratio). In promulgating the rule, the SEC adopted a largely flexible approach that it regarded as satisfying Dodd-Frank's statutory requirements while taking due consideration of the high compliance costs for companies. The report further discusses potential challenges that may be brought to the pay ratio disclosure requirement. Included in this discussion is a comparison between the pay ratio rule and the so-called "conflict minerals rule" and "resource extraction rule" the SEC previously promulgated pursuant to Dodd-Frank.

INTRODUCTION

From 2007-2009, the United States experienced what many commentators believe was the worst economic crisis since the Great Depression.[1] According to many observers, a principal cause of the crisis was the collapse of a bubble in the housing market that had developed in

[1] See Final Report of the Nat'l Comm'n on the Causes of the Fin. and Econ. Crisis in the U.S., v (2011) [hereinafter "Final Crisis Report"]; Jon Hilsenrath, Serena Ng & Damian Paletta, *Worst Crisis Since '30s, With No End Yet in Sight*, *Wall St. J.* (Sept. 18, 2008), https://www.wsj.com/articles/SB122169431617549947.

the early and mid-2000s.[2] As this bubble popped over the course of 2007 and 2008, many financial institutions began to experience large losses related to the subprime mortgage market.[3]

In particular, two of the nation's largest investment banks, Bear Stearns and Lehman Brothers, collapsed in 2008, leading to reverberations throughout the nation's financial markets. For instance, Lehman Brothers' bankruptcy in September 2008 led to a drop in the Dow Jones Industrial Average of more than 500 points, its worst single-day decline in seven years.[4] The fall of 2008 also witnessed the exposure of a $65 billion fraud perpetrated by Bernard Madoff, further impacting the financial markets.[5] As other large investment banks began experiencing considerable losses in value,[6] the government provided emergency funding to those institutions through the Emergency Economic Stabilization Act, signed into law in October 2008.[7] Specifically, the act created the Troubled Asset Relief Program (TARP),[8] pursuant to which the federal government would eventually disburse over $400 billion to financial institutions and the automotive industry, among others.[9]

The troubles in the financial system also spilled over to the real economy. Between the fourth quarter of 2007 and the second quarter of 2009, real GDP fell by an estimated 4.2 percent.[10] U.S. households lost an

---

[2] See, e.g., Christopher L. Foote, Kristopher S. Gerardi & Paul S. Willen, "Why Did So Many People Make So Many Ex Post Bad Decisions?: The Causes of the Foreclosure Crisis," in *Rethinking The Financial Crisis* 136, 136-40 (Alan S. Blinder, Andrew W. Lo & Robert M. Solow, eds. 2012).

[3] *Final Crisis Report*, *supra* note 1, at 279-91.

[4] Ben S. Bernanke, *The Courage to Act: A Memoir of A Crisis and Its Aftermath* 270 (2015).

[5] *See* Gregg Wirth, *Ponzi Schemes, the SEC, and the Myth of Investor Protection: A Q&A with Former SEC IG Kotz*, 18 NO. 12 wallstreetlawyer.com: SEC. ELEC. AGE 1, 1 (Dec. 2014); Felicia Smith, *Madoff Ponzi Scheme Exposes the "Myth of the Sophisticated Investor,"* 40 *U. Balt. L. Rev*. 215, 226, 236-39 (2010).

[6] *Id.*

[7] P.L. 110-343, 122 Stat. 3765 (2008).

[8] 12 U.S.C. § 5211.

[9] Jonathan Weisman, *U.S. Declares Bank and Auto Bailouts Over, and Profitable*, N.Y. TIMES (Dec. 19, 2014), https://www.nytimes.com/2014/12/20/business/us-signals-end-of-bailouts-of-automakers-and-wall-street.html; U.S. Dep't of the Treasury, *TARP Tracker*, https://www.treasury.gov/initiatives/financial-stability/reports/Pages/TARPTracker.aspx (last accessed 4/12/18).

[10] Murat Tasci & Caitlin Treanor, *Labor Market Behavior during and after the Great Recession: Has It Been Unusual?*, Fed. Res. Bank of Cleveland (Oct. 13, 2015),

estimated 26 percent of their wealth ($17 trillion) between mid-2007 and early 2009.[11] And between January 2008 and December 2009, the economy lost an estimated 8.3 million jobs.[12]

In assessing the central impetus for the economic crisis that began in late 2007, a range of views have emerged.[13] Nonetheless, one view that, as discussed below, influenced certain legal changes that resulted in the aftermath of the financial crisis concluded that the financial institutions' losses that contributed to the economic downturn were largely caused by excessively risky investments in and exposure to housing markets, including through the mortgage securitization process.[14] Relatedly, some commentators further viewed executive compensation structures during this time period as incentivizing excessive risk-taking and encouraging investments that resulted in widespread economic losses.[15]

In the wake of the financial crisis, policymakers began working on legislation to reform the financial system, and in July 2010, Congress passed the Dodd-Frank Wall Street Reform and Consumer Protection Act (Dodd-Frank or the Act).[16] The Act's stated purposes, among others, are "[t]o promote financial stability in the United States by improving accountability and transparency in the financial system, to end 'too big to

---

https://www.clevelandfed.org/newsroom-and-events/publications/economic-trends/2015-economic-trends/et-20151013-labor-market-during-after-great-recession.aspx.

[11] William R. Emmons & Bryan J. Noeth, *Household Financial Stability: Who Suffered the Most from the Crisis?*, Fed. Res. Bank of St. Louis (July 2012), https://www.stlouisfed.org/publications/regional-economist/july-2012/householdfinancial-stability--who-suffered-the-most-from-the-crisis#endnotes.

[12] *Final Crisis Report*, *supra* note 1, at 390.

[13] See, e.g., Robert E. Litan, "The Political Economy of Financial Regulation after the Crisis," in *Rethinking the Financial Crisis* 269, 270 ("There are so many alleged 'causes' of the great financial crisis of 2007 to 2008 that it is easy to lose count."); *Final Crisis Report*, *supra* note 1 at 125-26, 187, 230, 255; "Dissenting Statement of Keith Hennessy, Douglas Holtz-Eakin & Bill Thomas", in *Final Crisis Report*, *supra* note 1, at 413-37; "Dissenting Statement of Peter Wallison," in *Final Crisis Report*, *supra* note 1, at 443-553.

[14] *Final Crisis Report*, *supra* note 1, at xviii-xix, 44-45, 279-91.

[15] *See, e.g.*, Andrew Dunning, *The Changing Landscape of Executive Compensation After Dodd-Frank*, 30 Rev. Banking & Fin. L. 64, 64-66 (2010) (discussing pre-Dodd-Frank executive compensation packages' focus on achieving short-term financial goals and disconnect between executive performance and corporate value); Michael diFilipo, Note, *Regulating Executive Compensation in the Wake of the Financial Crisis*, 2 DREXEL L. REV. 258, 280-86 (2009) (discussing the manner in which executive pay practices may have encouraged decisions that led to the financial crisis).

[16] P.L. 111-203, 124 Stat. 1376 (2010) [hereinafter "Dodd-Frank"].

fail,' to protect the American taxpayer by ending bailouts, [and] to protect consumers from abusive financial services practices."[17] Ten years after the financial crisis, Dodd-Frank's changes to the law continue to be the subject of significant litigation and debate.[18]

Title IX of Dodd-Frank, entitled "Investor Protections and Improvements to the Regulation of Securities," focuses on the powers and authorities of the Securities and Exchange Commission (SEC),[19] an independent agency created by the Securities and Exchange Act of 1934 to enforce federal securities law.[20] Title IX authorizes the SEC to promulgate certain rules intended to enhance corporate accountability and governance.[21] In the view of the Senate Report accompanying Dodd-Frank, "[s]ignificant aspects of the financial crisis involved securities."[22] Specifically, the Senate Report took the position that "[s]erious and far-reaching problems were caused by poor and risky securitization practices; erroneous credit ratings; ineffective SEC regulation of investment banks such as Lehman Brothers and broker dealers such as Madoff; and excessive compensation incentives that promoted excessive risk taking."[23] According to the Senate Report, two main goals of Title IX were to provide investors with better protections and to give shareholders more of a voice in corporate governance.[24]

This chapter discusses two aspects of Title IX that have seen significant developments in early 2018. First, in February 2018, the Supreme Court rendered a potentially significant decision with respect to a new SEC whistleblower program instituted by Dodd-Frank, resolving a dispute that had arisen among the lower courts as to the scope of individuals who could avail themselves of anti-retaliation protections provided by the Act.[25] The report discusses the SEC whistleblower program, the dispute as framed by a

---

[17] *Id.*

[18] For a high-level overview of Dodd-Frank, see CRS Report R41350, *The Dodd-Frank Wall Street Reform and Consumer Protection Act: Background and Summary*, coordinated by Baird Webel.

[19] Dodd-Frank §§ 901-991.

[20] *See* 15 U.S.C. §§ 78d(a), 78d-5.

[21] Dodd-Frank §§ 901-991.

[22] *See* S. REP. NO. 111-176, at 36 (2010) [hereinafter "Senate Report"].

[23] *Id.*

[24] Id.

[25] Dig. Realty Tr., Inc. v. Somers, 138 S. Ct. 767 (2018).

number of U.S. Courts of Appeals, the Supreme Court's decision and reasoning, and implications of the Court's decision. Second, in early 2018, companies began their compliance with a new SEC disclosure rule mandated by Dodd-Frank, which requires them to publicly disclose the ratio between the median annual total compensation of all of their employees to the annual total compensation of their Chief Executive Officer.[26] The report discusses the SEC's adoption of the rule, the rule's operation, and potential challenges that may be brought to the pay ratio disclosure requirement now that it is in operation.

DODD-FRANK'S WHISTLEBLOWER INCENTIVES AND PROTECTIONS: RECENT DEVELOPMENTS

To promote corporate compliance with federal securities law, Section 922 of Dodd-Frank creates a new whistleblower program at the SEC, providing both incentives and enhanced protections for securities law "whistleblowers."[27] In a ruling that narrows the scope of Section 922, on February 21, 2018, the Supreme Court issued a decision in *Digital Realty, Inc. v. Somers*.[28] Specifically, in *Digital Realty*, the Court held that Section 922's whistleblower protections do not apply to internal whistleblowers—that is, those who report violations within their organizations but *not* to the SEC. This section of the report provides background regarding the SEC whistleblower program created by Dodd-Frank and compares pre-Dodd-Frank anti-retaliation protections available to securities law whistleblowers to Section 922. It then discusses the circuit split that arose concerning whether internal reporters are protected by Dodd-Frank's anti-retaliation provisions, the Supreme Court's reasoning in *Digital Realty*, and implications of the case for securities law.

---

[26] *Final Rule: Pay Ratio Disclosure*, Release Nos. 33-9877; 34-75610, 80 Fed. Reg. 50,104 (Aug. 18, 2015), https://www.sec.gov/rules/final/2015/33-9877.pdf (specifying that "registrants must comply with the final rule for the first fiscal year beginning on or after January 1, 2017).

[27] 15 U.S.C. § 78u-6.

[28] Dig. Realty Tr., Inc. v. Somers, 138 S. Ct. 767 (2018).

Background: Dodd-Frank's SEC Whistleblower Provisions

Section 922 of Dodd-Frank establishes new incentives and protections for whistleblowers who report certain violations of securities laws. The Senate Report accompanying Dodd-Frank pointed to factors such as "ineffective SEC regulation of Madoff Securities, Lehman Brothers and other firms" as a significant aspect of the financial crisis. Through Title IX of Dodd-Frank, the Senate Report stated, "[t]he SEC would get more power, assistance and money at its disposal to be an effective securities markets regulator."[29] The report further stated, with respect to the Act's whistleblower provisions that, "[t]he SEC would have more help in identifying securities law violations through a new, robust whistleblower program designed . . . to motivate people who know of securities law violations to tell the SEC."[30] The new whistleblower program introduced by Dodd-Frank has two central aspects: (1) providing monetary incentives for whistleblowers through financial rewards, and (2) enhancing anti-retaliation protections for whistleblowers against adverse actions taken by their employers.

Financial Incentives for Whistleblowers

Under Dodd-Frank, eligible whistleblowers who voluntarily provide "original information" to the SEC,[31] resulting in a successful judicial or administrative enforcement action with monetary sanctions exceeding one million dollars, are entitled to financial awards.[32] The cash award for a qualifying whistleblower may range from 10 to 30 percent of the monetary sanctions collected in the enforcement action, to be paid from a congressionally authorized Investor Protection Fund (so as not to detract

---

[29] *See* Senate Report, *supra* note 22, at 37.

[30] *Id.* at 38.

[31] For purposes of Section 922, "original information" is defined to mean information that (1) is derived from the independent knowledge or analysis of a whistleblower, (2) is not known to the SEC from any other source, unless the whistleblower is the original source of the information, and (3) is not exclusively derived from an allegation made in a judicial or administrative hearing, in a governmental report, hearing, audit, or investigation, or from the news media, unless the whistleblower is the source of the information. 15 U.S.C. § 78u-6(a)(3).

[32] *Id.* § 78u-6(b)(1).

from any victims' recovery).[33] The precise amount of the award is left to the discretion of the SEC, determined based on factors such as the significance of the information to the success of the action and the degree of assistance the whistleblower provided.[34] Whistleblowers are generally defined under the statute to be individuals "who provide . . . information relating to a violation of the securities laws to the Commission, in a manner established, by rule or regulation, by the Commission."[35] Nonetheless, the incentives program does exclude some whistleblowers, including "any whistleblower who is convicted of a criminal violation related to the judicial or administrative action for which the whistleblower otherwise could receive an award under this section."[36]

The incentive program established by Section 922 of Dodd-Frank is now in its seventh year of operation.[37] The SEC reports that enforcement matters involving whistleblower information have yielded $975 million in monetary sanctions to date, much of which has been or will be returned to investors.[38] Since the program's inception through the end of September 2017, the SEC had awarded $160 million in whistleblower awards under the incentive program.[39] Moreover, the agency recently increased that figure by approximately 50% with its largest award yet—$83 million awarded to three whistleblowers in related investigations that, according to the whistleblowers' lawyers, involved tips concerning transactions that effectively commingled customer and company funds at Merrill Lynch in violation of customer protection rules.[40]

---

[33] *Id.* § 78u-6(g); Sec, *Whistleblower Program: 2017 Annual Report to Congress* 29 (Nov. 15, 2017), https://www.sec.gov/files/sec-2017-annual-report-whistle blower-program.pdf [hereinafter "Whistleblower Program Report"] ("No money has been taken or withheld from harmed investors to pay whistleblower awards.").

[34] 15 U.S.C. § 78u-6(b)-(c).

[35] *Id.* § 78u-6(a)(6).

[36] *Id.* § 78u-6(c)(2)(B).

[37] See *Whistleblower Program Report*, *supra* note 33, at 1.

[38] *Id.*

[39] *Id.*

[40] *See* Jenny Strasburg and David Michaels, "Whistleblowers Helped SEC Bring $415 Million Settlement with Bank of America," *Wall St. J.* (Mar. 19, 2018), https://www.wsj.com/articles/whistleblowers-helped-sec-bring-415-millionsettlement-against-bank-of-america-1521479445; Press Release, SEC, *SEC Announces Its Largest-Ever Whistleblower Awards* (Mar. 19, 2018), https://www.sec.gov/news/press-release/2018-44; Press Release, SEC, *Merrill Lynch to Pay $415 Million For Misusing Customer Cash and Putting*

The Financial CHOICE Act passed by the House of Representatives in June 2017 would exclude certain additional categories of whistleblowers from eligibility for a financial incentive award. As noted above, currently, the incentive program makes whistleblowers with a criminal conviction related to the underlying complaint ineligible for an award.[41] The CHOICE Act would further deny bounties to any whistleblower who was responsible for or complicit in—or who in certain circumstances failed to try to prevent—the misconduct being reported.[42] The bill defines these categories in terms of a person who (1) "procures, induces, or causes another person to commit the offense"; (2) "aids or abets another person in committing the offense"; or (3) "having a duty to prevent the violation, fails to make an effort the person is required to make."[43] Critics of the bill have noted that the legislation, in excluding a whistleblower who fails to "make an effort" to stop the complained of action, could significantly reduce the pool of potential whistleblowers and eliminate those who may be in the best position to report wrongdoing, particularly if the person is in a subordinate position to the primary wrongdoer.[44] Supporters of the provision, by contrast, argue that the program should not reward individuals who may have had a role, even passively, in the underlying wrongdoing of which they complain.[45]

Customer Securities at Risk (June 23, 2016), https://www.sec.gov/news/pressrelease/2016-128.html.

[41] 15 U.S.C. § 78u-6(c)(2)(B).

[42] *See* H.R. 10, 115th Cong. § 828 (2017).

[43] *Id.*

[44] *See* John C. Coffee, Jr., *Hobson's CHOICE: The Financial CHOICE Act of 2017 and the Future of SEC Administrative Enforcement*, (June 22, 2017), https://www.sec.gov/spotlight/investor-advisory-committee-2012/coffeehobsons-choice-act.htm ("[S]uch persons will be disqualified from receiving any bounty, and this could chill the incentive to later blow the whistle. Subordinates should not be seen as complicit wrongdoers simply because they do not behave as heroes.").

[45] *See* Thomas Zaccaro, Nicolas Morgan, & Kyle Jones, *Congress Faces 'CHOICE' On Future Of SEC Enforcement*, LAW360 (Sept. 27, 2017), https://www.law360.com/articles/967996/congress-faces-choice-on-future-of-secenforcement ("Although this provision disqualifies individuals "convicted of a criminal violation" related to the conduct at issue, it still allows individuals who caused or allowed this conduct to occur to profit from these violations. Section 828 would fix this problem . . . .").

Whistleblower Anti-Retaliation Provisions

Section 922 also enhanced and strengthened anti-retaliation protections for whistleblowers in several respects[46]. The SEC has brought a number of actions against employers under the anti-retaliation provisions and a rule promulgated pursuant to it.[47] For example, in its enforcement efforts, the SEC has specifically focused on provisions in separation and severance agreements that restrict former employees' ability to report securities law violations to the SEC.[48] Most relevant to *Digital Realty,* the anti-retaliation provision further authorizes a private right of action, allowing individuals who experience retaliation as a result of activity protected by Section 922 to sue their employers in federal court for reinstatement, double back pay, with interest, and compensation for litigation costs and fees.[49]

The Sarbanes-Oxley Act (SOX), enacted in 2002 in the wake of the Enron and WorldCom accounting scandals,[50] contained the most significant whistleblower protection provision in federal securities law before Dodd-Frank. Because the anti-retaliation provision in Section 922 of Dodd-Frank contains certain references to SOX, it is important to understand the pre-existing protections that were available under SOX. The 2002 law's anti-retaliation provision generally protects an "employee" who provides information regarding a suspected violation of certain securities laws to: (1) a federal regulatory or law enforcement agency, (2) a Member or Committee of Congress, or (3) "a person with supervisory authority over the employee" working for the same employer.[51] Significantly, as related to the third category, SOX also mandated that public companies' audit committees establish procedures for internal complaints and reporting of suspected abuses within the company.[52] SOX and other laws further

---

[46] 15 U.S.C. § 78u-6(h).

[47] 17 C.F.R. § 240.21F-17(a). The relevant rule prohibits any person from "tak[ing] any action to impede an individual from communicating directly with the Commission staff about a possible securities law violation." *Id.*

[48] See *Whistleblower Program Report*, *supra* note 33, 2, 6-7, 19-21.

[49] 15 U.S.C. § 78u-6(h)(1)(B)(i), (1)(C).

[50] Jeffrey Golan and Chad Carder, *15 Years of SOX: The WorldCom and Enron Securities Cases*, LAW360 (July 31, 2017), https://www.law360.com/articles/947479/15-years-of-sox-the-worldcom-and-enron-securities -cases.

[51] 18 U.S.C. § 1514A.

[52] 15 U.S.C. § j-1(m)(4)(B).

require a company's auditors and attorneys to report suspected violations internally before reporting to an outside agency.[53] Commentators have noted that the internal reporting regime under SOX has been widely integrated into corporate compliance programs over the past 15 years.[54]

SOX allows employees who allege that they have been penalized for their reporting activity or for their assistance to law enforcement to file a complaint with the Secretary of Labor within 180 days of the alleged retaliatory conduct (or their awareness of such conduct), and they can bring an action in federal court only if the Secretary does not act on their complaint within 180 days of it being filed.[55] As for remedies, employees are entitled to reinstatement, backpay, and special damages (which may include, for example, damages for emotional injury).[56]

While SOX therefore afforded employees particular anti-retaliation protections for internal and external reporting prior to Dodd-Frank, the 2010 law provides certain more generous protections for individuals who are considered whistleblowers under that statute.[57] In contrast to SOX, Dodd-Frank does not require filing an administrative complaint before suing in court for retaliation, provides a longer statute of limitations (between six and ten years, depending on the circumstances), and offers reinstatement and *double* backpay as remedies.[58] In terms of protected activity, Dodd-Frank's anti-retaliation provision prohibits an employer from retaliating against a "whistleblower" "because of" three types of activity. First, the provision protects whistleblowers who provide information regarding securities law violations to the SEC.[59] Second, the

[53] *See id.* §§ 78j-1(b), 7245.

[54] Michael W. Peregrine, *Corporate Compliance and the Legacy of Sarbanes Oxley*, NYU Law Compliance & Enf't Blog (Aug. 3, 2017), https://wp.nyu.edu/compliance_enforcement/2017/08/03/corporate-compliance-and-the-legacyof-sarbanes-oxley/.

[55] 18 U.S.C. § 1514A.

[56] *Id.*

[57] 15 U.S.C. § 78u-6(a)(6).

[58] *Id.* § 78u-6(h).

[59] *Id.* § 78u-6(h)(1)(A)(i).

Table 1. Comparing the Anti-Retaliation Provisions in SOX and Dodd-Frank

	SOX	**Dodd-Frank**
Who Qualifies for the Anti-Retaliation Protections	*Employee* of public company who: (1) provides information relating to alleged securities fraud violations to: (A) a federal regulatory or law enforcement agency, (B) A Member or Committee of Congress, or (C) a person with supervisory authority over the employee working for the same employer; or (2) files, testifies in, or participates in a proceeding relating to an alleged violation of any rule or law relating to alleged securities fraud violations.[60]	*Whistleblower* who: (1) provides information to the SEC in accordance with Section 922; (2) initiates, testifies in, or assists in any investigation or judicial or administrative action of the SEC basedupon or related to such information; or (3) makes disclosures that are required or protected under [SOX], this chapter . . . and any other law, rule, or regulation subject to the jurisdiction of the SEC.[61]
Exhaustion Requirement	*Yes;* Must file a complaint with Secretary of Labor prior to suing in federal court[62]	*No*
Statute of Limitations for Private Right of Action	*180 days* Complaint with Secretary of Labor: Not later than 180 days after the date on which the violation occurs (or after the date on which the employee became aware of the violation)[63] Federal court complaint: Within 180 days of filing the complaint with the Secretary of Labor, if the Secretary has not issued a final decision[64]	*6-10 years* Not more than 6 years after the date on which the violation occurred; or Not more than three years after the date when facts material to the right of action are known or reasonably should have been known to the employee, but in no circumstances more than 10 years after the date on which the violation occurs[65]
Remedies Available	All relief necessary to make the employee whole, including: (1) Reinstatement; (2) *Back pay,* with interest; (3) *Special damages,* including litigation costs and fees.[66]	Relief for an individual prevailing in an action brought under Section 922 shall include: (1) Reinstatement; (2) *Double back pay,* with interest; (3) Litigation costs and fees.[67]

Source: Created by CRS.

---

[60] 18 U.S.C. § 1514A(a).
[61] 15 U.S.C. § 78u-6(h)(1).
[62] 18 U.S.C. § 1514A(b)(2)(D).
[63] Id.
[64] Id. § 1514A(b)(1)(B).
[65] 15 U.S.C. § 78u-6(h)(1)(B)(iii).
[66] 18 U.S.C. § 1514A(c).
[67] 15 U.S.C. § 78u-6(h)(1)(C).

provision also applies to whistleblowers who assist the SEC in an investigation or proceeding.[68] Third, and most relevant to *Digital Realty*, the anti-retaliation provision further specifies that it protects whistleblowers who "mak[e] disclosures that are required or protected under [SOX]," among other laws.[69]

Table 1 provides a comparison between the anti-retaliation provisions in SOX and Dodd-Frank.

Digital Realty and the Scope of Dodd-Frank's Whistleblower Protections

Dispute Regarding Interpretation of Dodd-Frank's Anti-Retaliation Provision

The third category of protected activity under Dodd-Frank, which includes the reference to SOX, does not itself suggest that the whistleblower needs to have made any disclosures *to the SEC* in order to recover.[70] And because SOX, in turn, protects an employee from retaliation for internal reporting,[71] it seems plausible that the Dodd-Frank provision could encompass internal reporters. However, the definition of the term "whistleblower" in Section 922 of Dodd-Frank complicates reaching a conclusion that internal whistleblowers are protected under the Act. The definition refers to individuals who provide "information relating to a violation of the securities laws *to the Commission*, in a manner established, by rule or regulation, by the Commission,"[72] suggesting that an individual must report to the SEC to benefit from the subsection's protections.

---

[68] *Id.* § 78u-6(h)(1)(A)(ii).

[69] *Id.* § 78u-6(h)(1)(A)(iii).

[70] *Id.* § 78u-6(h)(1) (protecting whistleblowers who "mak[e] disclosures that are required or protected under the Sarbanes-Oxley Act of 2002 (15 U.S.C. 7201 et seq.), this chapter, including section 78j-1(m) of this title, section 1513(e) of title 19, and any other law, rule, or regulation subject to the jurisdiction of the Commission").

[71] *Id.* § 78u-6(h)(1) (protecting whistleblowers who "mak[e] disclosures that are required or protected under the Sarbanes-Oxley Act of 2002 (15 U.S.C. 7201 et seq.), this chapter, including section 78j-1(m) of this title, section 1513(e) of title 19, and any other law, rule, or regulation subject to the jurisdiction of the Commission").

[72] 15 U.S.C. § 78u-6(a)(6) (emphasis added).

This tension between Dodd-Frank's definition of the term "whistleblower" and its incorporation of SOX in the anti-retaliation provision is at the heart of *Digital Realty*. That case began when Paul Somers, as a Vice President at Digital Realty, a publicly traded real estate investment trust,[73] complained internally to the company's management regarding alleged securities law violations.[74] Digital Realty fired Somers soon afterwards, an adverse action that Somers alleged violated Section 922.[75] Somers filed a lawsuit in the U.S. District Court for the Northern District of California, which dismissed the suit because he did "not report any alleged law violations to the SEC."[76] On appeal to the U.S. Court of Appeals for the Ninth Circuit (Ninth Circuit),[77] the appellate court ruled that Somers was entitled to sue under Dodd-Frank, even though he did not take the additional step of reporting his concerns to the SEC.[78] The Second Circuit reached the same result in a similar case in 2015.[79] But the Fifth Circuit took a different view in 2013, ruling that a "whistleblower" must have reported a complaint to the SEC in order to recover under Dodd-Frank's whistleblower provisions.[80] These decisions created a circuit split over the proper reading of Dodd-Frank, setting the stage for Supreme Court review.

The lower court in *Digital Realty* reasoned that Section 922's specific reference to SOX, and the overall purpose of the statute, indicated Congress's intent to protect internal whistleblowers as well as those who report to the SEC.[81] Specifically, the Ninth Circuit reasoned that a strict application of the "whistleblower" definition would effectively read the third category of protected activity of the anti-retaliation provision out of

---

[73] Digital Realty Trust, Inc. and Digital Realty Trust, L.P., *Annual Report* (Form 10-K) (Mar. 1, 2018), https://www.sec.gov/Archives/edgar/data/1297996/000129799618000026/dlr12311710k.htm.

[74] Somers v. Dig. Realty Tr., Inc., 850 F.3d 1045, 1047 (9th Cir. 2017).

[75] *Id.*

[76] Somers v. Dig. Realty Tr., Inc., 119 F. Supp. 3d 1088, 1094 (N.D. Cal. 2015).

[77] For purposes of brevity, references to a particular circuit in the body of this report (e.g., the Ninth Circuit) refer to the U.S. Court of Appeals for that particular circuit.

[78] *Somers*, 850 F.3d at 1050-51.

[79] *See* Berman v. Neo@Ogilvy LLC, 801 F.3d 145 (2d Cir. 2015).

[80] *See* Asadi v. G.E. Energy (USA), L.L.C., 720 F.3d 620 (5th Cir. 2013).

[81] *Somers*, 850 F.3d at 1049-50.

the statute because that class of protected individuals would be narrowed to the point of meaninglessness.[82] In implementing the Dodd-Frank anti-retaliation provision through regulations, the SEC had defined the term "whistleblower" to encompass internal whistleblowers, explaining that a more limited reading would chill employees' use of valuable internal reporting processes.[83] The Ninth Circuit agreed with the Second Circuit that the SEC's reading of the anti-retaliation provision was entitled to deference under *Chevron* principles,[84] even if the statute's definition of the term "whistleblower" cast some doubt on that interpretation.[85]

The Fifth Circuit, on the other hand, ruled in *Asadi v. G.E. Energy (USA), L.L.C.* that in order to qualify as a "whistleblower" under Dodd-Frank, an individual must report a suspected violation to the SEC.[86] In analyzing the statutory language, the Fifth Circuit determined that the reference to SOX in the anti-retaliation provision does not expand the definition of a "whistleblower" and concluded that it would be inappropriate to read the words "to the Commission" out of the definition.[87] The Fifth Circuit hypothesized at least one scenario in which the third category of Dodd-Frank whistleblower protections would apply under a more limited reading of the definition. Specifically, the appellate court reasoned that an employee who reports both internally *and* to the SEC, but is retaliated against only "because of" the internal report (e.g., if the employer was unaware of the report to the SEC) would qualify as a "whistleblower" under the Fifth Circuit's interpretation of Section 922.[88] The Fifth Circuit further reasoned that the anti-retaliation scheme for internal reporting that exists under SOX would essentially be rendered

---

[82] *Id.* at 1049.

[83] *See* 17 C.F.R. § 240.21f-2; Sec, Interpretation of the Sec's Whistleblower Rules Under Section 21f of the Securities Exchange Act of 1934, 80 Fed. Reg. 47,829, 47,830 (Aug. 10, 2015).

[84] *See* Chevron, U.S.A. v. Natural Resources Defense Council, Inc., 467 U.S. 837, 842-44 (1984) (holding that courts should defer to an agency's "construction of the statute which it administers" as long as the statute is ambiguous and the agency regulations are "based on a permissible construction of the statute"). For more on the *Chevron* doctrine, see CRS Report R44954, *Chevron Deference: A Primer*, by Valerie C. Brannon and Jared P. Cole.

[85] *Somers*, 850 F.3d at 1047, 1050.

[86] Asadi v. G.E. Energy (USA), L.L.C., 720 F.3d 620 (5th Cir. 2013).

[87] *Id.* at 626-27, 628.

[88] *Id.* at 627-28.

"moot" if the Dodd-Frank anti-retaliation provisions were to apply because whistleblowers would be more inclined to take advantage of Dodd-Frank's stronger protections.[89]

The Supreme Court's Digital Realty Decision

In ruling in favor of Digital Realty and resolving the circuit split, the Supreme Court unanimously held that the definition of "whistleblower" provided "an unequivocal answer" that resolved the case, affirming the principle that "[w]hen a statute includes an explicit definition, we must follow that definition."[90] The Court distinguished the case from prior instances in which it did not hold a statutory definition to control because, unlike those cases, the results in *Digital Realty* would not be incongruous with Congress's regulatory scheme.[91] Namely, the Court emphasized several times throughout its opinion that the purpose of the enhanced whistleblower provision was "to motivate people who know of securities law violations *to tell the SEC*," quoting Dodd-Frank's Senate Report.[92]

---

[89] *Id.* at 628.

[90] Dig. Realty Tr., Inc. v. Somers, 138 S. Ct. 767, 776-77 (2018) (quoting Burgess v. United States, 553 U.S. 124, 130 (2008)).

[91] *Id.* at 778. Specifically, the Court distinguished two prior Supreme Court decisions that had been raised by Somers. In the first case, *Lawson v. Suwannee Fruit & Steamship Company*, the Court found that applying the statutory definition of the term "disability" to the worker compensation provision at issue in *Lawson* would have caused "obvious incongruities in the language" of the statute and "destroy[ed] one of the major purposes" of the provision. 336 U.S. 198, 201-02 (1949). However, in *Digital Realty*, the Court rejected Somers's argument that a reading of the anti-retaliation provision to exclude internal reporting was at odds with congressional intent or the overall statutory scheme. *Digital Realty*, 138 S. Ct. at 778. Second, in contrast to *Utility Air Regulatory Group v. EPA*, where the Court held that the term "air pollutant" had a narrower meaning in one portion of the Clean Water Act than its statute-wide definition (because that the term was routinely interpreted with a "narrower, context-appropriate meaning" throughout individual portions of the statute, including by the EPA), 134 S. Ct. 2427, 2439 (2014), in *Digital Realty* the definition of "whistleblower" was located within Section 922 of Dodd-Frank itself and stated that it was applicable to the entire section. *Dig. Realty*, 138 S. Ct. at 778 (citing 15 U.S.C. § 78u-6(a)(6)).

[92] *See, e.g., Dig. Realty*, 138 S. Ct. 777, 780 (quoting S. REP. No. 111-176, at 37 (2010)). The citation to the Senate Report prompted significant debate amongst the concurring justices in *Digital Realty*. Justice Thomas, joined by Justices Alito and Gorsuch, wrote separately regarding their disagreement with the Court opinion's reliance on the Senate Report in interpreting the definition of whistleblower. *Id.* at 783 (Thomas, J., concurring in part and concurring in the judgment). They "join[ed] the Court's opinion only to the extent it relies on the text of Dodd-Frank," elaborating that the language of a statute enacted by Congress—rather than potentially unreliable documents explaining congressional intent—

Moreover, the Court rejected Somers's arguments that requiring reporting to the SEC to qualify as a "whistleblower" would lead to results incompatible with Congress's intent.[93] For example, echoing the Fifth Circuit's reasoning, the Court reasoned that the Dodd-Frank anti-retaliation provision's reference to SOX would still be meaningful under the narrower definition because it would protect those who report *both* internally and to the SEC, but incur retaliation for the internal report.[94] The Court observed that such a scenario may in fact be commonplace because, as data from the SEC presented to the Court showed, approximately 80% of those receiving SEC whistleblower awards in 2016 had indeed reported internally before making their complaints to the SEC.[95]

Implications of Digital Realty

With regard to the ruling's impact on the enforcement of federal securities law, *Digital Realty* eliminated a potential avenue of relief for internal whistleblowers, a population which, according to recent SEC and other statistics, appears to be historically larger than the pool of external whistleblowers.[96] The *Digital Realty* decision clarifies that internal reporters must rely on the protections in SOX, which, as discussed above, are in significant respects less advantageous than those provided under Dodd-Frank. While internal and external whistleblower reporting are each still protected under federal law, some commentators note that the decision, particularly when combined with large incentive awards coming

---

should ultimately control. *Id.* Justice Sotomayor, on the other hand, authored another concurring opinion, joined by Justice Breyer, in which she argued that it is appropriate to look to legislative history as an interpretive aid, "even when, as here, a statute's meaning can clearly be discerned from its text." *Id.* (Sotomayor, J., concurring). In such cases, Justice Sotomayor contended, inquiries into legislative intent can confirm and enhance the Court's understanding of the language. *Id.*

[93] *Id.* at 779-80 (majority opinion).

[94] *Id.* at 779.

[95] *Id.*

[96] See *Whistleblower Program Report*, *supra* note 33, at 17 (noting that 83% of whistleblower award recipients reporting to the SEC in 2017 who were employees or former employees of the subject entities first reported their complaints internally); *see also Ethics Res. Ctr.*, *Inside the Mind of a Whistleblower: A Supplemental Report of the 2011 National Business Ethics Survey* 2 (2012), http://www.corporate complianceinsights.com/wpcontent/uploads/2012/05/inside-the-mind-of-a-whistleblower-NBES.pdf (estimating that only one in six whistleblowers "ever chooses to report externally.").

out of the SEC whistleblower program, tips the scale towards incentivizing reporting of securities law violations to the authorities rather than deferring to public companies' internal compliance efforts,[97] which some commentators argue will lead to greater risk of noncompliance with federal law.[98]

Digital Realty's ultimate impact on corporations that are subject to Dodd-Frank's whistleblower provisions is unclear. In supporting the petitioner's arguments in *Digital Realty*, notable *amici* like the U.S. Chamber of Commerce favored the narrower "whistleblower" definition because, in its view, an expansive definition encompassing internal reporters would have increased costs for companies faced with more whistleblower actions in federal court, while spurning internal and administrative processes set up by SOX that it argued are often more efficient in weeding out non-meritorious claims.[99] Nonetheless, while *Digital Realty* will protect public companies against federal lawsuits under Dodd-Frank from internal whistleblowers, there may be other externalities created by the decision. Specifically, because, as commentators have noted, the Court's ruling may have the practical effect of increasing whistleblower reports made directly to the SEC over attempted internal resolutions, the ruling could potentially lead to increased regulatory action and greater costs for companies.[100] Whether these costs outpace any increased litigation costs that could have resulted from a different ruling in *Digital Realty* remains to be seen.

---

[97] *See* Dunstan Prial, *Incentives Get Weaker for Internal Whistleblower Reporting,* LAW360 (March 23, 2018), https://www.law360.com/articles/1025665/incentives-get-weaker-for-internal-whistleblower-reporting.

[98] *See* Stephen Kohn, *Digital Realty Trust v. Somers May Kill Corporate Compliance,* LAW360 (Sept. 21, 2017), https://www.law360.com/articles/964208/digital-realty-trust-v-somers-may-kill-corporate-compliance.

[99] Brief for United States Chamber of Commerce as Amicus Curiae Supporting Petitioner at 9-11, Digital Realty, Inc. v. Somers, 138 S. Ct. 767 (2018) (No. 16-1276).

[100] Dustin Prial, Companies May Find High Court Whistleblower Ruling Costly, LAW360 (Feb. 21, 2018), https://www.law360.com/securities/articles/1014744/companies-may-find-high-court-whistleblower-ruling-costly.

DODD-FRANK PAY RATIO DISCLOSURE RULE: RECENT DEVELOPMENTS

Section 953(b) of Dodd-Frank directs the SEC to promulgate a rule requiring reporting companies[101] to disclose in certain public filings the ratio of (a) the median annual total compensation of all of its employees (i.e., the median employee's compensation) to (b) the annual total compensation of its chief executive officer.[102] The SEC adopted the final pay ratio disclosure rule (the Rule)[103] on August 5, 2015 by a 3-2 vote of the Commissioners.[104] The vote followed a notice and comment process which drew nearly 300,000 comment letters[105] following release of the proposed rule in September 2013.[106] Because the SEC required compliance with the Rule to begin for the first fiscal year beginning on or after January 1, 2017,[107] the first wave of companies made their pay ratio disclosures earlier this year in annual statements and in proxy materials in advance of annual shareholder meetings. While the first major disclosure (in which Honeywell

---

[101] Section 953(b) specifies that companies must disclose the pay ratio in SEC filings required under 17 C.F.R. § 229.10(a), which include registration statements and annual and quarterly financial reports, among others. For ease of reference, this report may refer to companies subject to these rules as "reporting companies" or "registrants" (the term employed by the SEC in the final pay ratio disclosure rule, 17 C.F.R. § 229.402(u)).

[102] *See* Dodd-Frank § 953(b) ("The Commission shall amend section 229.402 of title 17, Code of Federal Regulations, to require each issuer to disclose in any filing of the issuer described in section 229.10(a) of title 17, Code of Federal Regulations (or any successor thereto)—(A) the median of the annual total compensation of all employees of the issuer, except the chief executive officer (or any equivalent position) of the issuer; (B) the annual total compensation of the chief executive officer (or any equivalent position) of the issuer; and (C) the ratio of the amount described in subparagraph (A) to the amount described in subparagraph (B).").

[103] 17 C.F.R. § 229.402(u). The rule was an addition to Item 402 of the SEC's Regulation S-K.

[104] Dennis R. Honabach and Mark A. Sargent, *The Final "Pay Ratio Disclosure Rule,"* PROXY RULES HDBK. § 4:25, (2017).

[105] Final Rule: Pay Ratio Disclosure, Release Nos. 33-9877; 34-75610, 80 Fed. Reg. 50,104, 50,108 (Aug. 18, 2015), https://www.sec.gov/rules/final/2015/33-9877.pdf [hereinafter "Adopting Release"].

[106] Proposed Rule: Pay Ratio Disclosure, Release Nos. 33-9452; 34-70443, Fed. Sec. L. Rep. P. 80356 (Sept. 18, 2013), https://www.sec.gov/rules/proposed/2013/33-9452.pdf.

[107] Adopting Release, *supra* note 105, at 1.

reported a 333:1 pay ratio)[108] drew considerable media attention,[109] companies have disclosed a very wide range of ratios to date.[110]

Background: Dodd-Frank's Accountability and Executive Compensation Provisions

The pay ratio provision is contained within Title IX of Dodd-Frank, in a subtitle concerning "Accountability and Executive Compensation." This subtitle includes several provisions geared towards transparency and shareholder involvement in matters of executive compensation.[111] Perhaps most notably, Section 951, the so-called "say on pay" provision, requires that shareholders be given the opportunity to cast advisory votes as to executive compensation at annual shareholder meetings at least once every three years.[112] Moreover, Section 953(a) mandates that issuers further make an executive "pay versus performance" disclosure in their annual proxy statements,[113] which would require disclosure of executive

---

108 Honeywell International Inc., Preliminary Proxy Statement (Schedule 14A) (Feb. 16, 2018), https://www.sec.gov/Archives/edgar/data/773840/000093041318000526/c89618_pre14a.htm.

109 *See, e.g.*, Jena McGregor, *As Companies Reveal Gigantic CEO-to-Worker Pay Ratios, Some Worry How Low-Paid Workers Might Take the News*, WASH. POST (Feb. 21, 2018), https://www.washingtonpost.com/news/on-leadership/wp/2018/02/21/as-companies-reveal-gigantic-ceo-to-worker-pay-ratios-some-worry-how-low-paid-workers-might-take-the-news/?noredirect=on&utm_term=.83eb25a5d659.

110 *Compare, e.g.*, Aptiv PLC, Definitive Proxy Statement (Schedule 14A) (Mar. 12, 2018), https://www.sec.gov/Archives/edgar/data/1521332/000119312518079291/d527278ddef14a.htm (disclosing a pay ratio of 2,526:1), *with* Dorchester Minerals, L.P., Preliminary Proxy Statement (Schedule 14A) (Feb. 26, 2018), https://www.sec.gov/Archives/edgar/data/1172358/000143774918003337/dmlp20180223_pre14a.htm (disclosing a pay ratio of 0.9:1).

111 Dodd-Frank §§ 951-957.

112 *Id.* § 951. The SEC adopted rules implementing the "say-on-pay" provision in 2011. *See* 17 C.F.R. § 240.14a-21(a). Title IX of Dodd-Frank further contains provisions requiring enhanced compensation structure reporting (Dodd-Frank § 956), that directors serving on a board's compensation committee be independent (Dodd-Frank § 952), and the clawback of executive incentive compensation that result from the firm's issuing erroneous financial statements that later need to be restated in compliance with accounting standards (Dodd-Frank § 954).

113 Dodd-Frank § 953(a).

compensation alongside the company's total shareholder return as a measure of performance.[114]

Title IX's legislative history arguably reflects that the law's various provisions on executive compensation were propelled by the view that compensation arrangements incentivized risky behavior by executives, contributing to the 2007-2009 financial crisis.[115] While the legislative history for Dodd-Frank's pay ratio disclosure provision is sparse, the SEC, in adopting the Rule, concluded that a major purpose of the Rule is to better enable shareholders to cast their "say on pay" votes.[116] This conclusion finds a measure of support in the legislative history for the rest of the subtitle, most notably, the "pay versus performance" disclosure requirements found in Section 953(a) of the Act.[117] The Senate Report's discussion of the "pay versus performance" disclosure specifies that the rule is intended to "show[] the relationship between executive compensation and the financial performance of the issuer" as a metric to assist shareholders in their evaluation of executive pay.[118] The Senate Report further states that the Committee on Banking, Housing, and Urban Affairs believed that the disclosure will "add to corporate responsibility as firms will have to more clearly disclose and explain executive pay" and "allow shareowners to evaluate the performance of the compensation committee and board in setting executive pay, to assess pay-for-performance links and to optimize their role of overseeing executive compensation through such means as proxy voting."[119] The legislative history of the "pay versus performance" provision could be viewed as

---

[114] The SEC proposed a rule implementing the "pay versus performance" provision in April 2015, followed by a notice and comment period. *See* Press Release, SEC, *SEC Proposes Rules to Require Companies to Disclose the Relationship Between Executive Pay and a Company's Financial Performance* (Apr. 29, 2015), https://www.sec.gov/news/press release/2015-78.html. However, no further action has been taken, and the rule was placed on the SEC's "long term" agenda in its Regulatory Flexibility Agenda released in January 2018. *See* Regulatory Flexibility Agenda, 83 Fed. Reg. 2022 (Jan. 12, 2018).

[115] Senate Report, *supra* note 22, at 36 ("Serious and far-reaching problems were caused by . . . excessive compensation incentives that promoted excessive risk taking. . . .").

[116] Adopting Release, *supra* note 105, at 9.

[117] For more on the use of legislative history in statutory interpretation, see CRS Report R45153, *Statutory Interpretation: Theories, Tools, and Trends*, by Valerie C. Brannon, at 35-40.

[118] Senate Report, *supra* note 22, at 135.

[119] *Id.*

providing insights into the meaning of its neighboring provision concerning the pay ratio disclosure.[120]

The SEC Commissioners who voted on the Rule, public commenters, and other commentators have differed in how they have interpreted the motivations for and value of the pay ratio disclosure rule. Former SEC Chairwoman Mary Jo White recognized that "[t]o say that the views on the pay ratio disclosure requirement are divided is an obvious understatement,"[121] while former SEC Commissioner Luis Aguilar remarked that the requirement is either "a boon or a bane, depending on one's perspective."[122] In addition to helping to inform "say on pay" votes, some public commenters noted that they supported the Rule because they believed it would deter executive pay practices that led to the financial crisis, and that the Rule would reduce inequitable wealth distribution in the United States.[123]

By contrast, the dissenting Commissioners issued statements in which they argued that the Rule would have no apparent shareholder benefits,[124] especially given the information already available on CEO pay.[125] The dissenting Commissioners viewed the Rule as merely a "name and shame"

---

[120] *See, e.g.*, Sprint Telephony PCS, L.P. v. County of San Diego, 311 F. Supp. 2d 898, 907-08 (S.D. Cal. 2004) (finding legislative history of surrounding provisions of statute, as well as of section more generally, persuasive in interpreting statutory provision); *cf.* EEOC v. Commercial Office Prods. Co., 486 U.S. 107, 116, 121 (1988) (noting that an interpretation of one provision in a statute can be supported by the legislative history of other, related sections of the same statute); *see also* Danskin, Inc. v. Comm'r, 331 F.2d 360, 361 (2d Cir. 1964) (looking to "language and legislative history of a related section" of the tax code to assist in determining classification of expenditures at issue).

[121] Mary Jo White, *Statement at Open Meeting on Security-based Swap Rules Under Title VII and on Pay Ratio Disclosure Rule*, SEC (Aug. 5, 2015), https://www.sec.gov/news/statement/statement-at-open-meeting-on-sbs-and-payratio-disclosure.html.

[122] Luis A. Aguilar, *The CEO Pay Ratio Rule: A Workable Solution for Both Issuers and Investors*, SEC (Aug. 5, 2015), https://www.sec.gov/news/statement/statement-on-open-meeting-on-pay-ratio-aguilar.html.

[123] Adopting Release, *supra* note 105, at 20-21.

[124] *See* Michael S. Piwowar, *Dissenting Statement at Open Meeting on Pay Ratio Disclosure*, SEC (Aug. 5, 2015), https://www.sec.gov/news/statement/dissenting-statement-at-open-meeting-on-pay-ratio-disclosure.html [hereinafter "Piwowar Dissenting Statement"]. This comment was generally echoed by various public commenters. Adopting Release, *supra* note 105, at 23 (discussing the comments filed by various commenters).

[125] *See* Daniel M. Gallagher, Dissenting Statement at an Open Meeting to Adopt the "Pay Ratio" Rule, SEC (Aug. 5, 2015), https://www.sec.gov/news/statement/dissenting-statement-at-open-meeting-to-adopt-the-pay-ratio-rule.html [hereinafter "Gallagher Dissenting Statement"].

exercise,[126] pointing unfavorably to an AFL-CIO statement indicating that the organization believed that "[d]isclosing this pay ratio will shame companies into lowering CEO pay."[127] One of the dissenting Commissioners expressed concern about further steps that may be taken at various levels of government, such as state efforts to tie their corporate tax rates or awards of public contracts to company pay ratios.[128] Other commenters focused on the costs of compliance with the Rule.[129] In this regard, the SEC estimated that initial compliance costs would total approximately $1.3 billion, given, for example, the complexities involved in collecting payroll and accounting information for all relevant employees, particularly those residing in other countries.[130]

What Does the Pay Ratio Disclosure Rule Entail?

The pay ratio disclosure rule requires that reporting companies disclose the ratio of their median worker's pay to their CEO's pay in certain public SEC filings, including registration statements, proxy and information statements, and annual reports.[131] Certain issuers are exempted from the Rule, including emerging growth companies[132] and smaller reporting companies.[133] In setting forth the "formula" for the pay ratio calculation, as discussed in more detail below, the SEC opted for a largely flexible

---

[126] *See* Piwowar Dissenting Statement, *supra* note 124.

[127] *See* Gallagher Dissenting Statement, *supra* note 125.

[128] *Id.* n. 22 & 23.

[129] Adopting Release, *supra* note 105, at 23-24.

[130] *Id.* at 194-203.

[131] Dodd-Frank § 953(b); 17 C.F.R. § 229.10(a). According to the SEC's Adopting Release, "in addition to potential liability under Section 18 of the Securities Exchange Act, 15 U.S.C. § 78r, "registrants that fail to comply with the final rule could . . . be violating Exchange Act Sections 13(a) and 15(d), as applicable, and would also be subject to potential liability under Exchange Act Section 10(b) and Rule 10b-5, promulgated thereunder, for any false or misleading material statements in the information disclosed pursuant to the rule." Adopting Release, *supra* note 105, at 146-47; 15 U.S.C. §§ 78m, 78o, 78j; 17 C.F.R. § 240.10b-5.

[132] 17 C.F.R. § 229.402(u), Instruction 8.

[133] *Id.*, Instruction 7.

approach that it regarded as being compliant with applicable statutory requirements while taking due consideration of compliance costs.[134]

Annual Total Compensation of All Employees

Calculation of Annual Total Compensation

Issuers are already required to use particular standards in calculating and disclosing executive pay, which the SEC has set forth in Item 402(c) of Regulation S-K.[135] Section 953(b) of Dodd-Frank and the Rule specify that the same method should be used to determine the "annual total compensation" of an employee for purposes of calculating the pay ratio disclosure.[136] Registrants are permitted to use reasonable estimates of annual total compensation, other than for the CEO.[137]

Employees

The statutory language in Dodd-Frank states that the median worker-CEO pay ratio is to be calculated using the annual total compensation of "*all* employees of the registrant."[138] The Rule therefore takes an inclusive approach, requiring registrants to include part-time, temporary or seasonal employees, as well as employees situated in the U.S. or abroad, employed by the company or any of its consolidated subsidiaries in its calculations.[139] Annualizing the pay of part-time or temporary/seasonal employees—that is, to reflect full-time or full-year equivalents—is not permitted, although the pay of a permanent employee who only worked part of the year (e.g., a new

---

134 Adopting Release, *supra* note 105, at 9.

135 17 C.F.R. § 229.402. Reporting companies had not previously been required to disclose median employee pay.

136 Dodd-Frank § 953(b) ("[T]he total compensation of an employee of an issuer shall be determined in accordance with section 229.402(c)(2)(x) of title 17, Code of Federal Regulations."); 17 C.F.R. § 229.402(u)(2)(i). Item 402(c)(2)(x) includes the following components of an executive's compensation, to be disclosed in a summary table: salary, bonus, stock awards, option awards, non-equity incentive plan compensation, change in pension value and non-qualified deferred compensation earnings, and all other compensation.

137 17 C.F.R. § 229.402(u), Instruction 4.

138 Dodd-Frank § 953(b) (emphasis added).

139 17 C.F.R. § 229.402(u)(3); Adopting Release, *supra* note 105, at 45, 49-50.

hire) may be annualized.[140] The "employee" definition does not include contractors that are employed by and whose compensation is determined by an unaffiliated third party.[141]

As to foreign employees, in recognition of certain difficulties that may arise in including such workers' compensation in the pay ratio calculation, the Rule provides for two potential exemptions:

- *Data Privacy Exemption*: A registrant may exclude employees located in countries whose data privacy laws make it impossible to obtain, process or disclose workers' compensation information without violating the data privacy laws of that country. To rely on this exemption, the registrant needs to have first made reasonable efforts to obtain the information, including under applicable exemptions to the privacy laws, and must file a legal opinion supporting their non-disclosure.[142]
- *De minimis Exemption*: A registrant may also exclude up to 5% of its non-U.S. employees. If certain employees in a particular non-U.S. jurisdiction are excluded, all employees from that jurisdiction need to be excluded without violating the 5% maximum.[143] Any exclusion of non-U.S. employees under this exemption must be disclosed, including the jurisdiction(s) and approximate number of employees at issue.[144]

Overall, the Rule's definition of "employee" is quite broad. In his dissenting statement, one of the Commissioners, Daniel Gallagher, stated that he would have limited the definition to full-time U.S. employees, arguing that the SEC had the authority to interpret the statutory language in such a manner.[145] One difficulty voiced by registrants has been that the

---

[140] 17 C.F.R. § 229.402(u), Instruction 5.

[141] *Id.*

[142] *Id.* § 229.402(u)(4)(i).

[143] A company with less than 5% non-U.S. employees that excludes any non-U.S. employees from their calculation must exclude all foreign employees. *Id.* § 229.402(u)(4)(ii).

[144] *Id.*

[145] *See* Gallagher Dissenting Statement, *supra* note 125. Moreover, for example, the National Retail Federation has argued that including part-time workers distorts the ratio in their

"employee" definition under the Rule does not match up in all respects with the definition of "employee" for other purposes under the law,[146] making it difficult to use existing records and classification systems as a basis for pay ratio calculations. In particular, commenters and registrants were concerned that the Rule appeared to define "contractor" more narrowly than that term is traditionally defined under employment and tax law.[147] However, more recent SEC guidance has clarified that registrants may use their existing payroll and tax records as a basis for determining their employee pool, at least for purposes of excluding independent contractors.[148]

Identifying the Median Employee and Providing Additional Information

Method of Identifying the "Median Employee"

Under the SEC pay ratio rule, the registrant may choose a "reasonable method" to identify the median employee that is appropriately tailored to their business, including using reasonable estimates both to identify the median employee and to calculate the annual total compensation of employees (other than the CEO).[149] Such methods may include using a statistical sampling of employees or any consistently applied compensation measure (e.g., using payroll or tax records),[150] even if those records do not include every element of annual total compensation.[151] Regardless,

industry, given that "about 30% of retail workers are classified as part-time." National Retail Federation, *SEC Pay Ratio Rule*, https://nrf.com/advocacy/ policy-agenda/secpay-ratio-rule.

[146] Sec, Interpretation: Comm'n Guidance on Pay Ratio Disclosure, Release Nos. 33-10415, 34-81673, 3 (Sept. 21, 2017), https://www.sec.gov/rules/interp/2017/33-10415.pdf [hereinafter "Comm'n Guidance"].

[147] *See, e.g.*, IRS, *Publication 15-A Employer's Supplemental Tax Guide* (2018), https:// www.irs.gov/pub/irspdf/p15a.pdf.

[148] Comm'n Guidance, *supra* note 146, at 3.

[149] 17 C.F.R. § 229.402(u), Instruction 4.

[150] *Id.*

[151] Comm'n Guidance, *supra* note 146, at 3.

registrants must disclose the methodology that they use in their public filing.[152]

Calculation Date

A registrant is able to select a determination date within the last three months of a company's fiscal year for identifying the median employee.[153] While the initial proposed rule contained a date certain (i.e., the last date of the company's fiscal year), the Rule departed from the proposal due to considerations such as disproportionate effects the date certain may have on registrants who employ a large portion of seasonal workers at the end of the year.[154] The Rule also incorporated a flexible date in order to leave sufficient time for companies to conduct the disclosure calculations at year-end.[155] The date chosen must be disclosed in public filings, and if companies change the date used from one year to the next, they must describe the reason for the change.[156]

Calculation of Median Every Three Years

Registrants need to identify the median employee every three years, rather than every year, if "during a registrant's last completed fiscal year there has been no change in its employee population or employee compensation arrangements that it reasonably believes would result in significant change to its pay ratio disclosure."[157] The pay ratio disclosure itself (including that median employee's compensation and the CEO's compensation), however, must be calculated each year.[158]

---

[152] 17 C.F.R. § 229.402(u), Instruction 4(5).

[153] *Id.* at Instruction 1.

[154] *Securities Regulation – Dodd-Frank Wall Street Reform and Consumer Protection Act – SEC Finalizes Regulations Requiring Companies to Disclose Pay Ratio Between the CEO and Median Employee*, 129 HARV. L. REV. 1144, 1147 (Feb. 2016) [hereinafter "HARV. L. REV."]. Some argue, however, that this flexibility does appear to leave such companies a way to potentially "skew" the median to exclude seasonal workers that would otherwise be included in the Rule's definition of "employee." *See* Adopting Release, *supra* note 105, at 55.

[155] Adopting Release, *supra* note 105, at 56.

[156] 17 C.F.R. § 229.402(u), Instruction 1.

[157] *Id.* at Instruction 2.

[158] *Id.*; *see id.* § 229.402(a).

Cost of Living Adjustments

In identifying the median employee and calculating their annual total compensation, the registrant may adjust the annual total compensation of its employees in jurisdictions other than the jurisdiction in which the CEO resides to account for the cost of living in the CEO's jurisdiction. If such adjustments are used, the registrant must also disclose in its public filings non-adjusted figures for the median employee's annual total compensation and the pay ratio.[159]

Additional Information

Registrants are permitted, but not required, to supplement the pay ratio disclosure required by the Rule with additional information or supplemental ratios, such as, for example, a version of the ratio using only U.S. employees.[160] The supplemental information cannot be misleading or displayed with more prominence than the mandated ratio.[161]

The main practical problem identified with the Rule's flexible approach is that the resulting pay ratio figures may not necessarily allow for easy "apples to apples" comparisons between companies, potentially making it a less useful metric for shareholders.[162] However, the SEC explicitly stated in formulating the Rule that it believed the ratio should be "designed to allow shareholders to better understand and assess *a particular registrant's compensation and pay ratio disclosures* rather than to facilitate a comparison of this information from one registrant to another."[163] In any event, commentators have begun to advise, given that public analysis may indeed focus on comparisons to peer companies, that registrants take advantage of permitted methods to contextualize their disclosure (such as providing additional ratios or information) and carefully consider how to use their permitted discretion under the Rule,[164] suggesting that certain best practices

---

159 *Id.* at Instruction 4(4).
160 Adopting Release, *supra* note 105, at 30.
161 17 C.F.R. § 229.402(u), Instruction 9.
162 *See, e.g.*, HARV. L. REV., *supra* note 154, at 1149.
163 Adopting Release, *supra* note 105, at 12 (emphasis added).
164 *See, e.g.*, David Martin, *The CEO-to-Employee Pay Ratio Rule: Begin Thinking About Messaging Now*, BLOOMBERG LAW (Aug. 7, 2017), https://www.bna.com/ceotoemployee-pay-ratio-n73014462845/.

may develop over time. However, the lack of purely comparable ratios among registrants may factor into potential challenges relating to the Rule,[165] although this would likely also need to be weighed against the cost savings to registrants that are gained from having greater flexibility in applying the rule.[166]

Potential Challenges to the Pay Ratio Rule

Given the split of opinions regarding the pay ratio rule highlighted through the SEC's adoption of the Rule, public comments, and further commentary, the pay ratio rule may become the subject of a challenge in court.[167] Potential challenges to the Rule would likely be based on requirements for agency rulemaking under the Administrative Procedure Act (APA) and securities law requirements for SEC rulemaking.[168] Under the APA, a court can "hold unlawful and set aside agency action, findings, and conclusions found to be...arbitrary, capricious, an abuse of discretion, or otherwise not in accordance with law."[169] Under this standard, a court may invalidate agency determinations that fail to "examine the relevant data and articulate a satisfactory explanation for its action including a 'rational connection between the facts found and the choice made.'"[170] Under federal securities laws, the SEC is also required to "consider, in addition to the protection of investors, whether the action will promote efficiency, competition, and capital formation."[171] These two principles

---

[165] *See infra* "Potential Challenges to the Pay Ratio Rule."

[166] *See id.*

[167] *See, e.g.*, HARV. L. REV., *supra* note 154, at 1151.

[168] As discussed in the next section, the First Amendment may be a further ground for challenge, based on the D.C. Circuit's 2015 decision invalidating a portion of the so-called "conflict minerals rule." *See infra* "Other SEC Disclosure Rules under Dodd-Frank."

[169] 5 U.S.C. § 706(2)(A).

[170] Motor Vehicle Manufs. Ass'n v. State Farm Auto Mutual Ins. Co., 463 U.S. 29, 43 (1983) (quoting Burlington Truck Lines v. United States, 371 U.S. 156, 168 (1962)); *see generally* CRS Report R44699, *An Introduction to Judicial Review of Federal Agency Action*, by Jared P. Cole.

[171] 15 U.S.C. §§ 77b(b), 77c(f).

often work in tandem in a court's assessment of rulemaking by the SEC.[172] Several areas of potential challenge, identified by the dissenting Commissioners or other commentators, are discussed below.

First, one dissenting Commissioner, Michael S. Piwowar, posited that the SEC acted in an arbitrary and capricious manner in not adequately considering the quantitative impact of certain flexible approaches permitted under the Rule on the accuracy or quality of the pay ratio disclosure.[173] Specifically, Commissioner Piwowar questioned the effect of allowing for different methodologies in determining the median employee and the allowance for a 5% de minimis exception for foreign workers, among other aspects of the Rule.[174] In his view, the SEC should have assessed whether these allowances would result in material deviations from a strict "annual total compensation" approach under Item 402.[175] The SEC's Division of Economic and Risk Analysis did, however, perform a study to analyze the potential effects on the pay ratio calculation of excluding different percentages of employees.[176] For example, it concluded that an exclusion of 5% of employees could result, under certain assumptions, in a 6.9% range of deviation,[177] which the SEC analyzed and believed to confirm that the 5% exclusion for non-U.S. employees would have de minimis effects on the ratio calculation.[178]

Second, a plaintiff may challenge possible deficiencies in the SEC's analysis of the costs and benefits of the Rule. Under the APA and securities law principles, the D.C. Circuit has vacated rules where it found

---

[172] *See, e.g.,* Business Roundtable v. SEC, 647 F.3d 1144, 1148 (D.C. Cir. 2011).

[173] *See* Michael S. Piwowar, *Additional Dissenting Comments on Pay Ratio Disclosure*, SEC (Aug. 7, 2015), https://www.sec.gov/news/statement/additional-dissenting-statement-on-pay-ratio-disclosure.html [hereinafter "Piwowar Additional Dissenting Statement"].

[174] *Id.*

[175] *Id.*

[176] *See* Sec Div. Of Econ. And Risk Analysis, *Potential Effect on Pay Ratio Disclosure of Exclusion of Different Percentages of Employees at a Range of Thresholds* (June 4, 2015), http://www.sec.gov.comments/s7-07-13/s70713-1556.pdf [hereinafter "June 4 Analysis"]; Sec Div. Of Econ. And Risk Analysis, *Extension of the Analysis of the Potential Effect on Pay Ratio Disclosure of Exclusion of Different Percentages of Employees at a Range of Thresholds* (June 30, 2015), http://www.sec.gov.comments/s7-07-13/s70713-1559.pdf.

[177] June 4 Analysis, *supra* note 176.

[178] *See* Adopting Release, *supra* note 105, at 74-75, 228-29.

the SEC "acted arbitrarily and capriciously for having failed…adequately to assess the economic effects of a new rule."[179] While the SEC estimated the cost of compliance with the Rule at $1.3 billion, some argue, for example, that it should have further assessed the costs of specific portions of the Rule, such as the cost of allowing a flexible calculation date within three months of the end of the fiscal year.[180] At least one commentator is further critical that the SEC did not seek to quantify the *benefits* of the Rule in order to perform a quantitative cost-benefit analysis.[181] In this vein, courts have imposed different, situation-specific requirements concerning the extent to which an agency needs to have sought to quantify *benefits* of a proposed rule.[182]

Third, some have suggested that the Rule may also be vulnerable to challenge due to the SEC's lack of investor testing evaluating how investors planned to use the pay ratio information.[183] As pointed out by a dissenting Commissioner, Section 912 of Dodd-Frank allows specifically for such

---

[179] Business Roundtable v. SEC, 647 F.3d 1144, 1148 (D.C. Cir. 2011) (vacating rule requiring companies to include information on certain shareholder nominees in its proxy materials because SEC did not adequately assess costs to companies in doing so, including costs of the company's challenges to shareholder nominees); *see* Chamber of Commerce of U.S. v. SEC, 412 F.3d 133, 143 (D.C. Cir. 2005) (vacating rule requiring that mutual funds have 75% independent directors to engage in certain types of transactions otherwise prohibited by the Investment Company Act because agency failed to consider costs of compliance to mutual funds); *see also* Am. Equity Inv. Life Ins. Co. v. SEC, 613 F.3d 166, 177 (D.C. Cir. 2010) (vacating rule bringing fixed indexed annuities under the SEC's regulation because SEC did not adequately explain its reasoning regarding purported positive effects on competition, efficiency or capital formation, asserting only that the benefits of clarity of regulation and required disclosures to investors would have such impacts).

[180] *See, e.g.,* HARV. L. REV., *supra* note 154, at 1151; *see Business Roundtable,* 647 F.3d at 1148.

[181] HARV. L. REV., *supra* note 154, at 1151; *see* Adopting Release, *supra* note 105, at 176 ("While we believe that the pay ratio disclosure may provide an informational benefit to shareholders in their say-on-pay voting, we are unable to quantify this benefit.").

[182] *Compare, e.g.,* Nat'l Assoc. Manufs. v. SEC, 748 F.3d 359, 369 (D.C. Cir. 2014), *overruled on other grounds by* American Meat Institute v. U.S. Dept. of Agric., 760 F.3d 18 (D.C. Cir. 2014), (rejecting argument that, under the securities laws, the SEC, in promulgating conflict minerals rule, should have sought to quantify the benefits of the rule), *with Am. Equity Investments*, 613 F.3d at 177 (vacating an SEC rule which would have provided additional disclosures and information to investors regarding fixed indexed annuities, and criticizing the SEC for not assessing the current baseline of investor information available and whether an increase in such information would be efficient).

[183] HARV. L. REV., *supra* note 154, at 1149.

testing,[184] stating that "[f]or the purpose of evaluating any rule or program of the Commission…the Commission may…engage in such temporary investor testing programs as the Commission determines are in the public interest or would protect investors."[185] Without empirical testing, observers argue that it is impossible to know whether investors anticipated or wished to use the pay ratio for direct comparison purposes among registrants, which would make the flexible aspects of the Rule more problematic.[186] In *Chamber of Commerce v. SEC*, however, the D.C. Circuit declined to vacate a rule for the SEC's failure to develop empirical data to assess the benefits of a mutual fund having independent (as opposed to inside) chairpersons of their boards of directors, recognizing that "an agency need not–indeed cannot–base its every action on empirical data."[187]

Legislatively, the Financial CHOICE Act passed by the House of Representatives in June 2017, which repeals many Dodd-Frank provisions, would also eliminate the pay ratio provision in Section 953(b) of Dodd-Frank.[188] A repeal is not contemplated, however, by the version of the Economic Growth, Regulatory Relief, and Consumer Protection Act passed by the Senate in March 2018.[189] At the Commission level, on February 6, 2017, the SEC called for further comments on difficulties in complying with the Rule so that the SEC staff could promptly "reconsider" its implementation,[190] but it is currently unclear what, if any, action the SEC will take in response to the further comments.

---

184 Piwowar Dissenting Statement, *supra* note 124.

185 15 U.S.C. § 77s(e).

186 HARV. L. REV., *supra* note 154, at 1149.

187 *Chamber of Commerce*, 412 F.3d at 142 ([A]lthough we recognize that an agency acting upon the basis of empirical data may be more readily able to show it has satisfied its obligations under the APA . . . we are acutely aware that an agency need not–indeed cannot–base its every action upon empirical data; depending upon the nature of the problem, an agency may be 'entitled to conduct . . . a general analysis based on informed conjecture.'") (citations omitted). Note, however, as noted above, the court in *Chamber of Commerce* did invalidate the relevant rule due to the SEC's lack of consideration of costs. *Id.* at 143.

188 *See* H.R. 10, 115th Cong. § 857 (2017). Individual bills have also been introduced in past Congresses to repeal the provision. *See* H.R. 414, 114th Cong. (2015); S. 1722, 114th Cong. (2015).

189 *See* S. 2155, 115th Cong. (2018).

190 Michael S. Piwowar, *Reconsideration of Pay Ratio Rule Implementation,* SEC (Feb. 6, 2017), https://www.sec.gov/news/statement/reconsideration-of-pay-ratio-rule-implementation.html.

Comparing the Pay Ratio Rule with Other SEC Disclosure Rules Under Dodd-Frank

Apart from the disclosures required by Title IX, Dodd-Frank requires the SEC to promulgate and enforce certain other disclosure rules, which may provide further insight on how the pay ratio rule would be considered if challenged. Specifically, Title XV, entitled "Miscellaneous Provisions," provides for the so-called "conflict minerals"[191] and "resource extraction" rules.[192] These rules generally require disclosures regarding, respectively, the source of certain minerals used in a company's products and payments made to governments relating to commercial natural resource development.[193] Each of the rules was intended to prompt social and political change in foreign countries,[194] with the "conflict minerals" rule addressing the impact of mineral extraction on armed conflict in the Democratic Republic of the Congo (DRC) and the "resource extraction" rule aimed at reducing government corruption in resource-rich nations. Over the past several years since being promulgated by the SEC, the two rules have been met with some skepticism by courts. Nonetheless, as discussed below, distinctions exist between these disclosure rules and the pay ratio disclosure rule that may make a true comparison inapt.

Conflict Minerals Rule

The conflict minerals rule was intended to address "the exploitation and trade of conflict minerals originating in the Democratic Republic of the Congo…helping to finance conflict characterized by extreme levels of violence…and contributing to an emergency humanitarian situation

---

[191] Dodd-Frank § 1502.

[192] *Id.* § 1504.

[193] 17 C.F.R. §§ 240.13p-1, 249b.400.

[194] *See, e.g.*, Nat'l Ass'n of Manufs. v. SEC, 800 F.3d 518, 522 (D.C. Cir. 2015) [hereinafter "*NAM II*"] (noting that the SEC acknowledged in the rulemaking process that the conflict minerals rule is "directed at achieving overall social benefits" and is not "intended to generate measurable, direct economic benefits to investors or issuers," making the regulatory requirements "quite different from the economic or investor protection benefits that our rules typically strive to achieve.").

therein."[195] The rule requires companies that manufacture products that include tin, tungsten, tantalum, or gold as necessary components to conduct a reasonable "country of origin inquiry" for these minerals.[196] If the minerals originated in the DRC or adjoining countries, the rule requires the further step of conducting due diligence to determine the minerals' source and chain of custody, to be disclosed on a Form SD (or specialized disclosure report).[197] While not affecting these first two parts of the rule, the D.C. Circuit has ruled that another part of the regulation—one that required companies to state whether the relevant minerals in their supply chains were "DRC conflict free," "not found to be DRC conflict free," or "DRC conflict undeterminable"—violated the First Amendment in a challenge brought in *National Association of Manufacturers v. SEC ("NAM")*.[198]

As an initial matter, the *NAM* case presented the question of what level of First Amendment scrutiny a court should apply to compelled speech like the conflict minerals rule.[199] While courts generally apply strict scrutiny to content-based compelled speech,[200] an intermediate level of scrutiny applies to commercial speech under the test set forth by the Supreme Court in *Central Hudson Gas & Electric Corp. v. Public Service Commission.*[201] To overcome a First Amendment challenge, *Central Hudson* requires a

---

195 Dodd-Frank §1502(a) (codified at 15 U.S.C. § 78m).

196 17 C.F.R. §§ 240.13p-1, 249b.400 (Form SD).

197 17 C.F.R. § 249b.400.

198 *NAM II*, 800 F.3d at 525-27, 530. The court entered final judgment in the suit, ending the case, in April 2017. NAM v. SEC, No. 1:13-cv-00635, 2017 WL 3503370 (D.D.C. Apr. 3, 2017). Note that the SEC had already stayed the portion of the rule requiring that companies label their products as "DRC conflict free," "not found to be 'DRC conflict free,'" or "DRC conflict undeterminable" in 2014 pending a final outcome in the case. Press Release, SEC, *SEC Issues Partial Stay of Conflict Minerals Rules* (May 2, 2014), https://www.sec.gov/news/press-release/2014-89.

199 *NAM v. SEC*, 748 F.3d 359, 370-72 (D.C. Cir. 2014) [hereinafter "*NAM I*"]

200 *See* Turner Broad. Sys., Inc. v. FCC, 512 U.S. 622, 642 (1994) (We "apply the most exacting scrutiny to regulations that suppress, disadvantage, or impose differential burdens upon speech because of its content."); Wooley v. Maynard, 430 U.S. 705 (1977) ("We must . . . determine whether the State's countervailing interest is sufficiently compelling to justify requiring appellees to display the state motto on their license plates."); Frudden v. Pilling, 742 F.3d 1199, 1207 (9th Cir. 2014) ("Because [school uniform policy] compels students to endorse a particular viewpoint, strict scrutiny applies—that is, inclusion of the written motto on the . . . uniform shirts must be 'a narrowly tailored means of serving a compelling state interest.'").

201 447 U.S. 557, 564-66 (1980).

"substantial" government interest that is "directly and materially advanced" by a "narrowly tailored" restriction on speech.[202] As a further caveat, however, the Supreme Court has also ruled in *Zauderer v. Office of Disciplinary Counsel* that a rule regulating a lawyer's deceptive advertisement merited an even lower level of scrutiny.[203] The D.C. Circuit in *NAM* applied *Central Hudson's* intermediate test to the conflict minerals rule in a 2014 decision, reasoning that the *Zauderer* test only applied to cases involving corrections to deceptive advertising.[204] But, an *en banc* (i.e., full court) panel of the D.C. Circuit overruled that portion of the *NAM* decision in 2015 in *American Meat Institute v. U.S. Department of Agriculture*, holding that *Zauderer* scrutiny can apply in broader circumstances to disclosures required to serve other government interests.[205]

In light of *American Meat Institute*, the D.C. Circuit reevaluated its initial *NAM* decision.[206] In a 2015 decision, a three-judge panel of the D.C. Circuit still held that *Central Hudson* scrutiny applied to the conflict minerals rule because it viewed *Zauderer* as still being limited to cases at least involving voluntary advertising.[207] However, the court further justified its decision under *Zauderer's* level of scrutiny given the "flux and uncertainty of the First Amendment doctrine of commercial speech."[208] In a *Zauderer* analysis, a court looks to whether the speech at issue is effective in meeting an adequate government objective and whether the compelled language is of a "purely factual and uncontroversial" nature.[209] The D.C. Circuit determined that neither Congress nor the SEC had attempted to determine whether or to what extent the conflict minerals disclosure would "in fact alleviate" the humanitarian crisis in the DRC.[210] It also concluded that the labels required by the rule went beyond the

---

[202] *See NAM I*, 748 F.3d at 372 (citing *Central Hudson*, 447 U.S. at 564-66).
[203] 471 U.S. 626, 651 (1985).
[204] *NAM I*, 748 F. 3d at 372.
[205] Am. Meat Institute v. U.S. Dept. of Agric., 760 F.3d 18, 22-23 (D.C. Cir. 2014).
[206] *NAM II*, 800 F.3d at 522-23.
[207] *Id.* at 524.
[208] *Id.*
[209] *Id.* at 525, 527.
[210] *Id.* at 525-27.

presentation of purely factual, uncontroversial information, instead requiring issuers to use language that may imply that their products were "ethically tainted."[211]

As with the conflict minerals rule, any First Amendment challenge to the pay ratio disclosure rule would likely raise as an initial matter the question of what level of scrutiny applies. The pay ratio disclosure does not directly relate to advertising, as the *NAM* court would require for *Zauderer* scrutiny,[212] suggesting that *Central Hudson* may apply to the pay ratio rule. On the other hand, the *American Meat Institute en banc* ruling's broader view of when *Zauderer* scrutiny applies could suggest an application to "factual and uncontroversial" disclosures mandated by the government for purposes beyond advertising.[213] Moreover, prior to *NAM,* the D.C. Circuit recognized that the federal "government's powers to regulate the securities industry" subject the "exchange of information regarding securities" to a more "limited First Amendment scrutiny."[214] Nonetheless, the precise contours of that limitation or how it would apply to the pay ratio rule are not perfectly defined.[215]

In terms of its stated goals and the nature of the disclosure required, the pay ratio rule does share certain similarities with the rule upheld in *American Meat Institute*. In *American Meat Institute*, the court upheld against a First Amendment challenge a Department of Agriculture regulation requiring meat producers to disclose "country of origin" information for their meat products. The court held that the relationship between the rule's means and its ends—"enabling customers to make informed choices based on characteristics of the products they wished to purchase"—was adequate under *Zauderer*.[216] The purpose behind the rule

---

[211] *Id.* at 530.

[212] *Id.* at 522-23.

[213] *See* Am. Meat Institute v. U.S. Dept. of Agric., 760 F.3d 18, 22-23 (D.C. Cir. 2014); *see also* *NAM II*, 800 F.3d at 533 (Srinivasan, J., dissenting).

[214] *See, e.g.,* SEC v. Wall St. Publ'g Inst., 851 F.2d 365, 372-73 (D.C. Cir. 1988).

[215] *See NAM I*, 748 F. 3d at 372 (concluding that *Wall Street Publishing* did not apply to evaluation of conflict minerals rule and further stating that "[i]t is not entirely clear what would result if *Wall Street Publishing* did apply to this case.").

[216] *Am. Meat Institute*, 760 F.3d at 24-26 ("[B]y acting only through a reasonably crafted disclosure mandate, the government meets its burden of showing that the mandate advances its interest in making the 'purely factual and uncontroversial information' accessible to the

at issue in *American Meat Institute* may be viewed by a court as similar to the SEC's stated goal of providing further information to investors,[217] in a manner that uses seemingly neutral numerical figures. On the other hand, there are reasons why the rule might be viewed as similar to conflict minerals rule at issue in *NAM.* For instance, with some viewing the underlying purpose of pay ratio rule to be "naming and shaming,"[218] the nature of the disclosure at issue with the pay ratio rule could be viewed as being more value-laden than factual and uncontroversial like the rule at issue in *American Meat Institute*.

Since the D.C. Circuit's decision in *NAM*, the SEC has issued statements announcing that it is reevaluating the conflict minerals rule[219] and that it will *not* take enforcement action against companies that comply with the rule's country of origin inquiry requirements, but forgo the second step of conducting further due diligence if the source of the minerals is found to be the DRC or adjoining countries.[220] The Financial CHOICE Act of 2017 would repeal the section of Dodd-Frank authorizing the conflict minerals rule.[221] However, the rule is not addressed by the Economic Growth, Regulatory Relief, and Consumer Protection Act passed by the Senate.[222]

---

recipients…[T]his particular method of achieving a government interest will almost always demonstrate a reasonable means-ends relationship, absent a showing that the disclosure is 'unduly burdensome' in a way that 'chill[s] protected commercial speech.'") (internal citations omitted).

[217] Adopting Release, *supra* note 105, at 9.

[218] Gallagher Dissenting Statement, *supra* note 125 ("We've seen from our Conflict Minerals rule that naming-andshaming rules can fall afoul of the First Amendment, and so the question is raised in my mind whether pay ratio disclosures are constitutional.").

[219] Public Statement, Acting Chairman Michael S. Piwowar, *Reconsideration of Conflict Minerals Rule Implementation* (Jan. 31, 2017), https://www.sec.gov/news/statement/reconsideration-of-conflict-minerals-rule-implementation.html.

[220] Public Statement, SEC DIVISION OF CORPORATE FINANCE, *Updated Statement on the Effect of the Court of Appeals Decision on the Conflict Minerals Rule* (April 7, 2017), https://www.sec.gov/news/public-statement/corpfin-updatedstatement-court-decision-conflict-minerals-rule ("[T]he Division of Corporation Finance has determined that it will not recommend enforcement action to the Commission if companies, including those that are subject to paragraph (c) of Item 1.01 of Form SD, only file disclosure under the provisions of paragraphs (a) and (b) of Item 1.01 of Form SD.")

[221] *See* H.R. 10, 115th Cong. § 862 (2017).

[222] *See* S. 2155, 115th Cong. (2018).

Resource Extraction Rule

Section 1504 of Dodd-Frank directs the SEC to promulgate a rule requiring companies to disclose payments they make to the U.S. or foreign governments relating to the commercial development of oil, natural gas, or minerals.[223] The purpose of the rule was to increase transparency and combat global corruption, addressing the "mineral curse" often experienced by resource-rich nations whose governments may divert funds obtained from resource extraction and development without accountability to their citizens.[224] As discussed below, the rule was vacated by a court in 2013 before being legislatively repealed in early 2017.

In 2013, the federal district court for the District of Columbia vacated an initial version of the resource extraction rule.[225] The court concluded that the SEC had misinterpreted the statutory language of Dodd-Frank as requiring issuers to *publicly* disclose the reports of their government payments, as opposed to simply filing them with the SEC.[226] The court further found that the SEC acted "arbitrarily and capriciously" in violation of the APA in not providing for any exemptions to the disclosure rule.[227] For example, industry participants had advocated for an exemption as to countries in which disclosing payments would be illegal under foreign law, claiming they would otherwise need to exit the market in those countries, losing billions of dollars.[228] While the SEC believed that any exemptions would undermine the rule's purpose, the court focused on Congress's specific authorization for exemptions[229] as well as the statutory text's focus on practicability[230] in rejecting the SEC's argument.

---

[223] Dodd-Frank § 1504 (codified at 15 U.S.C. § 78m(q)).

[224] *See id.;* Andrew L. Magner, *Drilling for Disclosure: Resource Extraction Issuer Disclosure and* American Petroleum Institute v. SEC, 40 J. CORP. L. 521, 523 (2015).

[225] *See* Am. Petroleum Inst. v. SEC, 953 F. Supp. 2d 5 (D.D.C. 2013).

[226] *Id.* at 11. For example, because another provision in Section 1504 provided for the SEC making public a *compilation* of data collected under the rule, as opposed to individual companies' reports, the court favored a reading of the statute that the individual reports themselves need not be made public. *Id.* at 17-19.

[227] *Id.* at 20.

[228] *Id.* at 21.

[229] *See* 15 U.S.C. § 78l(h).

[230] *See, e.g.,* 15 U.S.C. § 78m(q)(2)(E) (providing that the rule should support the government's efforts to promote international transparency "to the extent practicable").

The SEC passed another version of the rule in 2016, which again required public disclosure but allowed companies to apply for exemptions on a case-by-case basis.[231] However, the rule was revoked by Congress under the Congressional Review Act[232] via a joint resolution of disapproval, which the President signed in February 2017.[233] Unless Section 1504 of Dodd-Frank itself is repealed, however, the SEC retains the power to formulate a rule that is not "substantially the same" as the revoked version.[234] Nonetheless, the SEC has not identified doing so as a priority.[235] The Financial CHOICE Act would repeal Section 1504 altogether,[236] but such a repeal is not included in the Economic Growth, Regulatory Relief, and Consumer Protection Act passed by the Senate.[237]

---

[231] Final Rule: Disclosure of Payments by Resource Extraction Issuers, Exchange Act Release No. 34-78167, 81 Fed. Reg. 49359 (July 27, 2016).

[232] 5 U.S.C. §§ 801-808.

[233] P.L. 115-4, 131 Stat. 9 (Feb. 14, 2017).

[234] 5 U.S.C. § 801(b)(2).

[235] The rule was placed on the SEC's "long term" agenda in its Regulatory Flexibility Agenda released in January 2018. *See* Regulatory Flexibility Agenda, 83 Fed. Reg. 2022 (Jan. 12, 2018).

[236] *See* H.R. 10, 115th Cong. § 862 (2017).

[237] *See* S. 2155, 115th Cong. (2018).

In: Financial Crises and Programs
Editor: Patricia Hall
ISBN: 978-1-53614-159-7

Chapter 4

REGULATORY REFORM 10 YEARS AFTER THE FINANCIAL CRISIS: SYSTEMIC RISK REGULATION OF NON-BANK FINANCIAL INSTITUTIONS*

Jay B. Sykes

SUMMARY

When large, interconnected financial institutions become distressed, policymakers have historically faced a choice between (1) a taxpayer-funded bailout, and (2) the destabilization of the financial system—a dilemma that commentators have labeled the "too-big-to-fail" (TBTF) problem. The 2007-2009 financial crisis highlighted the significance of the TBTF problem. During the crisis, a number of large financial institutions experienced severe distress, and the federal government committed hundreds of billions of dollars in an effort to rescue the financial system. According to some commentators, the crisis underscored the inadequacy of existing prudential regulation of large financial institutions, and of the bankruptcy system for resolving the failure of such institutions.

* This is an edited, reformatted and augmented version of a Congressional Research Service report, R45162, dated April 12, 2018.

In response to the crisis, Congress passed and President Obama signed the Dodd-Frank Wall Street Reform and Consumer Protection Act (Dodd-Frank) in 2010. Titles I and II of Dodd-Frank are specifically directed at minimizing the systemic risk created by TBTF financial institutions. In order to minimize the risks that large financial institutions will fail, Title I of Dodd-Frank establishes an enhanced prudential regulatory regime for certain large bank holding companies and non-bank financial companies. In order to "resolve" (i.e., reorganize or liquidate) systemically important financial institutions, Title II establishes a new resolution regime available for such institutions outside of the Bankruptcy Code.

The Title I regime applies to (1) all bank holding companies with total consolidated assets of $50 billion or more, and (2) any non-bank financial companies that the Financial Stability Oversight Council (FSOC) designates as systemically important. To date, FSOC has designated four non-bank financial companies for enhanced supervision: AIG, GE Capital, Prudential, and MetLife. However, FSOC has rescinded its designations of AIG and GE Capital as a result of changes to those companies, and MetLife successfully challenged its designation in federal court, leaving Prudential as the sole remaining designee as of the publication of this chapter.

Legislation that would repeal FSOC's authority to designate non-banks for enhanced supervision has passed the House of Representatives (H.R. 10), and a bill that would alter FSOC's designation process and standards in more limited ways has also been introduced in the House (H.R. 4061).

Title II of Dodd-Frank creates an "Orderly Liquidation Authority" (OLA) pursuant to which the Federal Deposit Insurance Corporation (FDIC) can serve as the receiver for failing financial companies that pose a significant risk to the financial stability of the United States. The OLA, which was developed as an alternative to the Bankruptcy Code, is similar to the mechanisms the FDIC uses to resolve failed commercial banks. The OLA grants the FDIC broad powers to manage the liquidation or sale of a failed financial company, and Title II includes provisions that offer financial institutions more robust protections against "runs" by their derivatives counterparties than they would have under the Bankruptcy Code. The FDIC, Federal Reserve, and Office of the Comptroller of the Currency have promulgated a number of rules that have important consequences for the OLA concerning the FDIC's powers as receiver, its general strategy for resolving failed institutions, "loss-absorbing capacity" requirements for certain bank holding companies, and derivatives contracts.

There have also been a number of proposals to reform Title II. A bill that would (among other things) repeal Title II passed the House in June 2017, and bills to amend the Bankruptcy Code to allow it to deal more effectively with the failure of large financial institutions have been introduced in the House and the Senate (H.R. 10 (115th Cong.), H.R. 1667 (115th Cong.), S. 1840 (114th Cong.)).

INTRODUCTION

The prospect of a large financial institution's failure often presents policymakers with a stark choice. Regulators can "bailout" a distressed institution, risking taxpayer money and arguably creating incentives for management, shareholders, and creditors of similar institutions to take excessive risks. Alternatively, the government can allow the institution to fail, running the risk of financial destabilization.[1] Before the 2007-2009 financial crisis, regulators relied on a variety of prudential regulations, federal deposit insurance, and the Federal Reserve's emergency lending power to limit the risk of commercial bank failures.[2] Commercial banks are also subject to a special insolvency regime administered by the Federal Deposit Insurance Corporation (FDIC), in which the FDIC has robust authorities to rapidly resolve failed banks outside of the Bankruptcy Code.[3]

However, many non-bank financial institutions fall outside the ambit of these regulations despite facing risks similar to those confronting commercial banks. Many commentators viewed the distress and failure of a number of these institutions during the 2007-2009 crisis as highlighting the inadequacy of existing prudential regulations for such firms, and of the Bankruptcy Code for resolving their failure.[4] The Dodd-Frank Wall Street Reform and Consumer Protection Act of 2010 (Dodd-Frank) adopted two general solutions to these perceived problems.[5] First, Title I of the Act created the Financial Stability Oversight Council (FSOC) and granted it the authority to designate systemically important non-bank financial companies for enhanced prudential regulation by the Federal Reserve.[6] Second, Title II of Dodd-Frank established the Orderly Liquidation Authority (OLA), a

---

[1] *See* "The "Too-Big-To-Fail" Problem" *infra*.

[2] *See* "Title I: Enhanced Prudential Standards for Systemically Important Financial Institutions" *infra*.

[3] *See* "Pre-Dodd-Frank Resolution Mechanisms: Bankruptcy vs. FDIC Resolution" *infra*.

[4] *See* Ben S. Bernanke, *Why Dodd-Frank's Orderly Liquidation Authority Should be Preserved*, The Brookings Inst. (Feb. 28, 2017), https://www.brookings.edu/blog/ben-bernanke/2017/02/28/why-dodd-franks-orderly-liquidationauthority-should-be-preserved/; *Financial Regulatory Reform: A New Foundation*, U.S. Dep't Of The Treasury 20 (Oct. 8, 2009), https://www.treasury.gov/initiatives/Documents/Final Reportweb.pdf.

[5] P.L. 111-203, 124 Stat. 1376 (2010).

[6] *See* "Designation of Non-Banks for Enhanced Prudential Regulation" *infra*.

special resolution regime outside of the Bankruptcy Code that can be invoked for systemically important financial institutions.[7]

As discussed in more detail below, federal regulatory agencies have pursued a number of measures to implement Titles I and II of Dodd-Frank.[8] And 10 years after the crisis, legal commentators continue to debate whether these provisions have improved the resiliency of the financial system.[9] This chapter provides an overview of how regulatory agencies have implemented Dodd-Frank's systemic risk provisions concerning non-bank financial institutions, and the legal debates surrounding proposals to repeal or change those provisions. In order to provide necessary background, the first two sections of the report discuss the nature of the "too big-to-fail" problem and the 2007-2009 financial crisis.[10] The report then provides an overview of Titles I and II,[11] their implementation by the relevant federal agencies,[12] criticisms of those provisions and responses,[13] and legislative proposals to change them.[14] An *Appendix* to this chapter contains a glossary that defines certain key terms in the report.[15]

THE "TOO-BIG-TO-FAIL" PROBLEM

When large, interconnected financial institutions become distressed, policymakers often face a choice between (1) a taxpayer-funded bailout, and (2) the destabilization of the financial system—a dilemma that

[7] *See* "Title II and the Orderly Liquidation Authority" *infra.*
[8] *See* "Dodd-Frank Section 113 and FSOC Guidance" and "Administrative Rules" *infra.*
[9] *See* "Criticisms of Title I and Responses" and "Criticisms of Title II and Responses" *infra.*
[10] *See* "The "Too-Big-To-Fail" Problem" and "TBTF Financial Institutions During the 2007-2009 Financial Crisis" *infra.*
[11] *See* "Designation of Non-Banks for Enhanced Prudential Regulation" and "Title II and the Orderly Liquidation Authority" *infra.*
[12] *See* "Non-Bank Designations to Date" and "Administrative Rules" *infra.*
[13] *See* "Criticisms of Title I and Responses" and "Criticisms of Title II and Responses" *infra.*
[14] *See* "Proposals to Alter Title I" and "Proposals to Alter Title II" *infra.*
[15] *See Appendix.*

commentators have labeled the "too-big-to-fail" (TBTF) problem.[16] Two features of the financial system help explain the origin of the TBTF problem. First, banks and certain other financial institutions are almost always highly leveraged, meaning that their shareholder equity is a small fraction of their total assets, and that they accordingly fund their assets with large amounts of borrowing.[17] Second, banks and certain other financial institutions often fund themselves with large amounts of short-term debt, while investing in longer-term loans and other illiquid assets—a practice called "maturity transformation."[18] While commentators generally

---

[16] Randall D. Guynn, Framing the TBTF Problem: The Path to a Solution, in *Across the Great Divide: New Perspectives on the Financial Crisis* 281, 291 (Martin Neil Baily & John B. Taylor eds., 2014). See also Richard Scott Carnell, Jonathan R. Macey & Geoffrey P. Miller, *The Law of Financial Institutions* 38 (6th ed. 2017); CRS Report R42150, *Systemically Important or "Too Big to Fail" Financial Institutions*, by Marc Labonte; *Too Big to Fail: The Path to a Solution*, Bipartisan Policy Center (May 2013), http://bipartisanpolicy.org/wp-content/uploads/sites/default/files/TooBigToFail.pdf [hereinafter "Bipartisan Policy Center Report"].

[17] *See* Harry DeAngelo & René Stulz, *Why High Leverage is Optimal for Banks*, Harv. L. Sch. Forum on Corp. Gov. and Fin. Reg. (June 27, 2013), https://corpgov. law.harvard.edu/2013/06/27/why-high-leverage-is-optimal-for-banks/.

[18] *See* Guynn, *supra* note 16 at 291; Lawrence J. White, The Basics of Too Big to Fail, in *Perspectives in Doddfrank and Finance* 25, 26 (Paul H. Schultz ed., 2014); Daniel R. Fischel, Andrew M. Rosenfield & Robert S. Stillman, The Regulation of Banks and Bank Holding Companies, 73 *Va. L. Rev.* 301, 306-07 (1987); Douglas W. Diamond & Philip H. Dybvig, Bank Runs, Deposit Insurance, and Liquidity, 91 J. *Pol. Econ.* 401, 403 (1983).

Customer deposits, many of which are payable on demand (as in most checking accounts), represent major liabilities of commercial banks, which make loans to businesses and individuals. *See* Carnell, et al., *supra* note 16 at 67-78. And many large investment banks that deal in securities and derivatives obtain short-term financing from commercial paper and repurchase agreements (repos). White, *supra* note 18 at 26; Darrell Duffie, *How Big Banks Fail and What to Do About It* 29 (2011).

Commercial paper is a short-term, unsecured corporate IOU. Carnell, et al., *supra* note 16 at 152. By contrast, repos are transactions pursuant to which one party sells securities to another party for cash, while simultaneously agreeing to repurchase the same or similar securities at some time in the future at a premium. *See* Jeanne L. Schroeder, Repo Madness: The Characterization of Repurchase Agreements under the Bankruptcy Code and the U.C.C., 46 *Syracuse L. Rev.* 999, 1004-1006 (1996). The economic function of a repo is accordingly similar to that of a secured loan. *Id.* at 1006. Large investment banks often make heavy use of "overnight repos" with a term of one day in order to benefit from their flexibility and low financing rates. Duffie, *supra* note 18 at 29-30; *Final Report of the Nat'l Comm'n on the Causes of the Fin. And Econ. Crisis In The U.S.* 296-97 (2011) [Hereinafter "Financial Crisis Report"].

Although commentators generally agree that insurance companies "are less likely to pose systemic risk than similar-sized banks" because they are "less vulnerable to runs or other liquidity problems," Carnell, et al., *supra* note 16 at 671, insurance companies may pose systemic risk when they offer products that allow customers to withdraw assets with

agree that maturity transformation is socially valuable,[19] the process makes financial institutions vulnerable to liquidity "runs."[20] That is, when a financial institution's short-term creditors become concerned about its solvency or liquidity, they have incentives to demand immediate conversion of their claims into cash,[21] or to reduce their exposure in other ways that force the institution to sell its illiquid assets at significantly discounted prices.[22]

A "run" on one financial institution can spread to other institutions that do business with it.[23] Small banks typically hold deposit balances at larger banks, and large banks, securities firms, and insurance companies often face significant exposure to one another through their over-the-counter

---

minimal penalties, engage in securities lending and certain other capital markets activities, or when they have significant financial-guarantee businesses. *See* Daniel Schwarcz & Steven L. Schwarcz, Regulating Systemic Risk in Insurance, 81 U. *Chi. L. Rev.* 1569, 1571 (2014); Robert P. Bartlett III, *Inefficiencies in the Information Thicket: A Case Study of Derivatives Disclosures during the Financial Crisis*, 36 J. CORP. L. 1, 1-42 (2010).

19 *See* Edward Simpson Prescott, Introduction to the Special Issue on the Diamond-Dybvig Model, 96 *Fed. Res. Bank Richmond Econ. Q.* 1, 1-2 (2010).

20 *See* Guynn, *supra* note 16 at 291; Jonathan R. Macey & Geoffrey P. Miller, Bank Failures, Risk Monitoring, and the Market for Bank Control, 88 *Colum. L. Rev.* 1153, 1156-59 (1988); Fischel, et al., *supra* note 18 at 307-10; Diamond & Dybvig, *supra* note 18 at 401-02.

21 Guynn, *supra* note 16 at 291; Bipartisan Policy Center Report, *supra* note 16 at 38-39; Robert E. Litan & Jonathan Rauch, *American Finance for the 21st Century* 98-112 (1997); Fischel, et al., *supra* note 18 at 307-10.

Commentators have argued that short-term creditors face a classic "prisoner's dilemma" in which creditors as a group are often harmed by mass withdrawals that force a financial institution to take value-reducing actions, such as liquidating loans or securities at distressed prices. Macey & Miller, *supra* note 20 at 1156-57; Fischel, et al., *supra* note 18 at 307-10. However, individual creditors have incentives to withdraw their assets from a troubled institution to avoid being left with nothing. Fischel, et al., *supra* note 18 at 307-10. Fearing that other creditors will withdraw funds from a troubled institution, creditors "may rationally adopt a 'me-first' attitude and demand payment as soon as possible," precipitating a "run." *Id.* at 308.

22 In the case of a large investment bank, these exposure-mitigating activities may include, among other things: (1) repo lenders demanding increased collateral or declining to renew their positions altogether, (2) derivatives counterparties requesting that other investment banks assume the obligations of a troubled bank (an act referred to as a "novation"), resulting in the transfer of cash collateral out of the troubled bank, and (3) hedge funds and other prime-brokerage clients of a troubled bank withdrawing cash from their free credit balances at the bank. *See* Duffie, *supra* note 18 at 23- 42.

23 White, *supra* note 18 at 27; Litan & Rauch, *supra* note 21 at 98-112; Helen A. Garten, Banking on the Market: Relying on Depositors to Control Bank Risks, 4 *Yale J. On Reg.* 129, 160-63 (1986).

derivatives portfolios.[24] Accordingly, troubles at one financial institution can spread to others, resulting in additional "runs" and a "contagious panic throughout the financial system that causes otherwise solvent financial institutions to become insolvent."[25] This type of financial "contagion" can cause asset price implosions as institutions liquidate assets in order to meet creditor demands, further impairing their ability to lend and the ability of businesses to raise capital.[26] Faced with a choice between bailouts and economic collapse, policymakers have generally opted for bailouts,[27] arguably creating incentives for financial institutions to take excessive risks and grow larger than is socially optimal.[28]

---

[24] Litan & Rauch, *supra* note 21 at 98-112. A "derivative" is a financial instrument whose value depends on the value of some other asset, such as a commodity, interest rate, currency, bond, or stock. Carnell, et al., *supra* note 16 at 871-72. An "over-the-counter" (OTC) derivative is a derivative contract that is "individually negotiated by parties dealing directly with one another," as opposed to a derivative contract that is traded on an organized exchange. *Id.* at 871.

Commentators have observed that the OTC derivatives market is highly concentrated, generating high levels of systemic risk. *See* Sheri M. Markose, Systemic Risk from Global Financial Derivatives: A Network Analysis of Contagion and Its Mitigation with Super-Spreader Tax, *International Monetary Fund* 8 (2012), https://www.imf.org/external/pubs/ft/wp/2012/wp12282.pdf (noting that according to a 2009 survey conducted by Fitch Ratings, "the top 12 counterparties [in the OTC derivatives market] comprised 78 percent of total exposure," and that "dependence on a limited number of counterparties looks to be a permanent feature of the market").

Moreover, as discussed in greater detail in "QFCs" *infra*, OTC derivatives often provide counterparties with "cross-default rights"—that is, rights to terminate the contract, set-off obligations, or liquidate collateral based on the bankruptcy of a party's parent, subsidiary, or affiliate. The bankruptcy of a financial holding company can accordingly trigger "runs" on its subsidiaries, and vice versa.

[25] Guynn, *supra* note 16 at 291. *See also* White, *supra* note 18 at 27; Bipartisan Policy Center Report, *supra* note 16 at 39; Litan & Rauch, *supra* note 21 at 98-112.

[26] *See* Litan & Rauch, *supra* note 21 at 98-112.

[27] Guynn, *supra* note 16 at 291 ("All indications from history suggest that when public policymakers, and even the public, are faced with the choice between bailout and collapse or destabilization, they typically choose bailouts rather than risk a collapse of the system."); *Bipartisan Policy Center Report*, *supra* note 16 at 19 ("Faced with a choice between bailout and fire-sale liquidations or value-destroying reorganizations that can result in a contagious panic and a collapse of the financial system, ... policymakers typically choose bailout as the lesser of two evils."). *See also* Michael M. Phillips, Government Bailouts: A U.S. Tradition Dating to Hamilton, *Wall St. J.* (Sept. 20, 2008), https://www.wsj.com/articles/SB122186662036058787.

[28] *See* DUFFIE, *supra* note 18 at 5 (arguing that knowledge that TBTF institutions will receive government support when distressed "provides an additional incentive to large financial institutions to take inefficient risks, a well-understood moral hazard," and that "[t]he creditors of systemically important financial institutions may offer financing at terms that reflect the likelihood of a government bailout, thus further encouraging these financial

TBTF FINANCIAL INSTITUTIONS DURING THE 2007-2009 FINANCIAL CRISIS

The 2007-2009 financial crisis highlighted the significance of the TBTF problem. During that time, the United States experienced what many commentators believe was the worst financial crisis since the Great Depression, triggering a severe recession.[29] According to many observers, a principal cause of the crisis was the collapse of a bubble in the housing market that had developed in the early and mid-2000s.[30] As this bubble popped over the course of 2007 and 2008, many financial institutions experienced large losses related to the real estate market.[31]

---

institutions to increase leverage."); Bipartisan Policy Center Report, *supra* note 16 at 43-44 (arguing that if shareholders expect a TBTF institution to be bailed out, they "will encourage the institutions to engage in excessive risk-taking," and that bailouts result in market distortions in the form of "an *implicit government subsidy* of funding costs," because "shareholders, long-term unsecured debt holders and the holders of other capital structure liabilities might accept below-market returns if they expect the institutions or their claims to be bailed out by the government.").

[29] *See* Jeff Madrick, The Real Lesson of Lehman, *The N.Y. Review of Books* (Oct. 4, 2014), http://www.nybooks.com/ daily/2014/10/04/real-lesson-lehman-bankruptcy/; Jon Hilsenrath, Serena Ng & Damian Paletta, Worst Crisis Since '30s, With No End Yet in Sight, *Wall St. J.* (Sept. 18, 2008), https://www.wsj.com/articles/SB122169431617549947; Heather Stewart, We Are in the Worst Financial Crisis Since Depression, Says IMF, *The Guardian* (Apr. 9, 2008), https://www.theguardian.com/business/2008/apr/10/useconomy.subprimecrisis.

[30] *Financial Crisis Report*, *supra* note 18 at 1-4. *See also* Carnell, et al., *supra* note 16 at 32; White, *supra* note 18 at 31; Christopher L. Foote, Kristopher S. Gerardi & Paul S. Willen, Why Did So Many People Make So Many Ex Post Bad Decisions?: The Causes of the Foreclosure Crisis, in *Rethinking the Financial Crisis* 136, 136-40 (Alan S. Blinder, Andrew W. Lo & Robert M. Solow, eds. 2012).
Commentators have debated the ultimate and proximate causes of the 2007-2009 financial crisis. In analyzing the crisis, observers have contested the relative roles of financial deregulation, easy monetary policy, government housing policy, the complexity and opacity of newly-popular financial products, predatory mortgage lending, the concentration of risk in institutions outside the ambit of traditional banking regulations (the so-called "shadow banking system"), and government bailout policy, among other things. *See* Robert E. Litan, The Political Economy of Financial Regulation after the Crisis, in *Rethinking the Financial Crisis* 269, 270 ("There are so many alleged 'causes' of the great financial crisis of 2007 to 2008 that it is easy to lose count."); Financial Crisis Report, supra note 18 at 125-26, 187, 230, 255; Dissenting Statement of Keith Hennessy, Douglas Holtz-Eakin & Bill Thomas, in *Financial Crisis Report*, *supra* note 18 at 413-37; Dissenting Statement of Peter Wallison, in *Financial Crisis Report*, *supra* note 18 at 443-553.

[31] *Financial Crisis Report*, *supra* note 18 at 279-91.

In March 2008, Bear Stearns—the fifth largest American investment bank at the time—informed the Federal Reserve that it was unable to refinance its short-term debt as a result of a "run" by its short-term creditors.[32] Believing that the bankruptcy of Bear Stearns raised "the potential for contagion to similarly situated firms," and the possibility of "serious[] disrupt[ions]" to the stability of financial markets, the Federal Reserve exercised its authority to lend to non-banks in "unusual and exigent circumstances" under Section 13(3) of the Federal Reserve Act.[33] According to then-Chairman of the Federal Reserve Ben Bernanke, policymakers "were reasonably sure that [Bear Stearns's] unexpected bankruptcy filing would ignite ... panic."[34] A bankruptcy proceeding, Bernanke explained, could seriously damage the money market funds that lent to Bear Stearns and other corporations, and "lock up the cash of many other creditors, potentially for years."[35] Likewise, according to Bernanke, unwinding Bear Stearns's derivatives portfolio would have "prove[n] chaotic" because of its size and complexity.[36] Moreover, a decision by JP Morgan, the "clearing bank" for Bear Stearns's repurchase agreements (repos),[37] to liquidate collateral on behalf of Bear Stearns's creditors could

---

[32] Bear Stearns, JP Morgan Chase, and Maiden Lane LLC, Bd. Of Gov. Of The Fed. Res. Sys., https://www.federalreserve.gov/regreform/reform-bearstearns.htm.

[33] *See id.*; 12 U.S.C. § 343(3) (2006).

[34] Ben Bernanke, *The Courage To Act: A Memoir Of A Crisis And Its Aftermath* 215 (2015).

[35] *Id.* Money market funds are funds that generally invest in high-quality, liquid, short-term securities and give their investors the right to withdraw their share of the fund's assets on demand. Carnell, et al., *supra* note 16 at 32. However, unlike commercial banks, money market funds are not required to obtain deposit insurance and do not enjoy access to the Federal Reserve's "discount window." William A. Birdthistle, Breaking Bucks in Money Market Funds, 2010 *Wisc. L. Rev.* 1155, 1160-62 (2010). Before the financial crisis, money market funds had become a major source of short-term financing for major financial institutions and non-financial corporations, accumulating more than $3 trillion in assets. *Id.* at 1157.

[36] Bernanke, *supra* note 34 at 215-16.

[37] For an explanation of repos, see note 18 *supra*. Bear Stearns borrowed heavily in the "tri-party" repo market, in which a clearing bank intermediates between repo lenders and borrowers. *Id.* at 216. *See also* Adam Copeland, Darrell Duffie, Antoine Martin & Susan McLaughlin, Key Mechanics of the U.S. Tri-Party Repo Market, *Fed. Res. Bank of New York Econ. Pol. Rev.* 17 (Nov. 2012), https://www.newyorkfed.org/medialibrary/media/research/epr/12v18n3/ 1210cope.pdf.
The role of clearing banks in the tri-party repo market consists primarily in shifting cash and securities back and forth between borrowers and lenders. *Id.* at 6. However, before and during the financial crisis, the two principal clearing banks (JP Morgan and Bank of New

drive securities prices down even further, "leading to a new wave of losses and write-downs" and possible "runs" on other investment banks.[38]

Accordingly, on March 14, the Federal Reserve Bank of New York (New York Fed) extended a bridge loan of $12.9 billion to Bear Stearns as it worked to orchestrate a deal to save the investment bank.[39] On March 17, the Federal Reserve shepherded an acquisition of Bear Stearns by JP Morgan.[40] In order to facilitate the acquisition, the Federal Reserve again exercised its Section 13(3) authority, creating an entity called Maiden Lane LLC and lending it roughly $29 billion to purchase certain mortgage assets from Bear Stearns.[41]

Although the Bear Stearns rescue temporarily calmed markets,[42] similar troubles surfaced later in 2008 at Lehman Brothers (Lehman), the

---

York Mellon) provided borrowers with several hours of "intraday" credit while arranging their transactions. *Id.* at 6. Commentators have observed that the large exposure of clearing banks to troubled repo dealers and to the possibility of sharp declines in the value of the securities that collateralize repos were major contributors to systemic risk. *Id.* at 6-7.

[38] Bernanke, *supra* note 34 at 216. *See also* Timothy F. Geithner, *Stress Test: Reflections on Financial Crises* 150 (2014) ("[Bear Stearns] was completely unmeshed in the fabric of the system. It had nearly four hundred subsidiaries. It had trading positions with five thousand counterparties around the world. And it had borrowed about $80 billion in the tri-party repo market, presenting ... risks of runs on money markets and investment banks.").

[39] *See* Bd. of Gov. of the Fed. Res. Sys., *supra* note 32. This bridge loan was extended to Bear Stearns through JP Morgan, the clearing bank between Bear Stearns and its repo lenders. *Id.*; Bernanke, *supra* note 34 at 214. The loan was secured by Bear Stearns assets valued at $13.8 billion and was repaid on March 17, 2008. Bd. of Gov. of the Fed. Res. Sys, *supra* note 32.

[40] *Id.*

[41] *Id.*; Bernanke, *supra* note 34 at 219 (explaining that JP Morgan CEO Jamie Dimon "had made clear" that without government assistance, "the deal would be too big and too risky for JP Morgan"); Geithner, *supra* note 38 at 153 (explaining that JP Morgan had refused to acquire Bear Stearns without government assistance).

The Maiden Lane transaction was formally structured as a loan to comply with Section 13(3) of the Federal Reserve Act. However, some commentators have argued that the transaction exceeded the scope of the Federal Reserve's Section 13(3) authority because "the primary goal of the transaction was to remove ... assets from Bear Stearns's balance sheet," meaning that it functioned more like an asset purchase (which is not allowed under Section 13(3)) than a loan. *See* Alexander Mehra, *Legal Authority in Unusual and Exigent Circumstances: The Federal Reserve and the Financial Crisis*, 13 U. Pa. J. Bus. L. 221, 238 (2010).

JP Morgan also extended a loan of roughly $1 billion to Maiden Lane LLC, which was subordinated to the loan made by the Federal Reserve. Bd. of Gov. of the Fed. Res. Sys, *supra* note 32. Maiden Lane LLC fully repaid its loans from the Federal Reserve on June 14, 2012. *See Maiden Lane Transactions*, Fed. Res. Bank of New York, https://www.newyorkfed.org/markets/maidenlane.html#tabs-1.

[42] Bernanke, *supra* note 34 at 226; *Financial Crisis Report*, *supra* note 18 at 292.

nation's fourth largest investment bank at the time.[43] Over the weekend of September 12, the New York Fed attempted to coordinate a private-sector solution that would avert a Lehman bankruptcy.[44] During these negotiations, regulators took the position that no government money would be committed to rescuing Lehman, unlike the case of Bear Stearns six months earlier.[45]

The government's attempts to broker an acquisition of Lehman ultimately failed. Bank of America, one of the potential acquirers, purchased the also-troubled investment bank Merrill Lynch instead.[46] British regulators of Barclays, another potential purchaser, refused to approve a proposed deal without a shareholder vote.[47] Unable to secure government support or find a private buyer, Lehman declared bankruptcy on September 15, 2008.[48]

Lehman's bankruptcy reverberated throughout financial markets. On September 15, the Dow Jones Industrial Average dropped more than 500 points, its worst single-day decline in seven years.[49] Shares of Goldman Sachs and Morgan Stanley, two of the largest remaining investment banks, lost an eighth of their value.[50] Lehman's bankruptcy also precipitated a "run" on money market funds.[51] The Reserve Primary Fund, a large fund that had invested in Lehman's commercial paper, "broke the buck,"

---

[43] *Financial Crisis Report*, *supra* note 18 at 327-31; David Teather, Andrew Clark & Jill Treanor, Barclays Agrees $1.75bn Deal for Core Lehman Brothers Business, *The Guardian* (Sept. 16, 2008), https://www.theguardian.com/business/2008/sep/17/barclay.lehmanbrothers1.

While troubles at Lehman did not boil over until September 2008, policymakers reportedly "had been pressing [it] to raise more capital for at least a year." Bernanke, *supra* note 34 at 252. However, because Lehman was an investment bank, neither the Federal Reserve nor the FDIC had the authority to compel it to raise capital. *Id.* ("If Lehman had been a midsize commercial bank, forcing [it] to raise more capital would have been straightforward: Either the company met the supervisor's expectations or the FDIC would have taken it over and paid off the depositors as necessary. But neither the Fed nor the FDIC had the authority to take over Lehman ... Legally, the government's only alternative, if Lehman couldn't find new capital, would have been trying to force the firm into bankruptcy.").

[44] Carnell, et al., *supra* note 16 at 35.

[45] Carnell, et al., *supra* note 16 at 35; Geithner, *supra* note 38 at 178; *Financial Crisis Report*, *supra* note 18 at 334.

[46] *Financial Crisis Report*, *supra* note 18 at 337.

[47] *Id.* at 335-37.

[48] Carnell, et al., *supra* note 16 at 35.

[49] Bernanke, *supra* note 34 at 270.

[50] *Id.*

[51] Carnell, et al., *supra* note 16 at 35.

meaning that its asset value per share fell below $1.[52] Because money market investors had come to expect that fund shares would always be worth $1, the troubles at the Reserve Primary Fund precipitated a $300 billion "run" on other funds, threatening a key source of short-term financing for large and medium-sized companies.[53]

Also in September 2008, American International Group (AIG)—the nation's largest insurance company at the time—came under heavy financial pressure.[54] During the real estate boom, one of AIG's affiliates had accumulated significant exposure to the housing market by selling "credit default swaps" (CDSs) on mortgage bonds, which provided their purchasers with credit protection in the event that the bonds defaulted.[55] On September 15, the day Lehman declared bankruptcy, AIG suffered a credit rating downgrade that required it to post margin on its CDS obligations.[56] Later that day, AIG informed the New York Fed that it was unable to access the commercial paper market in order to meet the margin call.[57] As it had done with Bear Stearns, the Federal Reserve invoked its

---

[52] *Id.*

[53] *Id.*; Geithner, *supra* note 38 at 195.

[54] Carnell, et al., *supra* note 16 at 35; *Financial Crisis Report*, *supra* note 18 at 344-52.

[55] Carnell, et al., *supra* note 16 at 35, 50. As an insurance company, AIG's operations were primarily overseen by state regulators—specifically, the New York State Insurance Department. *Financial Crisis Report*, *supra* note 18 at 345. However, AIG's holding company (including its foreign operations and non-insurance businesses) was not subject to oversight by insurance regulators. Bernanke, *supra* note 34 at 271-72. Rather, because AIG's holding company owned a small savings-and-loan company, it fell within the regulatory purview of the federal Office of Thrift Supervision (OTS). *Id.* Dodd-Frank eliminated the OTS, 12 U.S.C. § 5413, and transferred its functions and powers to the Office of the Comptroller of the Currency, the FDIC, and the Federal Reserve, *id.* § 5412.
In addition to losses on its CDS portfolio, AIG also experienced large losses related to its securities lending business. *See* Robert McDonald & Anna Paulson, *AIG in Hindsight*, Fed. Res. Bank of Chicago 10-12 (Oct. 2014), https://www.chicagofed.org/~/media/publications/working-papers/2014/wp2014-07-pdf.pdf. In a securities lending transaction, one party borrows a security (often as part of a short-selling strategy, or to deliver a security to a customer) from another party and deposits collateral (typically cash) with the securities lender. *Id.* at 10. The securities lender often invests the cash collateral in short-term, highly liquid securities because lending agreements are generally callable on demand. *Id.* at 10-11. However, AIG invested a substantial portion of its cash collateral in longer-term, illiquid assets such as mortgage-backed securities, making it vulnerable to a "run." *Id.* at 11. After AIG announced a large quarterly loss in August 2008, a number of its securities lending counterparties terminated their lending agreements, forcing AIG to liquidate its longer-term assets at significantly discounted prices. *Id.* at 11-12.

[56] Carnell, et al., *supra* note 16 at 35.

[57] *Financial Crisis Report*, *supra* note 18 at 349.

Section 13(3) authority to rescue AIG, reasoning that an AIG bankruptcy would have devastating effects on the financial system.[58] On September 16, the Federal Reserve announced that it would provide AIG with an $85 billion credit line in exchange for a 79.9 percent stake in the firm.[59]

---

[58] Bernanke, *supra* note 34 at 283 ("[AIG's] failure would create chaos in so many ways: by raising doubts about the solvency of its creditors and derivative counterparties ... ; by imposing losses on holders of its commercial paper ... ; and by draining available cash from state funds set up to protect customers of failing insurance companies."); Geithner, *supra* note 38 at 191 ("The more our Fed team studied AIG and the insolvency regime for insurers, the less confidence they had in the potential for an orderly resolution ... Virtually every major financial institution in the world had some exposure to AIG."); *Financial Crisis Report*, *supra* note 18 at 350 (quoting a press release from the Federal Reserve explaining that "a disorderly failure of AIG could add to already significant levels of financial market fragility and lead to substantially higher borrowing costs, reduced household wealth, and materially weaker economic performance.").

[59] *Financial Crisis Report*, *supra* note 18 at 350. David S. Hilzenrath & Glenn Kessler, U.S. Seizes Control of AIG With $85 Billion Emergency Loan, *Wash. Post.* (Sept. 17, 2008), http://www.washingtonpost.com/wp-dyn/content/article/2008/09/16/AR2008091602174_3.html. The Federal Reserve's loans to AIG were fully repaid in June 2012. *New York Fed Announces Full Repayment of its Loans to Maiden Lane LLC and Maiden Lane III LLC*, Fed. Res. Bank of New York (June 14, 2012), https://www.newyorkfed.org/newsevents/news/markets/2012/an120614.html.

The reasons why regulators allowed Lehman but not Bear Stearns or AIG to fail remain contested. In the weeks after Lehman filed for bankruptcy, Bernanke testified that while "[t]he failure of Lehman posed risks," the bank's difficulties "had been well known for some time," and the market was accordingly prepared to deal with its failure. *Financial Crisis Report*, *supra* note 18 at 340. Bernanke and then-President of the New York Fed Timothy Geithner have subsequently asserted that unlike Bear Stearns and AIG, Lehman did not have sufficient collateral to allow the Federal Reserve to lend pursuant to its Section 13(3) authority. *See id.*; Bernanke, *supra* note 34 at 226, 287-88; Geithner, *supra* note 38 at 185, 187, 206-07.

This claim has been the subject of much debate. *See* Laurence M. Ball, *The Fed And Lehman Brothers: Setting The Record Straight On A Financial Disaster* (forthcoming, 2018); James B. Stewart & Peter Eavis, Revisiting the Lehman Brothers Bailout That Never Was, *N.Y. Times* (Sept. 29, 2014), https://www.nytimes.com/2014/09/30/business/revisiting-the-lehman-brothers-bailout-that-never-was.html; *Financial Crisis Report*, *supra* note 18 at 340 41; James Surowiecki, Explaining the Decision to Let Lehman Fail, *The New Yorker* (Jan. 22, 2009), https://www. newyorker.com/business/james-surowiecki/explaining-the-decision-to-let-lehman-fail.

Critics of the decision to allow Lehman to fail note that by its terms, Section 13(3) requires only that loans to non-banks be "secured to the satisfaction of the Federal Reserve," as opposed to fully secured. *Financial Crisis Report*, *supra* note 18 at 340-41. The Financial Crisis Inquiry Commission, a ten-member commission charged with investigating the crisis by the Fraud Enforcement and Recovery Act, P.L. 111-21 (2009), concluded that regulators declined to rescue Lehman "for a variety of reasons, including the lack of a private firm willing and able to acquire it, uncertainty about Lehman's potential losses, concerns about moral hazard and political reaction, and erroneous assumptions that Lehman's failure would have a manageable impact on the financial system." *Financial Crisis Report*, *supra* note 18 at 343.

In the fall of 2008, troubles at other large institutions rocked financial markets. Fannie Mae and Freddie Mac—government-sponsored enterprises that purchased and guaranteed mortgage loans and securities—were placed into conservatorships.[60] The FDIC took over Washington Mutual, the nation's third largest mortgage lender, and sold it to JP Morgan.[61] Goldman Sachs and Morgan Stanley, the two largest remaining investment banks, converted to bank holding companies to assure themselves continued access to the Federal Reserve's "discount window," among other reasons.[62] Numerous European financial institutions suffered "runs."[63] In October 2008, President George W. Bush signed the Emergency Economic Stabilization Act.[64] The Act established the Troubled Asset Relief Program (TARP),[65] pursuant to which the federal government would eventually disburse over $400 billion in the form of investments in financial institutions and the automotive industry, among other things.[66]

The troubles in the financial system also spilled over to the real economy. U.S. households lost an estimated 26 percent of their wealth ($17 trillion) between mid-2007 and early 2009.[67] And between 2008 and December 2009, the economy lost an estimated 8.3 million jobs.[68]

---

[60] *Financial Crisis Report*, *supra* note 18 at 309.

[61] Carnell, et al., *supra* note 16 at 35.

[62] As Goldman and Morgan Shift, a Wall St. Era Ends, *N.Y. Times Dealbook* (Sept. 21, 2008), https://dealbook.nytimes.com/2008/09/21/goldman-morgan-to-become-bank-holding-companies/. The "discount window" is the program pursuant to which the Federal Reserve serves as a "lender of last resort," allowing banks to borrow in order to meet temporary liquidity needs, generally at a penalty rate of interest. *See* 12 U.S.C. § 343(2). During the crisis, the Federal Reserve opened the "discount window" to investment banks. *Id.* However, the Federal Reserve had indicated that such access was only temporary when Goldman Sachs and Morgan Stanley converted to bank holding companies. *Id.*

[63] Carnell, et al., *supra* note 16 at 35-6.

[64] P.L. 110-343, 122 Stat. 3765 (2008).

[65] 12 U.S.C. § 5211.

[66] Jonathan Weisman, U.S. Declares Bank and Auto Bailouts Over, and Profitable, *N.Y. Times* (Dec. 19, 2014), https://www.nytimes.com/2014/12/20/business/us-signals-end-of-bailouts-of-automakers-and-wall-street.html. *See also TARP Programs*, U.S. Dep't of the Treasury, https://www.treasury.gov/initiatives/financial-stability/TARPPrograms/Pages/ default.aspx.

[67] William R. Emmons & Bryan J. Noeth, *Household Financial Stability: Who Suffered the Most from the Crisis?*, Fed. Res. Bank of St. Louis (July 2012), https://www.stlouisfed. org/publications/regional-economist/july-2012/householdfinancial-stability—who-suffered-the-most-from-the-crisis#endnotes.

[68] *Financial Crisis Report*, *supra* note 18 at 390.

In response to the crisis, Congress passed and President Obama signed the Dodd-Frank Wall Street Reform and Consumer Protection Act of 2010 (Dodd-Frank),[69] legislation that some commentators characterized as "the most ambitious overhaul of financial regulation in generations."[70] Among other things, Dodd-Frank reformed certain aspects of securities and derivatives markets,[71] imposed a variety of requirements related to mortgage standards,[72] and created a new federal agency tasked with consumer financial protection (the Consumer Financial Protection Bureau).[73] Other portions of Dodd-Frank are specifically directed at the systemic risk created by TBTF financial institutions. In order to minimize the risks that large financial institutions like Lehman and AIG fail, Title I of Dodd-Frank establishes an enhanced prudential regulatory regime for certain large bank holding companies and non-bank financial companies.[74] And in order to resolve systemically important financial institutions in the event that they nevertheless experience financial distress, Title II establishes a new resolution regime available for such institutions outside of the Bankruptcy Code.[75] The remaining sections of this chapter discuss the legal issues raised by Titles I and II, their implementation by federal regulatory agencies, and proposals to reform them.

---

[69] P.L. 111-203, 124 Stat. 1376 (2010).

[70] Brady Dennis, Congress passes financial reform bill, *Wash. Post.* (July 16, 2010), http://www.washingtonpost.com/wp-dyn/content/article/2010/07/15/AR2010071500464.html.

[71] 15 U.S.C. § 78o-11; P.L. 111-203, tit. VII, XVI. *See also* CRS Legal Sidebar LSB10077, *The Half Trillion Dollar Ruling: Latest Dodd-Frank Case Narrows "Skin-in-the-Game" Rule*, by Jay B. Sykes.

[72] P.L. 111-203, tit. XIV.

[73] *Id.* tit., X. For a high-level overview of Dodd-Frank, *see* CRS Report R41350, *The Dodd-Frank Wall Street Reform and Consumer Protection Act: Background and Summary*, coordinated by Baird Webel.

[74] P.L. 111-203, tit. I.

[75] *Id.*, tit. II.

TITLE I: ENHANCED PRUDENTIAL STANDARDS FOR SYSTEMICALLY IMPORTANT FINANCIAL INSTITUTIONS

Regulators have traditionally relied upon a variety of tools to minimize the risks of financial institution failures. In order to reduce the risk of insolvency, regulators have imposed capital requirements on commercial and investment banks.[76] In order to reduce depositors' incentives to "run," regulators require all commercial banks to obtain minimum levels of deposit insurance from the Federal Deposit Insurance Corporation (FDIC).[77] In order to address liquidity problems, the Federal Reserve has the authority to serve as a "lender of last resort" by making "discount window" loans to commercial banks.[78] Moreover, the Federal Reserve can lend to non-banks in "unusual and exigent circumstances" pursuant to its authority under Section 13(3) of the Federal Reserve Act.[79] However, as

---

[76] *See* 12 C.F.R. part 3, appendix A (imposing capital requirements on national banks), § 208.4(a) (imposing capital requirements on members of the Federal Reserve System), part 217 (imposing capital requirements on bank holding companies), parts 324-325 (imposing capital requirements on institutions insured by the Federal Deposit Insurance Corporation); 17 C.F.R. § 240.15c3-1(a) (imposing capital requirements on securities brokers and dealers). *See also* Carnell, et al., *supra* note 16 at 204-14, 238-66.

Federal regulators have also imposed liquidity requirements on commercial banks. *See* 12 C.F.R. part 50 (imposing liquidity requirements on national banks), part 249 (imposing liquidity requirements on members of the Federal Reserve System), part 329 (imposing liquidity requirements on institutions insured by the Federal Deposit Insurance Corporation). Likewise, state insurance regulators have adopted capital requirements and limitations on permissible investments for insurance companies. *See* Carnell, et al., *supra* note 16 at 658-59.

[77] *See* 12 C.F.R. § 5.20(e)(3); Michael S. Barr, Howell E. Jackson & Margaret E. Tahyar, *Financial Regulation: Law And Policy* 166 (2016).

[78] *See* 12 U.S.C. § 343(2). Ordinarily, the volume of "discount window" lending is low because (1) the Federal Reserve generally charges a "penalty" interest rate, and (2) obtaining "discount window" loans from the Federal Reserve may be stigmatizing. *See* Carnell, et al., *supra* note 16 at 221. However, during a crisis, the Federal Reserve often lowers the penalty rate of interest and accepts collateral that it might reject in normal times. *Id.*

[79] *See* 12 U.S.C. § 343(3) (2006). While not the focus of this report, the Federal Reserve's use of its emergency lending power to lend to non-banks during the 2007-2009 financial crisis generated controversy, leading to certain changes to Section 13(3) of the Federal Reserve Act. *See generally* CRS Report R44185, *Federal Reserve: Emergency Lending*, by Marc Labonte; Mehra, *supra* note 41. Specifically, Dodd-Frank provides that (1) the Treasury Secretary must approve any loans made by the Federal Reserve pursuant to its Section 13(3) authority, (2) such loans may be made only as part of "a program or facility with broad-based eligibility," as opposed to only specific firms, and (3) the security for any such loans must be sufficient to protect taxpayers from losses. *See* 12 U.S.C. § 343(3).

the 2007-2009 financial crisis arguably demonstrated, sometimes these measures have proven insufficient to prevent financial institution failures.

In response to these concerns, Title I of Dodd-Frank establishes an enhanced prudential regulatory regime for certain large financial institutions.[80] Specifically, the Title I regime applies to (1) all bank holding companies with total consolidated assets of $50 billion or more, and (2) any non-bank financial companies[81] that the Financial Stability Oversight Council (FSOC)[82] designates as systemically important.[83] Section 165 of

---

[80] 12 U.S.C. § 5365.

[81] Title I defines a "nonbank financial company" as a "U.S. nonbank financial company" or "foreign nonbank financial company." *Id.* § 5311(a)(4)(C). A "U.S. nonbank financial company" is a company (other than a banking holding company, Farm Credit System institution, national securities exchange, clearing agency, security-based swap execution facility, security-based swap data repository, or derivatives clearing organization) that is (1) incorporated under the laws of the United States or any state, and (2) predominantly engaged in financial activities. *Id.* § 5311(a)(4)(B). A "foreign nonbank financial company" is a company (other than a bank holding company) that is (1) incorporated or organized in a country other than the United States, and (2) predominantly engaged in financial activities. *Id.* § 5311(a)(4)(A).

A company is "predominantly engaged" in financial activities if (1) the annual gross revenues derived by the company and all of its subsidiaries related to activities that are "financial in nature" represents 85 percent or more of the consolidated gross revenues of the company, or (2) the consolidated assets of the company and all of its subsidiaries related to activities that are "financial in nature" represent 85 percent or more of the consolidated gross revenues of the company. *Id.* § 5311(a)(6).

For purposes of this definition, the following activities (among others) are considered "financial in nature": (1) lending, exchanging, transferring, investing for others, or safeguarding money or securities, (2) insuring, guaranteeing, or indemnifying against loss, harm, damage, illness, disability, or death, or providing and issuing annuities, and acting as principal, agent, or broker for purposes of the foregoing, (3) providing financial, investment, or economic advisory services, (4) issuing or selling instruments representing interests in pools of assets permissible for a bank to hold directly, (5) underwriting, dealing in, or making a market in securities. *See id.* § 1843(k)(4).

[82] FSOC is an umbrella regulatory body created by Dodd-Frank, whose voting members consist of the heads of nine federal regulatory agencies and an independent insurance expert. *Id.* § 5321(a)-(b). FSOC's voting members are the heads of the Federal Reserve Board of Governors, Federal Deposit Insurance Corporation, Office of the Comptroller of the Currency, Commodity Futures Trading Commission, Securities and Exchange Commission, National Credit Union Administration, Federal Housing Finance Agency, Consumer Financial Protection Bureau, and an independent insurance expert. *Id.* § 5321(b)(1). FSOC also includes five non-voting members: the director of the Office of Financial Research, the director of the Federal Insurance Office, a state banking supervisor, a state insurance commissioner, and a state securities regulator. *Id.* § 5321(b)(2).

The statutory purposes of FSOC are to (1) identify risks to the financial stability of the United States, (2) promote market discipline by eliminating expectations of government bailouts, and (3) respond to emerging threats to the stability of the United States financial

Dodd-Frank directs the Federal Reserve to impose prudential standards on these institutions that "are more stringent than" those applicable to other bank holding companies and non-bank financial companies, and that "increase in stringency" based on certain statutorily-prescribed considerations.[84] These enhanced standards include

1. risk-based capital requirements and leverage limits;[85]
2. liquidity requirements;[86]
3. overall risk management requirements;[87]
4. a requirement that the relevant companies develop resolution plans (so-called "living wills") describing how they can be rapidly resolved in the event of material distress or failure;[88] and
5. credit exposure reporting requirements.[89]

Congress is currently considering whether to change the first basis for imposition of enhanced prudential regulations on financial institutions—the automatic $50 billion threshold for bank holding companies.[90] That policy question is addressed in another recent Congressional Research Service report.[91] This section of the report accordingly provides a legal

---

system. *Id.* § 5322(a)(1). For a more detailed overview of FSOC's structure and authorities, see CRS Report R45052, *Financial Stability Oversight Council (FSOC): Structure and Activities*, by Jeffrey M. Stupak.

[83] *Id.* § 5365(a)(1).

[84] *Id.*

[85] *Id.* § 5365(b)(1)(A)(i).

[86] *Id.* § 5365(b)(1)(A)(ii).

[87] *Id.* § 5365(b)(1)(A)(iii).

[88] *Id.* § 5365(d)(1).

[89] *Id.* § 5365(b)(1)(A)(iv). For an overview of the Federal Reserve's implementation of these enhanced prudential standards, and legislative proposals to change Dodd-Frank's $50 billion threshold for enhanced supervision for bank holding companies, see CRS Report R45036, *Bank Systemic Risk Regulation: The $50 Billion Threshold in the Dodd-Frank Act*, by Marc Labonte and David W. Perkins.

[90] The Economic Growth, Regulatory Relief, and Consumer Protection Act, S. 2155, 115th Cong. (2017), which passed the Senate on March 14, 2018, would raise this threshold to $250 billion.

[91] *See* Labonte & Perkins, *supra* note 89.

overview of (1) FSOC's process for designating non-banks as systemically important and FSOC's designations to date, (2) criticisms of FSOC's designation process and responses, and (3) proposals to reform FSOC's designation process.

Designation of Non-Banks for Enhanced Prudential Regulation Dodd-Frank Section 113 and FSOC Guidance

As discussed, during the 2007-2009 financial crisis, troubles at certain non-bank financial firms (such as Lehman and AIG) "contributed to a broad seizing up of financial markets and stress at other financial firms."[92] Accordingly, in the aftermath of the crisis, the Obama Administration proposed creating a council to identify non-bank financial companies whose failure could pose a threat to financial stability and subjecting them to consolidated supervision by the Federal Reserve irrespective of their legal structure.[93] Section 113 of Dodd-Frank implemented this recommendation, creating FSOC and granting it the authority to designate certain non-bank financial companies for enhanced supervision by the Federal Reserve.[94]

Section 113 provides that FSOC may, by a vote of at least two-thirds of its voting members (which must include the Treasury Secretary in the majority), designate non-bank financial companies as systemically important under either of *two standards*:

---

[92] *Final Rule and Interpretive Guidance, Authority to Require Supervision and Regulation of Certain Nonbank Financial Companies*, 70 Fed. Reg. 21,637, 21,637 (Apr. 11, 2012) [hereinafter "Non-Bank Designation Rule"].

[93] *Financial Regulatory Reform: A New Foundation*, U.S. Dep't of the Treasury 20 (Oct. 8, 2009), https://www.treasury.gov/initiatives/Documents/Final Report_web.pdf.

[94] 12 U.S.C. § 5323(a)(1). Dodd-Frank does not use the term "systemically important" to describe non-banks subject to enhanced supervision. However, for purposes of brevity, this report will refer to such institutions as "systemically important."

1. " at a non-bank financial company "could pose a threat to the financial stability of the United States," or
2. when the "nature, scope, size, scale, concentration, interconnectedness, or mix of the [non-bank financial company's] activities" could pose that same threat.[95]

In making such a designation, FSOC must consider, among any other risk-related factors that FSOC deems appropriate, the following factors:

- the company's leverage;
- the extent and nature of its off-balance-sheet exposures;
- the extent and nature of the transactions and relationships of the company with other significant nonbank financial companies and significant bank holding companies;
- the importance of the company as a source of credit for low-income, minority, or underserved communities, and the impact that the failure of such company would have on the availability of credit in such communities;
- the extent to which assets are managed rather than owned by the company, and the extent to which ownership of assets under management is diffuse;
- the nature, scope, size, scale, concentration, interconnectedness, and mix of the activities of the company;
- the degree to which the company is already regulated by 1 or more primary financial regulatory agencies;
- the amount and nature of the financial assets of the company;
- the amount and types of the liabilities of the company, including the degree of reliance on short-term funding.[96]

Dodd-Frank requires that FSOC provide a non-bank financial company with written notice of a proposed systemic risk designation, including an

[95] *Id.*
[96] *Id.* § 5323(a)(2).

explanation for the basis of the proposed determination.[97] A non-bank that receives a notice of a proposed determination has 30 days to request an opportunity for a written or oral hearing before FSOC to contest the proposed determination, and FSOC has 60 days after such hearing to notify the non-bank financial company of its final determination.[98] Once that determination is made, the designated non-bank is subject to the enhanced prudential regulatory regime.

A designated company can then seek judicial review of FSOC's final determination within 30 days in either the U.S. district court for the judicial district in which its home office is located, or in the U.S. District Court for the District of Columbia.[99] The court's review is limited to whether FSOC's determination was "arbitrary and capricious,"[100] a standard pursuant to which a court evaluates whether an agency:

> has relied on factors which Congress has not intended it to consider, entirely failed to consider an important aspect of the problem, offered an explanation for its decision that runs counter to the evidence before the agency, or is so implausible that it cannot be ascribed to a difference in view of the product of agency expertise.[101]

FSOC is required to annually re-evaluate systemic risk designations for non-bank financial companies and may rescind such designations upon a vote of two-thirds of its voting members that includes the Treasury Secretary.[102]

In April 2012, FSOC issued guidance concerning the Title I designation process and standards for non-banks.[103] In the guidance, FSOC

---

[97] *Id.* § 5323(e)(1).

[98] *Id.* § 5323(e)(2)-(3). Upon a two-thirds vote that includes the Treasury Secretary, FSOC may waive these requirements if it determines "that such waiver or modification is necessary or appropriate to prevent or mitigate threats posed by the nonbank financial company to the financial stability of the United States." *Id.* § 5323(f)(1).

[99] *Id.* § 5323(h).

[100] *Id*

[101] Motor Vehicles Mfrs. v. State Farm Mut. Auto. Ins., 463 U.S. 29, 43 (1983).

[102] 12 U.S.C. § 5323(d).

[103] Non-Bank Designation Rule, *supra* note 92.

organized the 10 statutory factors guiding systemic risk designations into six "categories" of considerations:

1. interconnectedness;
2. substitutability (i.e., the extent to which other firms could timely provide similar financial services at a similar price and quantity if a non-bank financial company withdrew from a particular market);
3. size;
4. leverage;
5. liquidity risk and maturity mismatch; and
6. existing regulatory scrutiny.[104]

FSOC explained that the first three categories "seek to assess the potential for spillovers from [[105]a] firm's distress," while the remaining three categories "seek to assess how vulnerable a company is to financial distress."

The guidance further provided that FSOC intends to assess how a non-bank's financial stress could be transmitted to other firms or markets through any of three "transmission channels":

1. exposure (i.e., the extent to which creditors, counterparties, investors, or other market participants are exposed to the company);
2. asset liquidation (i.e., whether the company holds assets that, if liquidated quickly, would cause a fall in asset prices); and
3. critical function or service (i.e., whether the company provides a critical function or service that is relied upon by market participants and for which there are no ready substitutes).[106]

---

[104] *Id.* at 21,641.
[105] *Id.*
[106] *Id.*

The FSOC guidance also outlined a three-stage process for systemic risk designations.[107] FSOC explained that during Stage 1, it will apply "a set of uniform quantitative metrics ... to a broad group" of non-bank financial companies in order to identify companies "for further evaluation."[108] According to the guidance, during Stage 2, FSOC will apply "a wide range of quantitative and qualitative information" about the companies identified in Stage 1, and "begin the consultation process" with the company's "primary financial regulatory agencies or home country supervisors."[109] After Stage 2 is completed, companies selected for additional review are notified that they are being considered for designation as systemically important.[110] Finally, during Stage 3, FSOC will evaluate information collected from the company under consideration, in addition to information considered during Stages 1 and 2, and will decide whether to make a proposed determination that the company be subject to enhanced supervision.[111]

Non-Bank Designations to Date

To date, FSOC has designated four non-bank financial companies for enhanced supervision: AIG, General Electric Capital Corporation (GE Capital), Prudential Financial (Prudential), and MetLife.[112] However,

---

107 *Id.* at 21,660.

108 *Id.*

109 *Id.*

110 *Id.*

111 *Id.* In February 2015, FSOC issued additional supplemental procedures relating to its designations of non-banks for enhanced supervision. *See* Fin. Stability Oversight Council Supplemental Procedures Relating to Nonbank Financial Company Determinations, U.S. Dep't of the Treasury (Feb. 4, 2015), https://www.treasury.gov/initiatives/fsoc/designations/Documents/Supplemental%20Procedures%20Related%20to%20Nonbank%20Financial%20Company%20Determinations%20-%20February%202015.pdf. FSOC indicated that pursuant to the supplemental procedures, it will notify a non-bank financial company within 30 days after it forms an analytical team to commence active review of a company in Stage 2 (as opposed to after the company is advanced to Stage 3). *Id.* at 2. A company under active review in Stage 2 may submit to FSOC any information it deems relevant, and may meet with FSOC's analytical team. *Id.* FSOC also indicated that it intends to publicly confirm a company's announcement that it is under active review in Stage 2, or that it has been advanced to Stage 3. *Id.* at 4.

112 *See Designations*, Fin. Stability Oversight Council, U.S. Dep't of the Treasury, https://www.treasury.gov/initiatives/fsoc/designations/Pages/default.aspx (last visited Apr. 9, 2018).

FSOC later rescinded the designations of two of these entities—AIG and GE Capital—based on changed circumstances at those companies.[113] Further, MetLife successfully challenged its designation by FSOC in federal district court, leaving Prudential as the only non-bank financial company subject to the enhanced prudential regulatory regime at the time of publication of this chapter.[114] The following subsections of the report discuss the designations of each of these institutions as illustrations of how FSOC has implemented its designation authority.

AIG

FSOC designated AIG for enhanced supervision in July 2013.[115] In designating AIG, FSOC explained that although a large number of the company's insurance products (such as life insurance and annuities) are intended to be long-term liabilities, many also contain "features that could make them vulnerable to rapid and early withdrawals by policyholders."[116] FSOC further explained that if AIG were to encounter sufficiently severe stress, "funds from products allowing for early withdrawals might be withdrawn regardless of the size of associated surrender charges or tax penalties," forcing AIG to "liquidate a substantial portion of its large portfolio of relatively illiquid corporate and foreign bonds, as well as asset-backed securities."[117] Such an asset liquidation could, in FSOC's view, have disruptive effects on financial markets and "cause financial contagion if the negative sentiment and uncertainty associated with material distress at AIG spread[] to other insurers."[118] FSOC also concluded (1) that "[a] large number of corporate and financial entities have significant exposures to AIG,"[119] (2) that because AIG was the leading commercial insurance underwriter in the U.S., its exit from the marketplace "could reduce the

---

[113] *See* "AIG" and "GE Capital" *infra*.

[114] *See* "Prudential" and "MetLife" *infra*.

[115] *Basis of the Financial Stability Oversight Council's Final Determination Regarding American International Group, Inc.*, U.S. Dep't of the Treasury (July 8, 2013), https://www.treasury.gov/initiatives/fsoc/designations/Documents/Basis%20of%20Final%20Determination%20Regarding%20American%20International%20Group,%20Inc.pdf.

[116] *Id.* at 2.

[117] *Id.*

[118] *Id.* at 2-3.

[119] *Id.* at 6.

availability and affordability of certain insurance products,"[120] and (3) that AIG's "highly complex" interstate and cross-border structure complicated its resolvability, further aggravating the effects that its financial distress could have on financial stability.[121] AIG did not contest FSOC's designation.[122]

After an annual re-evaluation required by Dodd-Frank, FSOC voted to rescind its designation of AIG in September 2017.[123] In rescinding its designation, FSOC explained that AIG had reduced the amounts of its total debt, short-term debt, derivatives portfolio, securities lending, repos, and total assets.[124] FSOC further indicated that additional analyses conducted for the purposes of its re-evaluation, "including additional consideration of the effects of incentives and disincentives for [AIG's] policyholders to surrender their life insurance policies and annuities," indicated "that there is not a significant risk that a forced asset liquidation by AIG would disrupt market functioning."[125] FSOC also noted that AIG had sold certain businesses, "reduced its multi-jurisdictional operations, simplified its legal structure, and reduced its size and global footprint," making it "notably different from the company as it existed leading up to the financial crisis."[126]

GE Capital

On the same day it designated AIG for enhanced supervision, FSOC similarly designated GE Capital, a savings-and-loan holding company and wholly owned subsidiary of the General Electric Company.[127] In

---

[120] *Id.* at 8.

[121] *Id.* at 10-11.

[122] *Id.* at 1.

[123] *Notice and Explanation of the Basis for the Financial Stability Oversight Council's Rescission of Its Determination Regarding American International Group, Inc. (AIG),* U.S. Dep't of the Treasury (Sept. 29, 2017), https://www.treasury.gov/initiatives/fsoc/designations/Documents/American_International_Group,_Inc._(Rescission).pdf.

[124] *Id.* at 5.

[125] *Id.*

[126] *Id.* at 5, 7.

[127] *Basis of the Financial Stability Oversight Council's Final Determination Regarding General Electric Capital Corporation, Inc.,* U.S. Dep't of the Treasury (July 8, 2013), https://www.treasury.gov/initiatives/fsoc/designations/Documents/Basis%20of%20Final%2

designating GE Capital, FSOC explained that the company was one of the largest financial holding companies in the United States and "a significant source of credit to the U.S. economy."[128] FSOC further observed that large global banks and non-bank financial companies had significant exposure to GE Capital through their purchase of its commercial paper and long-term debt, and provision of backup lines of credit.[129] Financial distress at GE Capital, FSOC reasoned, could trigger "runs" on money market funds that would in turn "impair the ability of financial and other firms to fund their operations."[130] FSOC also concluded that GE Capital's interstate and cross-border structure, coupled with its intercompany funding and shared service agreements, complicated its resolvability.[131] GE Capital did not contest FSOC's designation.[132]

After an annual re-evaluation required by Dodd-Frank, FSOC rescinded its designation of GE Capital in June 2016, explaining that since its designation, GE Capital had "fundamentally changed its business ... [t]hrough a series of divestitures, a transformation of its funding model, and a corporate reorganization."[133] Moreover, FSOC noted that since its designation, GE Capital had decreased its total assets by more than 50 percent, shifted away from short-term debt, and reduced its interconnectedness with large financial institutions.[134] Finally, FSOC observed that as a result of divestitures and changes to its business, GE Capital no longer owned any U.S. depository institutions, nor did it provide financing to consumers or small business customers.[135]

0Determination%20Regarding%20General%20Electric%20Capital%20Corporation,%20Inc.pdf.

128 *Id.* at 2.

129 *Id.*

130 *Id.*

131 *Id.* at 10-11.

132 *Id.* at 1.

133 *Basis of the Financial Stability Oversight Council's Rescission of Its Determination Regarding GE Capital Global Holdings, LLC*, U.S. Dep't of the Treasury (June 28, 2016), https://www.treasury.gov/initiatives/fsoc/designations/Documents/GE%20Capital%20Public%20Rescission%20Basis.pdf.

134 *Id.* at 2.

135 *Id.*

Prudential

Slightly less than two months after designating AIG and GE Capital, FSOC designated Prudential, a large financial services company and one of the largest U.S. insurers, for enhanced supervision.[136] In designating Prudential, FSOC explained that "[c]orporations, banks, and pension plans have exposures to Prudential through retirement and pension products, corporate- and bank-owned life insurance, and other group insurance products."[137] Moreover, FSOC reasoned that Prudential's capital market activities—specifically, its derivatives activities, use of credit lines from large banks, securities lending, and reverse repo portfolio—further "expand[ed] its connections to other financial firms and markets."[138] As with AIG, FSOC reasoned that if Prudential faced pressure to rapidly liquidate its illiquid assets to meet withdrawals, securities markets could face significant disruptions, and other insurance companies could face "runs" of their own triggered by heightened uncertainty.[139] FSOC also concluded that because of its multistate and cross-border operations, and because there was "no precedent for the resolution of an insurance company the size and scale of Prudential," the company would likely be difficult to resolve in an orderly fashion.[140] Prudential requested a hearing to contest FSOC's proposed determination, and FSOC made its final determination after reviewing Prudential's written submissions and holding an oral hearing.[141]

As a result of FSOC's rescission of its designations of AIG and GE Capital, and a decision by the U.S. District Court for the District of Columbia overturning MetLife's designation (discussed in "MetLife" *infra*), Prudential remains the only non-bank financial company designated for enhanced supervision as of the publication of this chapter. However, in

---

[136] *Basis of the Financial Stability Oversight Council's Final Determination Regarding Prudential Financial, Inc.*, U.S. Dep't of the Treasury (Sept. 19, 2013), https://www.treasury.gov/initiatives/fsoc/designations/Documents/Prudential%20Financial%20Inc.pdf.

[137] *Id.* at 2.

[138] *Id.*

[139] *Id.* at 2-3.

[140] *Id.* at 12.

[141] *Id.* at 1.

February 2018, Prudential announced that FSOC was in the process of conducting its annual review of its designation, and that the company intended to make its case that it does not meet the statutory standards for designation.[142]

MetLife

Over a year after its designation of Prudential, FSOC designated MetLife, another large insurance company, for enhanced supervision.[143] MetLife's designation came after a lengthy engagement process that reportedly included 12 meetings between FSOC and the company's representatives, the submission of over 21,000 pages of materials to FSOC, and an oral hearing challenging FSOC's proposed determination.[144] In designating MetLife, FSOC reasoned that MetLife's financial distress "could lead to an impairment of financial intermediation or financial market functioning that could be sufficiently severe to inflict significant damage on the economy."[145] Specifically, FSOC reasoned that large financial intermediaries had significant exposure to MetLife because of its institutional products and capital market activities, such as funding agreements, guaranteed investment contracts, pension closeouts, and securities lending agreements.[146] Moreover, as with AIG and Prudential, FSOC concluded that a large-scale forced liquidation of MetLife's assets could disrupt securities markets.[147] FSOC also reasoned that MetLife's interstate and cross-border operations complicated its resolvability, further exacerbating the effects its distress might have on financial stability.[148]

MetLife proceeded to challenge FSOC's decision before the U.S. District Court for the District of Columbia, which invalidated FSOC's

---

[142] Michelle Price & Pete Schroeder, U.S. Financial Regulatory Panel to Review Prudential Risk Designation, *Reuters* (Feb. 15, 2018), https://www.reuters.com/article/us-usa-fsoc/u-s-financial-regulatory-panel-to-review-prudential-riskdesignation-idUSKCN1FZ291.

[143] *Basis for the Financial Stability Oversight Council's Final Determination Regarding MetLife, Inc.*, U.S. Dep't of the Treasury (Dec. 18, 2014), https://www.treasury.gov/initiatives/fsoc/designations/Documents/MetLife%20Public%20Basis.pdf.

[144] *Id.* at 2-3.

[145] *Id.* at 15.

[146] *Id.* at 16.

[147] *Id.*

[148] *Id.* at 29-30.

determination in March 2016.[149] In holding that FSOC's determination was "arbitrary and capricious," the court explained that by assessing only the potential impact of MetLife's financial distress, and not MetLife's *vulnerability to* financial distress, FSOC had violated its April 2012 guidance, which indicated that FSOC would consider both issues and divided its "categories" of analysis accordingly.[150]

The court also concluded that FSOC had failed to abide by its April 2012 guidance—which provided that a non-bank financial company could threaten financial stability only "if there would be an impairment of financial intermediation or of financial market functioning that would be sufficiently severe to inflict significant damage on the broader economy"[151]—by failing to project "*what* the losses would be, *which* financial institutions would have to actively manage their balance sheets, or *how* the market would destabilize as a result" of MetLife's distress.[152] Instead, the court observed, FSOC had only "summed gross potential market exposures" to MetLife in conducting its "transmission channel" analysis, without analyzing the extent to which MetLife's creditors were secured or other mitigating factors.[153]

In arriving at this conclusion, the court acknowledged that counterparties' gross exposure to MetLife is relevant to the second statutory standard for designation—that a company's "nature, scope, size, scale, concentration, interconnectedness, or mix of ... activities" alone "could pose a threat to" financial stability.[154] However, it interpreted FSOC's explanation for its designation as relying on only the *first* statutory standard, which allows for designation when "material financial distress" at a non-bank financial company "could pose a threat to the financial stability of the United States."[155] Because FSOC's guidance had provided that this standard requires a finding that a firm's financial distress would impair financial market functioning to a degree sufficient to inflict

---

149 MetLife, Inc. v. Financial Stability Oversight Council, 177 F. Supp. 3d 219 (2016).
150 *Id.* at 233-36.
151 *Id.*
152 *MetLife, Inc.*, 177 F. Supp. 3d at 237.
153 *Id.*
154 *MetLife, Inc.*, 177 F. Supp. 3d at 238.
155 *Id.*

significant damage on the broader economy, and FSOC had not adequately supported that finding, the court held that its determination was arbitrary and capricious.[156]

Finally, the court held that FSOC's designation of MetLife was arbitrary and capricious because FSOC failed to consider the costs of its designation (which MetLife alleged ran in the "billions of dollars")—a consideration that it explained is "essential to reasoned rulemaking."[157]

Although FSOC initially appealed the district court's decision to the U.S. Court of Appeals for the D.C. Circuit, it filed a motion to dismiss the appeal in January 2018, which the court granted, ending the case.[158]

Criticisms of Title I and Responses

Title I and FSOC's process for designating non-banks as systemically important have attracted some criticism. Some commentators have criticized FSOC for failing to provide firms under consideration with meaningful, specific information about the criteria used in determining whether a firm is systemically important.[159] Relatedly, some observers have questioned the

---

[156] *Id.*

[157] *Id.* at 239-42.

[158] *See* MetLife, Inc. v. Financial Stability Oversight Council, No. 16-5086, 2018 WL 1052618 (D.C. Cir. Jan. 23, 2018).

[159] *See* Andy Winkler, *Primer: FSOC's SIFI Designation Process for Nonbank Financial Companies*, *Am. Action Forum* (Sept. 3, 2014), https://www.americanactionforum.org/research/primer-fsocs-sifi-designation-process-fornonbank-financial-companies/; Peter J. Wallison, *What the FSOC's Prudential Decision Tells Us About SIFI Designation*, Am. Enter. Inst. (Mar. 31, 2014), http://www.aei.org/publication/what-the-fsocs-prudential-decisiontells-us-about-sifi-designation/ (arguing that FSOC has "failed to develop or implement any intelligible standard for determining whether a particular firm is" systemically important).

Relatedly, in 2014, a group of plaintiffs challenged the constitutionality of the provisions in Title I allowing FSOC to designate non-banks as systemically important, arguing that the level of discretion afforded FSOC violated the separation of powers. *See* Second Amended Complaint for Declaratory and Injunctive Relief ¶ 8, State Nat. Bank of Big Spring v. Lew, 958 F. Supp. 127 (D.D.C. 2013). To establish standing, a plaintiff-bank contended that it was harmed by FSOC's designation of GE Capital (a competitor) for enhanced regulation because that designation allegedly conferred reputational benefits upon GE Capital. State Nat. Bank of Big Spring v. Lew, 795 F.3d 48, 55 (D.C. Cir. 2015). The U.S. Court of Appeals for the D.C. Circuit rejected that argument and affirmed an order dismissing the plaintiff's claims for lack of standing, reasoning that the doctrine of competitor standing

rigor of FSOC's analysis of companies under consideration for designation.[160] Others have raised concerns about the transparency of the designation process.[161] Finally, some commentators have criticized FSOC for not considering the costs of designations in conducting its analyses—a criticism echoed in the district court's decision overturning FSOC's designation of MetLife.[162]

In response, defenders of FSOC have argued that the "malleable standard[s]" FSOC applies in determining whether companies qualify as systemically important effectively deter companies from seeking out systemically risky activities.[163] According to this line of argument, the adoption of precise mathematical formulas for distinguishing between safe and risky companies would encourage companies to seek out activities

---

does not apply in cases where a challenged regulation increases a competitor's regulatory burdens. *Id.*

[160] *See* Wallison, *supra* note 159 (noting that in its designation of Prudential, FSOC concluded that Prudential's failure would have "significant" effects on financial markets and counterparties, but "made no effort to support its characterizations with the kind of numerical data that would give the word some meaning"); *Resolution Approving Final Determination Regarding Prudential Financial, Inc., Views of the Council's Independent Member having Insurance Expertise*, U.S. Dep't of the Treasury at 6 (Sept. 19, 2013), https://www.treasury.gov/initiatives/fsoc/council-meetings/Documents/September% 2019%202013%20Notational%20Vote.pdf (dissenting from FSOC's designation of Prudential, and contending that FSOC's explanation of its designation "does not contain any analysis that presents any findings as to severe impairment of financial intermediation; severe impairment of the functioning of U.S. and global financial markets; or resulting significant damage to the economy. No empirical evidence is presented; no data is reviewed; no models are put forward.").

[161] *See Dodd-Frank's Missed Opportunity: A Road Map for a More Effective Regulatory Architecture*, Bipartisan Policy Center at 41 (April 2014), https://bipartisanpolicy.org/ wp-content/uploads/sites/default/files/BPC%20DoddFrank% 20Missed%20Opportunity.pdf (concluding that "[t]he use of more open forums to discuss FSOC business would ... be helpful," and arguing that "FSOC should also consider releasing additional details about the closed-door conversations that occur during their regular meetings"); U.S. Gov't Accountability Office, GAO-12-886, *New Council And Research Office Should Strengthen The Accountability And Transparency Of Their Decisions* 55, (Sept. 2012), https://www. gao.gov/assets/650/648064.pdf (noting that public information on FSOC's decision-making is limited, and recommending that FSOC keep detailed records of closed-door sessions and develop a strategy for improving communication with the public).

[162] *See MetLife, Inc.*, 177 F. Supp. 3d at 238; Winkler, *supra* note 159.

[163] Daniel Schwarcz & David Zaring, *Regulation by Threat: Dodd-Frank and the Nonbank Problem*, 84 U. CHI. L. REV. 1813, 1834 (2017); Simon Johnson & Antonio Weiss, *The Financial Stability Oversight Council: An Essential Role for the Evolving US Financial System*, Peterson Inst. For Int'l Econ. 10 (May 2017), https://piie.com/system/ files/documents/pb17-20.pdf.

with risks that are not adequately reflected in such rigid standards.[164] These commentators contend that vesting FSOC with "broad discretion" to designate firms as systemically important is appropriate given the inherent difficulty of identifying systemic risks and the perils of failing to identify such risks.[165] Moreover, in responding to arguments that it should consider the costs of designations, FSOC has argued that because Dodd-Frank's statutory text does not require such analysis, it need not engage in that inquiry.[166]

Proposals to Alter Title I

Proposed Legislation

A number of bills that would alter FSOC's authority to designate non-banks for enhanced regulation have been introduced in the 115th Congress. The Financial CHOICE Act of 2017, as passed by the House of Representatives in June 2017, would repeal FSOC's authority to designate non-banks for enhanced regulation altogether.[167] H.R. 4061, the Financial Stability Oversight Council Improvement Act of 2017, which was reported out of the House Committee on Financial Services in March 2018, proposes more limited changes to FSOC's authority.[168] Specifically, H.R. 4061 would require FSOC to consider "the appropriateness of the imposition of prudential standards as opposed to other forms of regulation

---

[164] Schwarcz & Zaring, *supra* note 163 at 1856. *See also* Johnson & Weiss, *supra* note 163 at 10 ("[F]irms considered for designation are, by definition, large multifaceted financial institutions, and only a holistic approach to assessing risk can be effective. Any fixed list of criteria would be easy to game, and there are not likely to be one or two easy 'fixes' for avoiding designation.").

[165] Schwarcz & Zaring, *supra* note 163 at 1817. *See also Written Testimony of Adam J. Levitin, Hearing on The Administrative State v. The Constitution: Dodd-Frank at Five Years Before the Subcomm. on the Constitution of the S. Comm. on the Judiciary*, 114th Cong. 8 (July 23, 2015) (statement of Adam. J. Levitin, Professor of Law, Georgetown University Law Center), https://www.judiciary.senate.gov/imo/media/doc/07-23-15%20Levitin%20Testimony.pdf. ("SIFI designation is not an unfettered exercise of discretion. Instead, it requires consideration of no less than eleven detailed factors, as well as an ultimate finding about the nature of risks posed by a firm to the economy.").

[166] *See MetLife, Inc.*, 177 F. Supp. 3d at 238.

[167] H.R. 10, 115th Cong. § 151 (2017).

[168] H.R. 4061, 115th Cong. (2017).

to mitigate the identified risks" in determining whether to designate a non-bank as systemically important.[169] The bill would further require that FSOC provide designated companies with the opportunity to submit written materials contesting their designation during FSOC's annual reevaluation process.[170] If FSOC determines during a reevaluation that a designation should not be rescinded, the bill would require it to provide notice to the designated company "address[ing] with specificity" how it assessed the relevant statutory factors in light of the company's written submissions.[171]

The Trump Administration's Views

In November 2017, the Trump Administration's Treasury Department released a report outlining four general recommendations for reforming FSOC's process for designating non-banks as systemically important.[172] First, the report recommended that FSOC adopt an "activities-based" or "industry-wide" approach to assessing potential risks posed by non-banks.[173] Under this approach, FSOC would prioritize identifying specific financial activities and products that could pose risks to financial stability, work with the primary financial regulatory agencies to address those specific risks, and consider individual firms for designation as systemically important only as a matter of last resort if more limited actions aimed at mitigating discrete risks are insufficient to safeguard financial stability.[174]

Second, the Treasury Department recommended that FSOC "increas[e] the analytical rigor" of its designation analyses.[175] Specifically, the Report recommended that FSOC: (1) consider any factors that might mitigate the exposure of a firm's creditors and counterparties to its financial distress; (2) focus on "plausible" (and not merely "possible") asset liquidation risks; (3) evaluate the likelihood that a firm will experience financial distress

---

[169] *Id.* § 2.
[170] *Id.*
[171] *Id.*
[172] *Fin. Stability Oversight Council Designations*, U.S. Dep't of the Treasury (Nov. 17, 2017), https://www.treasury.gov/press-center/press-releases/Documents/PM-FSOC-Designations-Memo 11-17.pdf.
[173] *Id.* at 10.
[174] *Id.* at 19-21.
[175] *Id.* at 22.

before evaluating how that distress could be transmitted to other firms; (4) consider the benefits *and* costs of designations; and (5) collapse its three-stage review process into two steps, notifying companies that they are under active review during Stage 1 and voting on proposed designations after the completion of Stage 2.[176]

Third, the Treasury Department recommended enhancing engagement between FSOC and companies under review, and improving the designation process's transparency.[177] Specifically, the report recommended that FSOC: (1) engage earlier with companies under review and "explain ... the key risks" that FSOC has identified, (2) "undertake greater engagement" with companies' primary financial regulators, and (3) publicly release explanations of its designation decisions.[178]

Fourth, the Treasury Department recommended that FSOC provide "a clear off-ramp" for non-banks designated as systemically important.[179] The report recommended that FSOC: (1) highlight the key risks that led to a company's designation, (2) "adopt a more robust and transparent process for its annual reevaluations" that "make[s] clear how companies can engage with FSOC ... and what information companies should submit during a reevaluation," (3) "develop a process to enable a designated company to discuss potential changes it could make to address the risks it could pose to financial stability," and (4) "make clear that the standard it applies in its annual reevaluations is the same as the standard for an initial designation of a nonbank financial company."[180] FSOC has yet to act on these recommendations.

TITLE II: ORDERLY LIQUIDATION AUTHORITY

While Title I of Dodd-Frank is aimed at minimizing the likelihood that systemically important financial institutions experience financial distress,

---

[176] *Id.* at 22-29.
[177] *Id.* at 29.
[178] *Id.* at 29-34.
[179] *Id.* at 34.
[180] *Id.* at 34-36.

Title II is directed at resolving such institutions in a rapid and orderly fashion in the event that they nevertheless become distressed. To accomplish this goal, Title II establishes a new resolution regime available for systemically important financial institutions outside of the Bankruptcy Code.[181] The following sections of the report discuss Title II and proposals for its reform. First, the report provides an overview of the resolution mechanisms available for financial institutions before Dodd-Frank. Second, the report discusses Title II's legislative history and the new resolution authority that it establishes. Third, the report canvasses a variety of administrative rules with important implications for Title II. Fourth, the report discusses certain criticisms of Title II, and responses to those criticisms. Finally, the report discusses proposals to repeal or change Title II.

Pre-Dodd-Frank Resolution Mechanisms: Bankruptcy vs. FDIC Resolution

Commercial banks, broker-dealers, and insurance companies are subject to different insolvency regimes. Commercial banks must utilize a special resolution regime administered by the FDIC.[182] Before Dodd-Frank, broker-dealers and bank holding companies were limited to the Bankruptcy Code.[183] Finally, before Dodd-Frank, insurance companies were limited to state law insolvency proceedings.[184]

---

[181] P.L. 111-203, 124 Stat. 1376, tit. II. (2010).

[182] 12 U.S.C. § 1821(c)-(d). *See also* 11 U.S.C. § 109 (specifying which entities are eligible to declare bankruptcy under the Bankruptcy Code); Carnell, et al., *supra* note 16 at 397-446. Commentators have adduced a number of considerations favoring a special insolvency regime for commercial banks, including, among other things: (1) banks' importance to the nation's money supply, payments system, and macroeconomy, (2) banks' vulnerability to "runs," and (3) the fact that bank assets can be transferred quickly and cheaply. *See* Robert R. Bliss & George G. Kaufman, *U.S. Corporate and Bank Insolvency Regimes: A Comparison and Evaluation*, 2 Va. L. & Bus. Rev. 143, 147-48 (2007).

[183] *See* 11 U.S.C. §§ 741-753; Wolkowitz v. FDIC (*In re* Imperial Credit Indus., Inc.), 527 F.3d 959, 962 (9th Cir. 2008). Broker-dealers are not eligible for Chapter 11 reorganizations and may only be liquidated pursuant to Chapter 7. *Id.* § 109(d). Under the Securities Investor Protection Act of 1970, the Securities Investor Protection Corporation (SIPC) may file an application to stay bankruptcy proceedings of a broker that is an SIPC member to allow the

The purpose and mechanics of bankruptcy and the FDIC's resolution regime differ in important respects.[185] A non-bank corporation may generally file a voluntary bankruptcy petition with the clerk of a federal bankruptcy court,[186] or the company's creditors can file a petition for involuntary bankruptcy if certain conditions are met.[187] By contrast, a bank's chartering agency, primary federal regulator, or the FDIC initiates the bank resolution process based upon one or more statutorily-established grounds, including a bank's undercapitalization.[188] Accordingly, a bank need not have defaulted

---

SIPC liquidate the broker. 15 U.S.C. § 78eee. For an overview of differences between Chapter 7 liquidations and Chapter 11 reorganizations, see CRS Report R45137, *Bankruptcy Basics: A Primer*, by Kevin M. Lewis, at 9-14.

[184] *See* Carnell, et al., *supra* note 16 at 659-71.

[185] *See* Lewis, *supra* note 183; Richard M. Hynes & Steven D. Walt, *Why Banks are Not Allowed in Bankruptcy*, 67 Wash. & Lee L. Rev. 985, 987 (2010); Bliss & Kaufman, *supra* note 182 at 153-54.

[186] *See* 11 U.S.C. § 301; FED. R. BANKR. P. 1002(a). *But see* 11 U.S.C. § 109 (limiting which entities are eligible to be a debtor under the Bankruptcy Code).

[187] *See* 11 U.S.C. § 303; FED. R. BANKR. P. 1003.

[188] *See* 12 U.S.C. §§ 203(a), 1821(c). The Office of the Comptroller of the Currency serves as the chartering agency for national banks, while state banking agencies serve as the chartering agencies for state-chartered banks. *See* Bliss & Kaufman, *supra* note 182 at 156 n.44. State-chartered banks are required to obtain deposit insurance from the FDIC and can become members of the Federal Reserve System. *See* BARR ET AL., *supra* note 77 at 166; 12 U.S.C. § 321. Accordingly, the FDIC serves as the primary federal regulator for state-chartered banks that are not members of the Federal Reserve System. For a discussion of the architecture of bank regulation in the United States, see CRS Report R44918, *Who Regulates Whom? An Overview of the U.S. Financial Regulatory Framework*, by Marc Labonte.

The statutorily-established grounds for appointment of a receiver or conservator are: (1) the insufficiency of a bank's assets to service its obligations, (2) the "substantial dissipation" of assets due to a violation of law or "any unsafe or unsound practice," (3) "[a]n unsafe or unsound condition to transact business," (4) the willful violation of a final cease and-desist order, (5) concealment of the bank's books or records from its regulators, (6) likelihood that a bank will be unable to pay its obligations or meet its depositors' demands, (7) the incurring or likelihood that a bank will incur losses that will deplete all or substantially all of its capital, (8) any violation of law that is likely to cause insolvency or a substantial dissipation of assets, weaken the bank's condition, or otherwise seriously prejudice the bank's depositors or the Deposit Insurance Fund, (9) consent to the appointment of a conservator or receiver, (10) failure to maintain deposit insurance, (11) undercapitalization, with no reasonable prospect of becoming adequately capitalized, failure to become adequately capitalized when required to do so, failure to submit a required capital restoration plan, or material failure to implement a capital restoration plan, (12) "critical[]" undercapitalization or otherwise having "substantially insufficient capital," or (13) notification from the Attorney General that the bank has been found guilty of certain criminal money laundering offenses. 12 U.S.C. § 1821(c)(5).

on any outstanding obligations or be deemed insolvent for an involuntary resolution to begin.[189]

Corporate bankruptcies are usually resolved in special federal bankruptcy courts.[190] In a Chapter 7 bankruptcy, a court appoints an agent such as a trustee to coordinate the insolvency process.[191] In a bankruptcy reorganization, the insolvent corporation's management is generally allowed to continue operating the company[192] and has exclusive rights to develop a reorganization plan for a period of 120 days after the petition is filed, which may be extended under certain circumstances.[193] Many of the trustee or management's decisions—for example, to release collateral to secured creditors, pay employees, and obtain debtor-in-possession financing (i.e., financing used to keep the company operating as a going concern)—are subject to court approval.[194] Moreover, any reorganization plan is subject to the unanimous agreement of a company's creditors unless the court determines that certain conditions are met.[195] These and other decisions by the bankruptcy court are reviewable by higher courts.[196]

By contrast, bank resolutions are handled in administrative proceedings conducted by the FDIC.[197] When the FDIC commences administrative resolution proceedings, it generally removes a bank's senior management without notice or a hearing and assumes control of the bank.[198] The FDIC

---

[189] *See* Stanley V. Ragalevsky & Sarah J. Ricardi, *Anatomy of a Bank Failure*, 126 Banking L. J. 867, 870 (2009); Bliss & Kaufman, *supra* note 182 at 156.

[190] *See* Bliss & Kaufman, *supra* note 182 at 156. *But see* 28 U.S.C. § 157(b)(5), (c)(1), (d) (specifying bankruptcy-related matters that may or must be resolved by a federal district court rather than a bankruptcy court).

[191] 11 U.S.C. §§ 701-704. Corporate liquidations are governed by Chapter 7 of the Bankruptcy Code, *id.* § 701, while reorganizations are governed by Chapter 11, *id.* § 1101.

[192] *See id.* § 1107. *But see id.* §§ 1104, 1108 (specifying circumstances under which a bankruptcy court may "order the appointment of a trustee" to administer a Chapter 11 debtor).

[193] *Id.* § 1121.

[194] *Id.* §§ 363-366.

[195] *See* Bliss & Kaufman, *supra* note 182 at 159-60; 11 U.S.C. § 1129.

[196] FED. R. APP. P. 6; 28 U.S.C. § 158.

[197] *See* Bliss & Kaufman, *supra* note 182 at 159-60; 11 U.S.C. §§ 109(b)(2), (d) (providing that banks are ineligible for bankruptcy).

[198] *See* Bliss & Kaufman, *supra* note 182 at 159-60. Although a bank's directors have the right to judicial review of a decision to appoint a conservator or receiver, 12 U.S.C. § 1821(c)(7), commentators have observed that "[t]his right appears to have been rarely exercised and never successfully," Bliss & Kaufman, *supra* note 182 at 160 n.62. *See also* Thomas W. Merrill & Margaret L. Merrill, *Dodd-Frank Orderly Liquidation Authority: Too Big for the*

unilaterally makes decisions related to the liquidation (pursuant to a receivership) or continued operation (pursuant to a conservatorship) of the failed bank.[199] For FDIC resolutions of a commercial bank, there is no separate oversight authority analogous to the relationship between the bankruptcy court and trustee or management, and there is no mechanism for creditors, management, or shareholders to participate in the resolution process beyond filing claims and providing requested information.[200] While some of the FDIC's decisions during this process are subject to judicial review, others—including decisions to disallow creditor claims that are not proved to the FDIC's satisfaction—are not reviewable.[201]

Bankruptcy and FDIC resolution also differ with respect to how creditors can be temporarily prevented from pursuing their claims against an insolvent debtor. In bankruptcy, creditors are temporarily barred from pursuing many of their claims by an "automatic stay" that is effective upon the filing of a bankruptcy petition,[202] and bankruptcy courts have the authority to impose certain additional stays to ensure an orderly reorganization.[203] However, a variety of financial contracts—including certain securities and commodities contracts, swaps, forwards, and repos—are exempt from the Bankruptcy Code's automatic stay.[204] Often, such

---

Constitution?, 163 U. Pa. L. Rev. 165, 179 (2014) (noting that although judicial review of the FDIC's decision to appoint a receiver is authorized by statute, it is "extremely difficult" to persuade a court to unwind a receivership).

199 *See* Bliss & Kaufman, *supra* note 182 at 159-60. While the FDIC can resolve a bank by a receivership (in which the FDIC liquidates and winds up of the affairs of a failed bank) or a conservatorship (in which the FDIC continues to operate a bank as a going concern), 12 U.S.C. §§ 1821(c)-(d), the FDIC has rarely used conservatorships to resolve failed banks, *see* Hynes & Walt, *supra* note 185 at 987 n.3.

200 *See* Hynes & Walt, *supra* note 185 at 989; Bliss & Kaufman, *supra* note 182 at 159-60.

201 *See* 12 U.S.C. § 1821(d)(5)(E) (providing that decisions to disallow creditor claims are not reviewable).

202 11 U.S.C. § 362. *See also* Lewis, *supra* note 183 at 6-8.

203 *Id.* § 105(a); *In re* Keene Corp., 164 B.R. 844, 849 (Bankr. S.D.N.Y. 1994).

204 11 U.S.C. §§ 362(b)(6), (7), (17), (27), 362(o), 555-56, 559-61. Commentators have proffered a variety of arguments for and against exempting such contracts from the automatic stay. *See* Mark D. Sherrill, *In Defense of the Bankruptcy Code's Safe Harbors*, 70 BUS. LAW. 1007 (2015); Stephen J. Lubben, *Derivatives and Bankruptcy: The Flawed Case for Special Treatment*, 12 U. PA. J. BUS. L. 61 (2009); Franklin R. Edwards & Edward R. Morrison, Derivatives and the Bankruptcy Code: Why the Special Treatment? 22 *Yale J. On Reg.* 91 (2005).

Some observers have argued that the legislative history behind the relevant safe-harbor provisions suggests that Congress was concerned that the inability of derivatives

contracts provide that certain rights—for example, to terminate the contract, net obligations, or liquidate collateral—are triggered by a party's entry into bankruptcy (direct default rights) or by the entry into bankruptcy of a party's parent or affiliate (cross-default rights).[205] Because of the Bankruptcy Code's "safe harbor" provisions, such rights can be exercised immediately upon the filing of a bankruptcy petition, notwithstanding the automatic stay.[206]

By contrast, while the FDIC lacks general power to stay enforcement of a failed bank's contracts,[207] it has broad power to disaffirm or repudiate certain contracts if it determines that performance would be "burdensome," and that disaffirmance or repudiation would "promote the orderly administration of the institution's affairs."[208] Moreover, counterparties to "qualified financial contracts" (QFCs)—a term defined to include certain securities or commodities contracts, swaps, forwards, and repos[209]—with a bank in an FDIC resolution are barred from exercising *direct* default rights against the bank based on its entry into resolution proceedings for one business day.[210] If the FDIC transfers a QFC to another party (as it often does when it sells a bank's assets to a healthy acquirer), default rights under the QFC are permanently stayed.[211] Accordingly, banks enjoy greater protection against "runs" by their derivatives counterparties in an FDIC resolution than do non-bank corporations in bankruptcy.

Finally, bankruptcy and FDIC resolution differ with respect to the legal priority of creditors. The Bankruptcy Code provides a list of priorities

---

counterparties to exit contracts with a bankrupt company contributed to systemic risk by preventing counterparties from mitigating their exposure to the company. Edwards & Morrison, *supra* note 204 at 107-08.

205 Final Rule, Restrictions on Qualified Financial Contracts of Certain FDIC-Supervised Institutions; Revisions to the Definition of Qualifying Master Netting Agreement and Related Definitions, 82 Fed. Reg. 50,228, 50,231 (Oct. 30, 2017).

206 11 U.S.C. §§ 362(b)(6), (7), (17), (27), 362(o), 555-56, 559-61.

207 *See* Bliss & Kaufman, *supra* note 182 at 157.

208 12 U.S.C. § 1821(e)(1).

209 *Id.* § 1821(e)(8)(D)(i).

210 *Id.* § 1821(e)(10)(B)(i)-(ii). This stay is limited to *direct* default rights—that is, rights against the bank in receivership triggered by its placement into receivership. There are no limitations on a counterparty's *cross-default* rights—that is, rights against a bank's affiliate triggered by the bank's entry into receivership.

211 *Id.*

specifying the order in which creditors are to be paid.[212] During a Chapter 11 reorganization, the "absolute priority rule" bars the approval of a reorganization plan that awards property to a junior class of unsecured creditors while failing to compensate a dissenting class of senior creditors in full.[213] A bankrupt firm can also obtain debtor-in-possession financing during a reorganization, which enjoys priority over certain pre-bankruptcy debts.[214]

By contrast, if the FDIC is unable to find a healthy bank to purchase a failing bank in a "purchase and assumption" transaction (the most common method of resolving a failed bank), it generally liquidates the bank, paying off insured depositors and issuing receivership certificates to uninsured depositors and other general creditors.[215] The FDIC pays uninsured depositors and general creditors according to a statutorily prescribed priority scheme.[216] In paying these creditors, the FDIC is required to use the "least costly" resolution method—that is, the resolution method that minimizes expenditures from the deposit insurance fund.[217] However, the FDIC can waive the least-cost resolution requirement if the Treasury Secretary (in consultation with the President and with the recommendation of the Federal Reserve) determines that adhering to that requirement "would have serious adverse effects on economic conditions or financial stability" and that alternative action "would avoid or mitigate such adverse effects."[218] Although there is no external debtor-in-possession financing

---

[212] 11 U.S.C. § 507.

[213] *See id.* § 1129(b)(2)(B)(ii); Norwest Bank Worthington v. Ahlers, 485 U.S. 197, 202 (1988). Some courts have recognized a "new value exception" to the absolute priority rule, according to which junior creditors can receive property in a reorganization plan when they provide new value to the debtor. *See In re* Abeinsa Holding, Inc., 562 B.R. 265, 277 (Bankr. D. Del. 2016).

[214] *See* Bliss & Kaufman, *supra* note 182 at 162.
A bankruptcy trustee can also claw back or "avoid" certain preferential pre-bankruptcy transfers. 11 U.S.C. §§ 546-47, 555-56, 559-61. By contrast, bank insolvency law does not contain a mechanism for clawing back preferential transfers. Bliss & Kaufman, *supra* note 182 at 164. However, the FDIC may claw-back fraudulent transfers made within five years of a bank's closure. 12 U.S.C. § 1821(d)(17).

[215] *See* Ragalevsky & Ricardi, *supra* note 189 at 876.

[216] 12 U.S.C. § 1821(d)(11).

[217] *Id.* § 1823(c)(4).

[218] *Id.* § 1823(c)(4)(G). The FDIC invoked this "systemic risk exception" multiple times during the 2007-2009 financial crisis. In September 2008, the FDIC announced that Citigroup

during an FDIC resolution, the FDIC can offer "open bank assistance" (OBA) to a troubled bank in the form of a loan, an assumption of some or all of its liabilities, a purchase of troubled assets, or a direct infusion of capital.[219] However, OBA is "rarely used" because of the least-cost resolution requirement, among other reasons.[220]

These differences between the Bankruptcy Code and FDIC resolution reflect the different priorities of their respective insolvency schemes. According to many commentators, corporate bankruptcy is principally focused on maximizing creditor recovery by preserving the "going-concern" value of a firm, or equitably distributing its assets in the event of a liquidation.[221] Accordingly, the Bankruptcy Code gives a firm's creditors a prominent role in the insolvency process, allowing them to vote on proposed reorganization plans if their interests are impaired,[222] and subjecting a trustee or management's decisions to judicial scrutiny.[223]

---

would acquire Wachovia's banking operations in a transaction assisted by the FDIC. *Crisis And Response: An Fdic History*, 2008-2013 69 (2017). Specifically, the FDIC agreed to share future losses with Citigroup on a pre-identified pool of $312 billion in loans, in exchange for $12 billion in preferred stock and warrants. *Id.* at 75. This deal was ultimately abandoned, however, when Wells Fargo agreed to acquire all of Wachovia's operations without FDIC assistance. *Id.* at 76.

The FDIC again invoked the "systemic risk exception" in November 2008 to assist Citigroup. *Id.* at 82. Pursuant to this authority, the FDIC (in conjunction with the Treasury Department, acting pursuant to a program established under the Troubled Asset Relief Program) issued an asset guarantee for a selected pool of $306 billion of Citigroup's assets, in exchange for $7 billion in preferred stock paying an 8 percent annual dividend. *Id.* at 83.

The FDIC invoked the "systemic risk exception" once more in January 2009 to assist Bank of America, which had acquired Merrill Lynch the previous September. *Id.* at 86. Pursuant to this authority, the FDIC (again in conjunction with the Treasury Department) issued an asset guarantee for a selected pool of $118 billion of loans, securities, and other assets, in exchange for $4 billion in preferred stock and warrants. *Id.* at 90-91.

In addition to invoking the "systemic risk exception" to assist individual troubled banks during the financial crisis, the FDIC also adopted the then-novel interpretation that the "systemic risk exception" allowed it to take actions to preserve the stability of the banking system more generally. *See id.* at 33-60. Pursuant to this interpretation of its authority, the FDIC implemented the Temporary Liquidity Guarantee Program, which (1) provided a limited-term guarantee for certain newly-issued debt of commercial banks, thrifts, and financial holding companies and eligible bank affiliates, and (2) fully guaranteed certain non-interest bearing transaction deposit accounts. *Id.* at 33.

[219] *See* Ragalevsky & Ricardi, *supra* note 189 at 882; Bliss & Kaufman, *supra* note 182 at 162.

[220] *See* Ragalevsky & Ricardi, *supra* note 189 at 882.

[221] *See* Bliss & Kaufman, *supra* note 182 at 153.

[222] 11 U.S.C. § 1126(a), (f); FED. R. BANKR. P. 3018.

[223] *See* Hynes & Walt, *supra* note 185 at 1006.

Table 1. Differences Between Bankruptcy and FDIC Resolution

	Bankruptcy	**FDIC Resolutions**
Where are proceedings held?	Bankruptcy court (with certain exceptions).	Administrative proceedings before the FDIC.
What are the bases for commencing an involuntary resolution?	Among other requirements, a debtor must be "generally not paying ... debts" as they become due.	The FDIC may involuntarily seize a bank for a variety of reasons, including a bank's undercapitalization.
What happens to old management?	In a Chapter 11 reorganization, management is generally permitted to continue running the company, and has exclusive rights to develop a reorganization plan for a period of 120 days after the bankruptcy petition is filed. In a Chapter 7 liquidation, a trustee generally replaces old management and liquidates the debtor.	The FDIC generally removes old management.
How can creditors participate?	Creditors have several avenues by which they can participate in a bankruptcy proceeding. Creditors can object if the debtor takes certain actions outside the ordinary course of business, and impaired creditors can generally vote on proposed reorganization plans.	Creditors are generally limited to submitting their claims and other requested information to the FDIC.
Are debtors protected against "runs" by derivatives counterparties?	Generally not. Certain derivatives contracts are exempt from the "automatic stay."	Yes. QFC counterparties are stayed from exercising direct default rights for one business day, and are permanently stayed from exercising such rights if the FDIC transfers a QFC to a third party.

Source: CRS.

Bank resolution, by contrast, arguably places greater emphasis on financial stability than does the Bankruptcy Code, making the speed of the resolution process especially important.[224] Accordingly, authority over

[224] *Id.* at 1007-08.

bank resolution is highly concentrated in one actor: the FDIC. With its considerable resolution powers, the FDIC is often able to seize a failed bank at the close of business on a Friday, sell many of its assets, and re-open many of its offices under the auspices of a healthy acquirer by the following Monday, minimizing negative effects on the financial system.[225]

This dual-track insolvency system, with the FDIC in charge of resolving commercial banks and bankruptcy courts tasked with non-bank insolvencies, arguably functioned effectively for much of the 20th century.[226] However, many commentators have contended that the bankruptcy system is ill-suited for the resolution of large, complex financial institutions.[227] Specifically, observers have noted that the dependence of such institutions on short-term, highly liquid funding leaves them susceptible to "runs"—a problem exacerbated by the Bankruptcy Code's "safe harbor" provisions for certain derivatives contracts.[228] Moreover, commentators have argued that the complicated legal structures of large financial institutions make their resolution in bankruptcy difficult, because such institutions often (1) have

---

[225] *Id.* at 989.

[226] *See Ending "Too Big to Fail": Title II of the Dodd-Frank Act and the Approach of "Single Point of Entry" Private Sector Recapitalization of a Failed Financial Company*, The Clearing House 12 (Jan. 2013), https://www.cov.com/ files/Publication/714f0b24-8047-4d79-825f-55f5d1e80bdc/Presentation/PublicationAttachment/f7462820-7d03-4ed2- 8b75-96b917418d8f/White_Paper_Ending_Too-Big-to-Fail.pdf. [hereinafter "Clearing House Report"] (arguing that the "bifurcated regimes worked well for a range of institutions" before the financial crisis, and that "the bank failure regime administered by the FDIC proved to be very effective in dealing in an orderly way with the wave of depository institution failures of the 1980s and 1990s"); Sheila Bair, Beyond Bankruptcy and Bailouts, *Wall St. J.* (Apr. 5, 2010), https://www.wsj.com/articles/SB10001424052702304871704575159643688328442 (asserting that "the FDIC has a well-established process that works for failing banks"); Thomas H. Jackson, Chapter 11F: A Proposal for the Use of Bankruptcy to Resolve Financial Institutions 217, 217 in *Ending Government Bailouts As We Know Them* (Kenneth E. Scott, George P. Schultz & John B. Taylor, eds. 2009) (asserting that "[b]ankruptcy reorganization is, for the most part, an American success story").

[227] See Adam J. Levitin, Bankruptcy's Lorelei: The Dangerous Allure of Financial Institution Bankruptcy, 97 N.C. L. Rev., (forthcoming); Paul L. Lee, Bankruptcy Alternatives to Title II of the Dodd-Frank Act—Part I, Banking L. J. 437, 442-44 (Oct. 2015); Ben S. Bernanke, *The Federal Reserve and the Financial Crisis* 86 (2013); Clearing House Report, supra note 226 at 11-17; Resolving Globally Active, Systemically Important, Financial Institutions, Bank Of England (Dec. 10, 2012), https://www.fdic.gov/ about/srac/2012/gsifi.pdf.

[228] U.S. Gov. Accountability Office, GAO-11-707, *Bankruptcy: Complex Institutions And International Coordination Pose Challenges* 28-30 (July 2011) [hereinafter "GAO Bankruptcy Report"].

regulated subsidiaries such as banks and insurance companies that are not themselves eligible for bankruptcy, and (2) operate their businesses without regard for the legal separateness of these entities.[229] Others have argued that reorganizing a large financial institution in bankruptcy (or continuing its subsidiaries' operations on a temporary basis until a buyer can be found) would be extraordinarily difficult, because such an institution would likely require billions of dollars of debtor-in-possession financing—a sum that "[p]rivate lending markets are not capable of providing" to a bankrupt firm, especially in a period of financial distress.[230] According to these observers, the 2007-2009 financial crisis highlighted these problems with the Bankruptcy Code, and the need to develop alternative resolution mechanisms for financial institutions not subject to the FDIC's supervision.[231]

Dodd-Frank and the Orderly Liquidation Authority

Legislative History

In March 2009, the Treasury Department released a legislative proposal for a new resolution authority "to address systemically significant financial institutions that fall outside of the existing resolution regime under the FDIC."[232] The Treasury Department argued that the financial crisis highlighted the inadequacy of the existing resolution options for large non-bank financial institutions.[233] According to the Obama Administration's Treasury Department, policymakers during the crisis were forced to choose between two untenable options for such institutions: (1) securing outside capital or committing government funds to rescue a

---

[229] Id. at 30-35.

[230] Levitin, supra note 227 at 18.

[231] See Ben S. Bernanke, Why Dodd-Frank's Orderly Liquidation Authority Should be Preserved, The Brookings Inst. (Feb. 28, 2017), https://www.brookings.edu/blog/ben-bernanke/2017/02/28/why-dodd-franks-orderly-liquidationauthority-should-be-preserved/; Merrill & Merrill, supra note 198 at 167; *GAO Bankruptcy Report*, supra note 228 at 28-35.

[232] See *Treasury Proposes Legislation for Resolution Authority*, U.S. Dep't of the Treasury (Mar. 25, 2009), https://www.treasury.gov/press-center/press-releases/ Pages/tg70.aspx.

[233] *Id.*

TBTF institution (as in the case of AIG), or (2) a destabilizing bankruptcy (as in the case of Lehman).[234]

The Obama Administration accordingly proposed supplementing these options with a resolution regime "modeled on the statutory framework that governs the FDIC's exercise of emergency resolution and other authority with respect to banks."[235] Instead of "subjecting a firm to bankruptcy" or "injecting taxpayers' funds with no real control," the Treasury Department's proposed legislation would enable the federal government to put a firm into a conservatorship or receivership managed by the FDIC, which could sell or transfer the firm's assets and liabilities, renegotiate or repudiate its contracts, and address its derivatives portfolio.[236] The proposed legislation would also allow the FDIC to make loans to a financial institution placed into conservatorship or receivership, purchase the institution's obligations or assets, assume or guarantee the institution's liabilities, or purchase an equity interest in the institution.[237]

The Obama Administration's proposal provided that the Board of Governors of the Federal Reserve and the Board of the FDIC, by two-thirds votes, were to provide the Treasury Secretary with a "recomm-endation" concerning actions that should be taken with respect to a troubled financial company, and that the Treasury Secretary make certain findings before commencing the conservatorship or receivership.[238] The Administration's proposal allowed a seized firm to file suit requesting that the conservatorship or receivership be set aside within thirty days.[239] The proposal did not restrict the issues that the reviewing court could consider or impose a time limit on the court's review.[240] In December 2009, the House of Representatives passed a version of the new resolution regime

---

[234] *Id.*

[235] *Id.*

[236] *Id.*

[237] *Id.*

[238] Exec. Office of the President, Resolution Authority for Large, Interconnected Financial Companies Act of 2009, tit. XII § 1203(a)-(c) (July 23, 2009).

[239] *Id.* § 1205.

[240] *Id.*

based on the Treasury Department's proposal.[241] Like the Treasury Department's proposal, the House bill provided for the appointment of a receiver after (1) two-thirds votes by the Board of Governors of the Federal Reserve and the Board of the FDIC, and (2) the Treasury Secretary made certain determinations.[242] The House bill also provided for a thirty-day period within which a seized firm could seek judicial review.[243] However, unlike the Treasury Department's proposal, the House bill did not grant the FDIC the authority to provide equity financing to companies during the resolution process.[244] Also in contrast to Treasury's proposal, the House bill required that any debt funding the government provided to a seized company be repaid from ex ante assessments on certain large financial institutions.[245]

A Senate bill introduced in April 2010 built on these proposals, but envisioned a slightly different process for appointing a receiver for non-bank financial institutions. The initial Senate bill required that a panel of three bankruptcy judges from the Bankruptcy Court for the District of Delaware approve the Treasury Secretary's decision to appoint a receiver for a troubled company.[246] However, this panel of bankruptcy judges would consider only one of the Treasury Secretary's various findings: that the relevant firm is in default or in danger of default.[247] The Senate bill also imposed a variety of secrecy requirements related to resolution proceedings. The bill provided that (1) the Treasury Secretary's petition to the bankruptcy panel would be filed under seal, (2) proceedings before the panel would be held "[o]n a strictly confidential basis," and (3) criminal penalties would be imposed on persons who disclosed information about the

---

[241] Wall Street Reform and Consumer Protection Act of 2009, H.R. 4173, 111th Cong. (as passed by the House of Representatives, Dec. 11, 2009)).

[242] *Id.* § 1603(a)(1).

[243] *Id.* § 1605.

[244] *See id.* § 1609.

[245] *Id.* §§ 1604(d) & 1609(n).

[246] Restoring American Financial Stability Act of 2010, S. 3217, 111th Cong. § 203 (as substituted Apr. 29, 2010).

[247] *Id.* § 202(b)(1)(A)(iii)-(iv).

proceedings.[248] The panel would be required to rule within 24 hours of receiving the petition.[249]

After the initial Senate bill was introduced, Senator Christopher Dodd proposed a series of amendments.[250] Among other things, the amendments provided that the Treasury Secretary would petition the U.S. District Court for the District of Columbia instead of a panel of bankruptcy judges for the appointment of a receiver.[251] The amendments further provided that the district court would review two of the Treasury Secretary's determinations: (1) that the firm to be placed into receivership satisfied the statutory definition of a "financial company," and (2) that the firm is in default or in danger of default.[252] The Senate passed the revised bill on May 20, 2010.[253]

A Conference Committee resolved the differences between the House and Senate bills.[254] Among other things, the Conference Committee report adopted an ex post assessment process on large financial institutions to repay any government funding providing during the resolution process, in place of the ex ante assessment in the House bill.[255] The House and Senate passed the Conference Committee report in late June and mid-July 2010, respectively,[256] and President Obama signed Dodd-Frank on July 21, 2010.[257]

Title II and the Orderly Liquidation Authority

These various legislative proceedings culminated in Title II of Dodd-Frank, which creates an "Orderly Liquidation Authority" (OLA) pursuant to which the FDIC can serve as the receiver for "failing financial

---

[248] *Id.* §§ 202(b)(1)(A)(ii)-(iii), 202(b)(1)(C).

[249] *Id.* § 202(b)(1)(A)(iii).

[250] 156 CONG. REC. S3139-40 (daily ed. May 5, 2010).

[251] Restoring American Financial Stability Act of 2010, H.R. 4173 § 202(a)(1)(A)(i) (111th Cong. (as substituted in the Senate, May 20, 2010)).

[252] *Id.* § 202(a)(1)(A)(i).

[253] 156 CONG. REC. S4708 (daily ed. May 20, 2010).

[254] H.R. REP. No. 111-517 (2010) (Conf. Rep.).

[255] H.R. REP. No. 111-517 § 210(n)(9).

[256] *See* Brady Dennis, Congress Passes Financial Reform Bill, *Wash. Post*. (July 16, 2010), http://www.washingtonpost.com/wp-dyn/content/article/2010/07/15/AR2010071500464.html.

[257] *See* Helene Cooper, Obama Signs Overhaul of Financial System, *N.Y. Times* (July 21, 2010), https://www.nytimes.com/2010/07/22/business/22regulate.html?hp.

companies that pose a significant risk to the financial stability of the United States."[258] Title II can be invoked only for "covered financial companies" and "covered brokers and dealers."[259] Title II defines a "covered financial company" as a "financial company"[260] that is not an insured depository institution, and for which a "systemic risk determination" has been made.[261] Title II defines a "covered broker or dealer" as a broker or dealer that is registered with the Securities and Exchange Commission (SEC) and is a member of the Securities Investor Protection Corporation.[262]

The Decision to Invoke Title II

Under Title II, certain designated federal regulators may recommend to the Treasury Secretary the appointment of the FDIC as receiver of a financial company.[263] The Federal Reserve and the SEC will make the recommendation if the company or its largest subsidiary is a broker or dealer.[264] The Federal Reserve and the Director of the Federal Insurance Office will make the recommendation if the company is an insurance

---

[258] 12 U.S.C. § 5384(a).

[259] *Id.* §§ 5384-85.

[260] The term "financial company" is defined to mean (1) "bank holding companies," as that term is defined in the Bank Holding Company Act (BHCA); (2) non-bank financial companies supervised by the Federal Reserve; (3) any company predominantly engaged in activities that the Federal Reserve has determined are financial in nature or incidental thereto for purposes of the BHCA; or (4) any subsidiary of any company in the three foregoing categories that is predominantly engaged in activities that the Federal Reserve has determined are financial in nature or incidental thereto for purposes of the BHCA, except if those subsidiaries are insured depository institutions or insurance companies. *Id.* § 5381(a)(11).

The Bank Holding Company Act defines a "bank holding company" as "any company which has control over any bank or over any company that is or becomes a bank holding company." *Id.* § 1841(a)(1). For purposes of this definition, a company "has control over a bank or over any company" if (1) the company directly or indirectly owns, controls, or has the power to vote 25 percent or more of any class of voting securities of the bank or company, (2) the company controls in any manner the election of a majority of the directors or trustees of the bank or company, or (3) the Federal Reserve determines that the company directly or indirectly exercises a controlling influence over the management or policies of a bank or company. *Id.* § 1841(a)(2).

[261] *Id.* § 5381(a)(8).

[262] *Id.* § 5381(a)(7).

[263] *Id.* § 5383(a)(1).

[264] *Id.* § 5383(a)(1)(B).

company.[265] The Federal Reserve and the FDIC will make the recommendation in all other cases.[266] Such a recommendation requires a vote of at least two-thirds of the members of the Board of Governors of the Federal Reserve, and (1) at least two-thirds of the SEC members then serving (in the case of a broker or dealer), (2) the Director of the Federal Insurance Office (in the case of an insurance company), or (3) two-thirds of the members of the FDIC's Board of Directors (in all other cases).[267] Any such recommendation shall contain

1. an evaluation of whether the financial company is in default or danger of default;
2. a description of the effect that the default of the financial company would have on financial stability in the United States;
3. a description of the effect that the default of the financial company would have on economic conditions or financial stability for low income, minority, or underserved communities;
4. a recommendation regarding the nature and the extent of actions to be taken regarding the financial company;
5. an evaluation of the likelihood of a private sector alternative to prevent the default of the financial company;
6. an evaluation of why a case under the Bankruptcy Code is not appropriate for the financial company;
7. an evaluation of the effects on creditors, counterparties, and shareholders of the financial company and other market participants; and
8. an evaluation of whether the company satisfies the definition of a "financial company."[268]

Upon a written recommendation, the Treasury Secretary shall seek appointment of the FDIC as receiver of the financial company if (in

[265] *Id.* § 5383(a)(1)(C).
[266] *Id.* § 5383(a)(1)(A).
[267] *Id.* § 5383(a)(1).
[268] *Id.* § 5383(a)(2).

consultation with the President) he makes a "systemic risk determination"—that is, if he makes the following seven determinations:

1. the financial company is in default or in danger of default;[269]
2. the failure of the financial company and its resolution under otherwise applicable federal or state law would have serious adverse effects on financial stability in the United States;
3. no viable private sector alternative is available to prevent the default of the financial company;
4. any effect on the claims or interests of creditors, counterparties, and shareholders of the financial company and other market participants as a result of actions to be taken under the relevant subchapter is appropriate, given the impact that any such action would have on financial stability in the United States;
5. the relevant action would avoid or mitigate such adverse effects, taking into consideration the effectiveness of the action in mitigating potential adverse effects on the financial system, the cost to the general fund of the Treasury Department, and the potential to increase excessive risk taking on the part of creditors, counterparties, and shareholders in the financial company;
6. a federal regulatory agency has ordered the financial company to convert all of its convertible debt instruments that are subject to the regulatory order; and
7. the company satisfies the definition of a "financial company."[270]

Upon making a "systemic risk determination," the Treasury Secretary must notify the financial company and the FDIC.[271] If the company's board

---

[269] For purposes of the relevant subchapter of Title II, a financial company is considered to be "in default or in danger of default" if (1) a case has been, or likely will promptly be, commenced with respect to it under the Bankruptcy Code, (2) the financial company has incurred, or is likely to incur, losses that will deplete all or substantially all of its capital, and there is no reasonable prospect for the company to avoid such depletion, (3) the assets of the financial company are, or are likely to be, less than its obligations to creditors and others, or (4) the financial company is, or is likely to be, unable to pay its obligations (other than those subject to a bona fide dispute) in the normal course of business. *Id.* § 5383(c)(4).

[270] *Id.* § 5383(b).

of directors consents to the appointment of the FDIC as receiver, the Treasury Secretary must appoint the FDIC as receiver.[272] If the company's board of directors does not consent to the appointment, the Treasury Secretary can petition the U.S. District Court for the District of Columbia for an order authorizing the appointment.[273] The court must then hold a "strictly confidential" hearing at which it reviews (under the "arbitrary and capricious" standard) two of the Treasury Secretary's determinations: (1) the company is in default or in danger of default, and (2) the company is a "financial company."[274]

If the court determines that these determinations are not arbitrary and capricious, it must issue an order immediately authorizing the Treasury Secretary to appoint the FDIC as receiver of the financial company.[275] If the court does not make a determination within 24 hours after receiving the petition, the petition is deemed granted by operation of law.[276] The court's determination is "final," and "not ... subject to any stay or injunction pending appeal."[277] Moreover, any appeal of the district court's decision must be considered "on an expedited basis."[278] Title II also imposes criminal penalties on persons who "recklessly disclose[]" a systemic risk determination by the Treasury Secretary or the pendency of court proceedings related to such a determination.[279]

The FDIC's Powers as Receiver

Upon its appointment as receiver, the FDIC succeeds to all rights, titles, powers, and privileges of the company and its assets, and of any

---

[271] *Id.* § 5382(a)(1)(A)(i).

[272] *Id.*

[273] *Id.*

[274] 12 U.S.C. § 5382(a)(1)(A)(iii).

[275] *Id.* § 5382(a)(1)(A)(iv)(I). If the court determines that these determinations are arbitrary and capricious, it must immediately provide the Treasury Secretary "a written statement of each reason supporting its determination, and afford the Secretary an immediate opportunity to amend and refile the petition." *Id.* § 5382(a)(1)(A)(iv)(II).

[276] *Id.* § 5382(a)(1)(A)(v).

[277] *Id.* § 5382(a)(1)(B).

[278] *Id.* § 5382(a)(2)(A)(iii). *See also id.* § 5382(a)(2)(B)(iii) (providing that the Supreme Court shall consider any appeals from the U.S. Court of Appeals from the D.C. Circuit "on an expedited basis").

[279] *Id.* § 5382(a)(1)(C).

stockholder, member, officer or director.[280] The FDIC may continue the company's business and "liquidate" and "wind-up" its affairs "in such manner as [it] deems appropriate."[281] Pursuant to this authority, the FDIC may sell the company's assets,[282] merge the company with another company,[283] transfer its assets or liabilities to another company,[284] or transfer the company's assets or liabilities to a newly created "bridge financial company."[285]

The creation of a bridge company allows the FDIC to continue the troubled company's critical businesses on a temporary basis until it can find a buyer or liquidate the company.[286] This new entity would "not be saddled with the shareholders, debt, senior executives or bad assets and operations that led to the failure of the covered financial company."[287] QFCs transferred to a bridge company cannot be terminated simply because they are assumed by the bridge company.[288] According to the FDIC, this provision "is an important tool to avoid market destabilization because, unlike the Bankruptcy Code, it can prevent the immediate and disorderly liquidation of collateral during a period of market distress."[289]

---

[280] *Id.* § 5390(a)(1)(A).
[281] *Id.* § 5390(a)(1)(D).
[282] *Id.*
[283] For mergers requiring approval by a federal agency, transactions may not be consummated before the 5th calendar day after the day of approval by the relevant agency. *Id.* § 5390(a)(1)(G)(ii)(I).
[284] *Id.* § 5390(a)(1)(D).
[285] *Id.* §§ 5390(a)(1)(D), 5390(a)(1)(F), 5390(h). Any judicial action to which a bridge financial company becomes a party by virtue of its acquisition of assets or assumption of liabilities of a financial company can be stayed for a period of up to 45 days, at the request of the bridge financial company. *Id.* § 5390(h)(6). A bridge company established by the FDIC terminates two years after it is granted its charter, unless the FDIC extends its status for up to three additional one-year periods. *Id.* § 5390(h)(12).
[286] Clearing House Report, *supra* note 226 at 23; Interim Final Rule, Orderly Liquidation Authority Provisions of the Dodd-Frank Wall Street Reform and Consumer Protection Act, 76 Fed. Reg. 4,207, 4,209 (Jan. 25, 2011).
[287] Orderly Liquidation Authority Provisions of the Dodd-Frank Wall Street Reform and Consumer Protection Act, 76 Fed. Reg. at 4,209. Title II exempts a bridge company created by the FDIC from all federal, state, and local taxes. 12 U.S.C. § 5390(h)(10). For a discussion of how the FDIC envisions transferring the assets of a failed company to a bridge company, and exchanging equity and debt in the bridge company for claims against the failed company, see "Single Point of Entry (SPOE) Resolution" *infra*.
[288] 12 U.S.C. § 5390(c)(10)(B)(i)(II).
[289] Orderly Liquidation Authority Provisions of the Dodd-Frank Wall Street Reform and Consumer Protection Act, 76 Fed. Reg. at 4,209. Along these lines, the FDIC has contended

Title II also specifies the priorities governing payment of unsecured claims, mandating that the costs of the receivership be paid first.[290] Claims owed to the United States are paid second, followed by a rank-ordering of other categories of unsecured claims.[291] However, Title II allows the FDIC to depart from this statutory priority list and make "additional payments" to "any claimant or category claimants" if it "determines that such payments ... are necessary or appropriate to minimize losses to the [FDIC]."[292] Title II also requires that the FDIC treat all similarly situated creditors similarly, except when the FDIC determines that not doing so is necessary to (1) maximize the assets of the covered financial company, (2) continue operations that are "essential to implementation of the receivership," (3) maximize the present value return from the sale or other disposition of covered financial company's assets, or (4) minimize the amount of any loss realized upon the sale or other disposition of the covered financial company's assets.[293] Despite granting these powers to the FDIC, Title II provides that "in no event" shall a creditor receive less than it would have received if the FDIC had not been appointed receiver and the company had instead been liquidated under Chapter 7 of the Bankruptcy Code.[294]

As in bank resolutions, the FDIC has the authority to disallow any claims not proved to its satisfaction.[295] A claimant may contest such determinations by filing suit in the federal district where the relevant

---

that "[t]he absence of funding for continuing valuable contracts and the rights of counterparties under the Bankruptcy Code to immediately terminate [QFCs] resulted in a loss of billions of dollars in market value to the bankruptcy estate in the Lehman insolvency." *Id.*

[290] 12 U.S.C. § 5390(b)(1).

[291] *Id.*

[292] *Id.* § 5390(d)(4)(A). This power is subject to the caveat that the FDIC may not make any "additional payments" to a claimant or category of claimants "that would result in any claimant receiving more than the face value amount of any claim." *Id.* § 5390(d)(4)(B).

[293] *Id.* § 5390(b)(4). *See also id.* § 5390(h)(5)(E) (imposing the same "equitable treatment" requirement and similar exceptions when the FDIC transfers assets or liabilities to a bridge financial company). If the FDIC exercises its authority to treat similarly situated creditors differently under any of these provisions, it must file a report with the Senate Committee on Banking, Housing, and Urban Affairs and the House of Representatives Committee on Financial Services identifying the claimants that have received special treatment, the amount of any additional payments, and the reason for such action. *Id.* § 5383(c)(3)(A)(vi).

[294] *Id.* § 5390(a)(7)(B), (d)(2).

[295] *Id.* § 5390(a)(3)(D).

financial company's principal place of business is located.[296] Title II also provides that the FDIC may disaffirm or repudiate any contract or lease of a company in receivership if it determines that performance would be "burdensome" and that doing so "will promote the orderly administration of the affairs of the covered financial company."[297] The FDIC may transfer its rights under a contract or lease to an acquirer of a financial company's assets, despite any contractual provisions excusing a counterparty from performance in the event of the financial company's insolvency, the appointment of a receiver, or similar circumstances.[298] The FDIC also has the authority to sue to avoid fraudulent transfers, preferences, and improper setoffs, like a trustee in bankruptcy.[299] Finally, Title II gives the FDIC the authority to "recover from any current or former senior executive or director substantially responsible for the failed condition of [a] covered financial company any compensation received during the 2-year period preceding" the FDIC's appointment as receiver.[300]

Although Title II gives the FDIC broad powers to resolve troubled companies, it also imposes a number of mandatory conditions on its conduct as a receiver. Specifically, Title II provides that the FDIC shall

1. determine that any actions it takes as receiver are "necessary for purposes of the financial stability of the United States, and not for the purpose of preserving the covered financial company;"
2. "ensure that the shareholders of a covered financial company do not receive payment until after all other claims and the [Orderly Liquidation] Fund are fully paid;"

---

[296] *Id.* § 5390(a)(4).

[297] *Id.* § 5390(c)(1). Damages for the disaffirmance or repudiation of a contract to which a company in receivership is a party are limited to "actual direct compensatory damages," and do not include "punitive or exemplary damages," "damages for lost profits or opportunity," or "damages for pain and suffering." *Id.* § 5390(c)(3)(A)-(B). However, damages for the disaffirmance or repudiation of a QFC are "deemed to include normal and reasonable costs of other reasonable measures of damages utilized in the industries for such contract and agreement claims." *Id.* § 5390(c)(3)(C).

[298] *Id.* § 5390(c)(13).

[299] *Id.* § 5390(a)(11)(A)-(B), 5390(a)(12).

[300] *Id.* § 5390(s)(1). In cases of fraud, "no time limit shall apply" to the FDIC's power to recoup executive or director compensation. *Id.*

3. ensure that unsecured creditors bear losses in accordance with statutorily prescribed priorities;
4. "ensure that management responsible for the failed condition of the covered financial company is removed;"
5. "ensure that the members of the board of directors ... responsible for the failed condition of the covered financial company are removed;" and
6. not take an equity interest in or become a shareholder of any covered financial company.[301]

Title II limits judicial review over the FDIC's actions as receiver. Specifically, Title II provides that except as otherwise provided, no court has jurisdiction over (1) claims for payment from or a determination of rights with respect to the assets of a company in receivership, or (2) any claim relating to acts or omissions of such companies or the FDIC as receiver.[302] Moreover, except as otherwise provided, "no court may take any action to restrain or affect the exercise of powers or functions of the receiver," and "any remedy against the [FDIC] or receiver shall be limited to money damages."[303]

Funding a Resolution Under Title II

Title II allows for the creation of an "Orderly Liquidation Fund" (OLF) funded with money the FDIC may borrow from the Treasury Department.[304] The FDIC's borrowing cannot exceed 10 percent of a financial company's total consolidated assets during the first 30 days of a receivership, or 90 percent of total consolidated assets that are available for repayment thereafter.[305] The FDIC can "in its discretion" and "as necessary and appropriate" make OLF funds "available to the receivership," including by making loans to the company in receivership or purchasing or

---

[301] *Id.* § 5386.
[302] *Id.* § 5390(a)(9)(D).
[303] *Id.* § 5390(e).
[304] *Id.* § 5390(n)(5).
[305] *Id.* § 5390(n)(6).

guaranteeing its assets.[306] However, the FDIC can use the OLF only after developing an orderly liquidation plan for a company in receivership "that is acceptable to" the Treasury Secretary.[307]

Despite granting the FDIC the authority to make loans to a company in receivership from the OLF, Title II provides that taxpayers "shall bear no losses" from an OLA resolution.[308] Any funds expended in the liquidation of a financial company must be "recovered from the disposition of assets of such financial company, or shall be the responsibility of the financial sector, through assessments."[309] Any loans the FDIC makes to a company in receivership from the OLF enjoy priority over all other unsecured creditors.[310] If a company's assets are insufficient to pay the sums borrowed from the Treasury Department within 60 months of their issuance, the FDIC must charge "one or more risk-based assessments" on any creditors that received "additional payments" from the FDIC pursuant to its authority to treat some creditors more favorably than similarly situated creditors.[311] If those funds are also inadequate to satisfy the FDIC's obligations to the Treasury Secretary, the FDIC must impose additional assessments on "eligible financial companies" and financial companies with total consolidated assets equal to or greater than $50 billion.[312]

---

306 *Id.* § 5384(d).

307 *Id.* § 5390(n)(9)(A).

308 *Id.* § 5394(c). *See also id.* § 5384(a)(1) (explaining that the purpose of Title II is "to provide the necessary authority to liquidate failing financial companies that pose a significant risk to the financial stability of the United States in a manner that mitigates such risk and minimizes moral hazard," and that "[t]he authority provided in this subchapter shall be exercised in the manner that best fulfills such purpose, so that ... creditors and shareholders will bear the losses of the financial company.").

309 *Id.* § 5394(b).

310 *Id.* § 5390(b)(1)(B).

311 *Id.* § 5390(o)(1)(B), 5390(o)(1)(D)(i). The FDIC may extend this period if it "determines that an extension is necessary to avoid a serious adverse effect on the financial system of the United States." *Id.* § 5390(o)(1)(C).

312 *Id.* § 5390(o)(1)(D)(ii). The term "eligible financial company" is defined to mean "any bank holding company with total consolidated assets equal to or greater $50 billion and any nonbank financial company supervised by the Board of Governors [of the Federal Reserve]." *Id.* § 5390(o)(1)(A). The FDIC must impose such assessments pursuant to a "risk matrix" that takes into account a variety of factors, including a financial company's risk to the financial system, the extent to which the company has benefitted or likely would benefit

Title II's Treatment of QFCs

Title II contains a number of provisions addressing QFCs, which are defined to encompass "any securities contract, commodity contract, forward contract, repurchase agreement, swap agreement, and any similar agreement that the [FDIC] determines by regulation, resolution, or order to be a [QFC] for purposes of this paragraph."[313] As in FDIC bank resolutions, Title II stays the exercise of any *direct* default rights under a QFC—that is, rights against the institution in receivership triggered by the institution's placement into receivership—for one business day.[314] If the FDIC transfers a QFC to a third party, including a bridge financial company, Title II permanently stays the exercise of direct default rights.[315] Moreover, unlike the rules governing FDIC resolutions, Title II addresses *cross-default* rights under QFCs using a similar procedure. Specifically, Title II empowers the FDIC to "enforce contracts of subsidiaries or affiliates" of a company in receivership that are guaranteed or otherwise support by or linked to the company, notwithstanding any cross-default rights.[316] If a QFC is supported by a guarantee or otherwise supported by a company in receivership, the FDIC must take certain steps to protect the QFC counterparty's interests by the end of the business day following the company's entry into receivership.[317]

Administrative Rules

The OLA has never been used. However, federal agencies have promulgated a number of rules that affect Title II in important ways. Section 209 of Dodd-Frank directs the FDIC, in consultation with FSOC, to "prescribe such rules or regulations as the [FDIC] considers necessary or appropriate to implement [Title II], including rules and regulations with

from the orderly liquidation of a company placed into receivership, and any other risk-related factors the FDIC determines to be appropriate. *Id.* § 5390(o)(4).

[313] *Id.* § 5390(c)(8)(D)(i).
[314] *Id.* § 5390(c)(10)(B)(i)(I).
[315] *Id.* § 5390(c)(10)(B)(i)(II).
[316] *Id.* § 5390(c)(16).
[317] *Id.*

respect to the rights, interests, and priorities of creditors, counterparties, security entitlement holders, or other persons with respect to any covered financial company."[318] A number of other provisions also direct the FDIC to promulgate rules addressing specific issues under Title II.[319] Moreover, other provisions in Dodd-Frank and federal statutes allow federal regulatory agencies to promulgate rules that have important implications for Title II.[320] This subsection provides a general overview of some of the key administrative rules related to Title II.

Early FDIC Rules

In January 2011, the FDIC promulgated a rule addressing a variety of discrete topics.[321] Among other things, the rule addressed the provisions in Title II that allow the FDIC as receiver to pay certain creditors more than similarly situated creditors if it makes certain findings related to maximizing recovery for the receivership.[322] Responding to criticism that the relevant statutory provision permitted it to bailout favored creditors,[323] the FDIC clarified that it will not use this authority to make such "additional payments" to creditors who hold certain unsecured senior debt with a term of more than 360 days or to holders of subordinated debt or shareholders.[324] The FDIC explained that it will evaluate whether to make "additional payments" to holders of shorter-term debt "on a case-by-case

---

318 *Id.* § 5389.

319 *See id.* §§ 5390(a)(7)(D) (directing the FDIC to promulgate regulations "to establish an interest rate for or to make payments of post-insolvency interest to creditors" of a receivership estate); 5390(b)(1)(C)-(D) (directing the FDIC to promulgate regulations regarding the inflation index for certain employee compensation and benefit claims); 5390(s)(3) (directing the FDIC to promulgate regulations implementing Title II's provision regarding claw-backs of executive and director compensation).

320 *See* 12 U.S.C. § 5365(a)(1) (allowing the Federal Reserve to impose enhanced prudential standards on bank holding companies with more than $50 billion in assets).

321 Interim Final Rule, Orderly Liquidation Authority Provisions of the Dodd-Frank Wall Street Reform and Consumer Protection Act, 76 Fed. Reg. 4,207, 4,209 (Jan. 25, 2011).

322 *See* 12 U.S.C. §§ 5390(b)(4), 5390(d)(4)(A), 5390(h)(5)(E).

323 *See* Statement of Republican Policy on H.R. 4173, the "Dodd-Frank Wall Street Reform and Consumer Protection Act" (June 30, 2010), https://repcloakroom.house.gov/news/documentsingle.aspx?DocumentID=193034.

324 Orderly Liquidation Authority Provisions of the Dodd-Frank Wall Street Reform and Consumer Protection Act, 76 Fed. Reg. at 4,211.

basis" and that such payments will be "very rare."[325] Possible examples of creditors who might receive such payments, the FDIC noted, include providers of "essential and necessary service[s]," and creditors with contract claims that are tied to performance bonds or other credit support needed for the company to continue other valuable contracts.[326]

In July 2011, the FDIC promulgated another rule addressing a variety of issues.[327] Among other things, the rule provided that for purposes of Title II's provision allowing the FDIC to recover compensation from executives and directors "substantially responsible" for the failure of a covered financial company, a person will be deemed "substantially responsible" if "he or she failed to conduct his or her responsibilities with the degree of skill and care of an ordinarily prudent person in a like position would exercise under similar circumstances."[328] In establishing a negligence standard for recovery of executive or director compensation, the FDIC rejected proposals to adopt a stricter standard such as gross negligence.[329] The FDIC's rule further provided that a senior executive or director will be presumed to be "substantially responsible" for the failure of a covered financial company in certain circumstances.[330]

Single Point of Entry (SPOE) Resolution (FDIC Notice for Public Comment)

Arguably, the FDIC's most prominent refinement of its Title II authorities has involved its general strategy for resolving a financial company in receivership.[331] In December 2013, the FDIC proposed for

---

325 *Id.* at 4,211-4,212. *See also id.* at 4,212 ("Short-term debt holders (including, without limitation, holders of commercial paper and derivatives counterparties) are highly unlikely to meet the criteria set forth in the statute for permitting payment of additional amounts.").

326 *Id.* at 4,212.

327 Final Rule, Certain Orderly Liquidation Authority Provisions under Title II of the Dodd-Frank Wall Street Reform and Consumer Protection Act, 76 Fed. Reg. 41,626 (July 15, 2011).

328 *Id.* at 41,631.

329 *Id.*

330 *Id.* The FDIC's rule also addressed issues concerning personal service agreements with a failed financial company, the treatment of insurance company subsidiaries, the treatment of fraudulent and preferential transfers, and the priority of certain claims, among other issues. *Id.* at 41,630-41,638.

331 *See* David A. Skeel, Jr., Single Point of Entry and the Bankruptcy Alternative in *Across the Great Divide: New Perspectives on the Financial Crisis* 311, 312-13 (Martin Neil Baily &

public comment a notice describing its "Single Point of Entry" (SPOE) strategy for implementing its Title II authority.[332] As background, in the United States, large financial institutions are generally organized under a holding company structure, with a top-tier parent company and sometimes hundreds or even thousands of subsidiaries spanning different countries.[333] Functions and business lines often are not aligned with the structures of individual subsidiaries, and funding is often allocated among subsidiaries as needed.[334] Moreover, many holding companies own bank and non-bank subsidiaries that are subject to different insolvency regimes, complicating their orderly resolution.[335]

Under its SPOE approach, the FDIC would be appointed as receiver of only the top-tier U.S. holding company of a troubled financial institution, and the institution's subsidiaries would remain open and continue operations.[336] The FDIC would create a bridge financial company into which it would transfer the assets of the holding company.[337] Certain liabilities of the holding company (principally, the company's long-term debt) would remain in the receivership, and losses would be allocated among the holding company's creditors according to the statutory priorities established under Title II.[338] In exchange for their claims, the holding company's creditors would receive debt, equity, or contingent securities

---

John B. Taylor eds., 2014) (characterizing the Single Point of Entry strategy as "remarkable" and "quite promising," and noting that it has generated "much enthusiasm among regulators"); Lee, *supra* note 227 at 466-67 (noting that the FDIC has "actively engaged" with the Bank of England, European Commission, Japan Financial Services Authority, and Swiss Financial Market Supervisory Authority in developing and promoting the Single Point of Entry strategy).

[332] Notice, Resolution of Systemically Important Financial Institutions: The Single Point of Entry Strategy, 78 Fed. Reg. 76,614 (Dec. 18, 2013).

[333] *Id.* at 76,615.

[334] *Id.* In this type of holding company structure, the top-tier parent company raises equity capital and then provides it to its subsidiaries. *Id.*

[335] Dafna Avraham, Patricia Selvaggi & James Vickery, *A Structural View of U.S. Bank Holding Companies*, Fed. Res. Bank of New York Econ. Pol. Rev. 65 (July 2012), https://www.newyorkfed.org/medialibrary/media/research/epr/ 12v18n2/1207avra.pdf.

[336] *Id.* at 76,616.

[337] *Id.*

[338] *Id.* Claims of critical vendors and guarantees related to the holding company's subsidiaries may be transferred to the bridge company. *Id.*

(such as warrants or options) in the newly established bridge company.[339] As a result of this process, the bridge company would no longer be burdened by certain debts of the holding company, leaving it with a stronger balance sheet.[340]

Under the SPOE approach, the FDIC would select new management for the bridge company, and the holding company's subsidiaries would continue operating, "allowing them to continue critical operations for the financial system and avoid the disruption that would otherwise accompany their closings."[341] While the FDIC indicated that it "intends to maximize the use of private funding" in a Title II resolution, it noted that it could provide guarantees of new debt issued by the bridge company, or provide the bridge company with funding from the OLF in order to facilitate an orderly resolution.[342]

In its December 2013 notice, the FDIC sought comment on a number of aspects of its SPOE strategy, including the level and types of capital and debt that large institutions should be required to maintain to optimize the SPOE resolution strategy, how the OLF should be used in a resolution, and the treatment of the foreign operations of a failed financial company under Title II.[343] The comment period ended on January 13, 2014, and the FDIC has yet to promulgate a final rule concerning its SPOE strategy.

Total Loss-Absorbing Capacity (TLAC) and "Clean Holding Companies"

In December 2016, pursuant to its authority under Section 165 of Dodd-Frank to impose enhanced prudential standards on large bank holding companies, the Federal Reserve finalized a rule imposing "total loss-absorbing capacity" (TLAC) and "clean holding company"

---

[339] *Id.* The FDIC explained that warrants or options (which would enable claimants to recover value in the event that a valuation underestimates the market value of the holding company) may be used to protect creditors of the holding company in lower priority classes against the possibility of undervaluation of their claims. *Id.* at 76,618.

[340] *Id.* at 76,616.

[341] *Id.*

[342] *Id.*

[343] *Id.* at 76,624. For a general summary of submitted comments, see Lee *supra* note 227 at 473-74.

requirements on such companies[344]—a rule that some commentators have described as "essential to the execution of the SPOE resolution strategy."[345] Under the rule, bank holding companies of U.S. global systemically important banks (G-SIBs)[346] and top-tier U.S. intermediate holding companies of foreign G-SIBs are required to maintain minimum levels of long-term debt and certain types of capital (which together represent a bank's TLAC).[347] The "clean holding company" requirements prohibit the relevant holding companies from (1) issuing short-term debt to third parties (i.e., to entities other than their subsidiaries), (2) entering into QFCs with third parties, (3) having liabilities that are guaranteed by their subsidiaries or subject to contractual offset rights for their subsidiaries' creditors, or (4) issuing certain guarantees of their subsidiaries liabilities, if the liabilities provide default rights based on the resolution of the holding company.[348]

The TLAC requirements supplement other regulatory capital requirements, which "are intended to ensure that a banking organization has sufficient capital to remain a going concern."[349] Like other regulatory capital requirements, the TLAC rule is directed at strengthening the resiliency of large bank holding companies in the event that they experience financial

---

[344] Final Rule, Total Loss-Absorbing Capacity, Long-Term Debt, and Clean Holding Company Requirements for Systemically Important U.S. Bank Holding Companies and Intermediate Holding Companies of Systemically Important Foreign Banking Organizations, 82 Fed. Reg. 8,266 (Jan. 24, 2017) [hereinafter "TLAC Rule"].

[345] *Orderly Liquidation Authority and Bankruptcy Reform*, U.S. Dep't of the Treasury 16 (Feb. 21, 2018), https://home.treasury.gov/sites/default/files/2018-02/OLA_REPORT.pdf. [hereinafter "OLA Treasury Report"].

[346] 346 Under the Third Basel Accord (Basel III), an international regulatory framework agreed upon by members of the Basel Committee on Banking Supervision, banks identified as G-SIBs are subject to enhanced prudential regulation. *See Global Systemically Important Banks: Assessment Methodology and the Additional Loss Absorbency Requirement*, Bank For Int'l Settlements, https://www.bis.org/bcbs/gsib/ (last updated Nov. 21, 2017). For purposes of the Federal Reserve's implementation of Basel III, whether a bank qualifies as a G-SIB is determined based on a methodology that considers the bank's size, interconnectedness, cross-jurisdictional activity, substitutability, and complexity. *See GSIB Framework Denominators*, Bd. of Gov. of the Fed. Res. Sys., https://www.federalreserve.gov/supervisionreg/basel/denominators.htm. (last updated Dec. 14, 2017).

[347] TLAC Rule, *supra* note 344 at 8,266.

[348] *Id.* at 8,272.

[349] *Id.* at 8,267.

distress.[350] However, the TLAC requirements also have the additional goal of improving the resolvability of such companies in the event of distress or failure.[351] The requirements attempt to accomplish this goal by requiring that large bank holding companies hold minimum levels of long-term debt, which can serve as the source of new capital in the event of financial distress.[352] Specifically, unlike regulatory capital (which is likely to be significantly depleted as a result of financial distress) and short-term debt (which must be continually refinanced or "rolled over," and is susceptible to "runs" in the event of financial distress), long-term debt can serve as the source of new capital because it can be reduced in a resolution or bankruptcy proceeding, increasing the ratio of a firm's assets to its liabilities and thereby increasing its equity.[353] Commentators have accordingly argued that because of the loss-absorbing capacity of long-term debt, the availability of TLAC at the holding company level "generate[s] market confidence to help avoid runs on deposits and other liabilities ... that could otherwise lead to financial contagion."[354] Similarly, the "clean holding company" requirements have the potential to help facilitate the orderly resolution of a financial institution by simplifying the holdings of its top-level holding company.[355]

QFCs

In 2017, the Federal Reserve, FDIC, and Office of the Comptroller of the Currency (OCC) finalized rules restricting the types of QFCs into which certain regulated banks and bank holding companies can enter.[356]

---

[350] *Id.* at 8,266.
[351] *Id.*
[352] *Id.* at 8,267.
[353] *Id.*
[354] OLA Treasury Report, *supra* note 345 at 16.
[355] *Id.*
[356] Final Rule, Mandatory Contractual Stay Requirements for Qualified Financial Contracts, 82 Fed. Reg. 56,630 (Nov. 29, 2017) [hereinafter "OCC QFC Rule"]; Final Rule, Restrictions on Qualified Financial Contracts of Certain FDIC-Supervised Institutions; Revisions to the Definition of Qualifying Master Netting Agreement and Related Definitions, 82 Fed. Reg. 50,228 (Oct. 30, 2017) [hereinafter "FDIC QFC Rule"]; Restrictions on Qualified Financial Contracts of Systemically Important U.S. Banking Organizations and the U.S. Operations of Systemically Important Foreign Banking Organizations; Revisions to the Definition of

The rules were directed at plugging gaps in provisions of the Bankruptcy Code, FDIC receivership authority, and Title II involving default rights under QFCs.

As discussed above, the Bankruptcy Code generally subjects creditors to an automatic stay that prevents them from enforcing certain rights (for example, to terminate a contract, set-off obligations, or liquidate collateral) upon the filing of a bankruptcy petition.[357] However, the Bankruptcy Code also provides a "safe harbor" that allows counterparties to a variety of financial contracts—including certain securities and commodities contracts, swaps, forwards, and repos— to exercise their rights against a debtor that are triggered by its entry into bankruptcy.[358] Moreover, the Bankruptcy Code does not stay the exercise of cross-default rights (i.e., rights against a company triggered by the entry of a company's parent, subsidiary, or affiliate into bankruptcy).[359] These "safe harbors" potentially exacerbate the risk of "runs" against a company or its affiliates triggered by bankruptcy proceedings.[360]

By contrast, as noted above, in *non-Title II* bank resolutions under the Federal Deposit Insurance Act (FDIA), counterparties to QFCs—a term defined as encompassing many of the same financial contracts exempt from the Bankruptcy Code's automatic stay—are stayed from exercising *direct* default rights for one business day, and are permanently stayed from exercising such rights if the FDIC transfers QFCs to a third party.[361] However, there is no similar stay applicable to *cross-default* rights.[362] Accordingly, while derivatives counterparties are temporarily stayed from exercising default rights against a bank triggered by the bank's entry into a non-Title II FDIC resolution, they are not stayed from exercising default rights against a *parent or affiliate* of a bank triggered by the bank's entry into a non-Title II FDIC resolution. The absence of such a stay creates the

Qualifying Master Netting Agreement and Related Definitions, 82 Fed. Reg. 42,882 (Sept. 12, 2017) [hereinafter "Federal Reserve QFC Rule"].

[357] 11 U.S.C. § 362.

[358] *Id.* §§ 362(b)(6), (7), (17), (27), 362(o), 555-56, 559-61.

[359] FDIC QFC Rule, *supra* note 356 at 50,231.

[360] OCC QFC Rule, *supra* note 356 at 56,633.

[361] 12 U.S.C. § 1821(e)(10)(B)(i)-(ii).

[362] FDIC QFC Rule, *supra* note 356 at 50,231.

possibility that a bank's entry into a non-Title II FDIC resolution could trigger "runs" on its parent holding company or its affiliates.[363] Moreover, commentators have raised the possibility that foreign courts may not enforce the FDIA's stay-and-transfer provisions concerning direct default rights, disadvantaging domestic QFC counterparties relative to foreign QFC counterparties, and exacerbating the risk of "runs" against a bank's parent or affiliates.[364]

Finally, in a Title II resolution, QFC counterparties are stayed from exercising *direct* default rights for one business day, and are permanently stayed from exercising such rights if the FDIC transfers a QFC to a third party (as in *non-Title II* FDIC resolutions).[365] Moreover, the FDIC can "enforce contracts of subsidiaries or affiliates" of a company in receivership that are guaranteed or otherwise supported by or linked to the company, notwithstanding any *cross-default* rights.[366] However, as with non-Title II FDIC resolutions, commentators have raised the possibility that foreign courts may not enforce Title II's stay-and-transfer provisions.[367]

In promulgating its QFC rules, the Federal Reserve, FDIC, and OCC were concerned with plugging certain gaps the Bankruptcy Code, the FDIA, and Title II involving default rights under QFCs. Specifically, the agencies were concerned with scenarios in which the entry of one institution into bankruptcy, a non-Title II FDIC resolution, or a Title II resolution would prompt a "run" by its derivatives counterparties or by the derivatives counterparties of its parent, subsidiary, or affiliate.[368]

---

[363] *Id.* at 50,234.

[364] OCC QFC Rule, *supra* note 356 at 56,635; FDIC QFC Rule, *supra* note 356 at 50,243; Federal Reserve QFC Rule, *supra* note 356 at 42,885-42,890.

[365] 12 U.S.C. § 5390(c)(10), 5390(c)(16).

[366] *Id.*

[367] OCC QFC Rule, *supra* note 356 at 56,635; FDIC QFC Rule, *supra* note 356 at 50,243; Federal Reserve QFC Rule, *supra* note 356 at 42,885-42,890.

[368] OCC QFC Rule, *supra* note 356 at 56,631-56,632; FDIC QFC Rule, *supra* note 356 at 50,230; Federal Reserve QFC Rule, *supra* note 356 at 42,882-42,886.

Table 2. QFCs Under the Bankruptcy Code, Federal Deposit Insurance Act, and Title II

	Bankruptcy Code	Federal Deposit Insurance Act	Title II
Direct default rights	Certain derivatives contracts are exempt from the "automatic stay," allowing counterparties to immediately exercise rights against a debtor triggered by the debtor's entry into bankruptcy. This leaves bankrupt debtors susceptible to "runs."	Counterparties to QFCs are stayed from exercising rights against a bank triggered by the bank's entry into resolution proceedings for one business day. Counterparties to QFCs are permanently stayed from exercising such rights if the FDIC transfers a QFC to a third party. However, it is possible that foreign courts may refuse to enforce these limitations.	Counterparties to QFCs are stayed from exercising rights against a financial company triggered by the financial company's entry into resolution proceedings for one business day. Counterparties to QFCs are permanently stayed from exercising such rights if the FDIC transfers a QFC to a third party. However, it is possible that foreign courts may refuse to enforce these limitations.
Cross-default rights	No limitations on rights against a debtor's parent, subsidiaries, or affiliates triggered by the debtor's entry into bankruptcy, leaving a debtor's parent, subsidiaries, and affiliates susceptible to "runs."	No limitations on rights against a bank's parent, subsidiaries, or affiliates triggered by a bank's entry into resolution proceedings, leaving a bank's parent, subsidiaries, and affiliates susceptible to "runs."	The FDIC can enforce contracts of a failed company's subsidiaries or affiliates that are guaranteed or otherwise supported by or linked to the failed company, notwithstanding any crossdefault rights. However, it is possible that foreign courts may refuse to enforce these limitations.

Source: CRS.

The QFC rules provide that certain institutions regulated by the agencies[369] may enter into a QFC only if (1) the QFC includes terms explicitly providing that, in the event that the institution enters into a Title II proceeding or a non-Title II resolution, any default rights or transfer restrictions under the QFC are subject to the stay-and-transfer limitations imposed under the relevant insolvency scheme, and (2) the QFC does not allow counterparties to exercise *cross-default* rights against the institution.[370] The QFC rules accordingly require QFCs entered into by the relevant institutions to affirmatively opt into the stay-and-transfer provisions of the FDIA and Title II, thereby minimizing the risk that a QFC counterparty in a foreign court would successfully challenge stay-and-transfer actions taken by the FDIC.[371] Moreover, the rule prohibits the relevant institutions from entering into QFCs that give counterparties cross-default rights against them, thereby minimizing the risk that the bankruptcy or resolution of the institutions' parents or affiliates will trigger "runs" against them.[372]

---

[369] The OCC's QFC rule applies to national banks or federal savings associations not under a bank holding company with more than $700 billion in assets, and national banks and federal savings associations that are subsidiaries of a G-SIB holding company, among other institutions. OCC QFC Rule, *supra* note 356 at 56,636-56,638. The FDIC's QFC rule applies to state-chartered banks that are not members of the Federal Reserve system and their subsidiaries. FDIC QFC Rule, *supra* note 356 at 50,234. The Federal Reserve's QFC rule applies to U.S. top-tier bank holding companies identified by the Federal Reserve as G-SIBs, the subsidiaries of any U.S. G-SIB (other than national banks, federal savings associations, state nonmember banks, and state savings associations), and the U.S. operations of any foreign GSIBs (other than national banks, federal savings associations, state nonmember banks, and state savings associations). Federal Reserve QFC Rule, *supra* note 356 at 42,882.

[370] OCC QFC Rule, *supra* note 356 at 56,645; FDIC QFC Rule, *supra* note 356 at 50,234; Federal Reserve QFC Rule, *supra* note 356 at 42,889. However, the final rules do not prohibit the relevant institutions from entering into QFCs that provide counterparties with *direct* default rights. OCC QFC Rule, *supra* note 356 at 56,647; FDIC QFC Rule, *supra* note 356 at 50,234; Federal Reserve QFC Rule, *supra* note 356 at 42,887.

[371] OCC QFC Rule, *supra* note 356 at 56,645; FDIC QFC Rule, *supra* note 356 at 50,234; Federal Reserve QFC Rule, *supra* note 356 at 42,889.

[372] *Id.*

Criticisms of Title II and Responses

Title II has attracted criticism and generated a number of alternative proposals concerning the resolution of large financial institutions. Some critics have argued that the broad powers that Title II grants the FDIC—both in determining whether to place a firm into receivership and in conducting a resolution—create uncertainty about creditors' rights, raising the cost of credit for financial institutions.[373] Other commentators have contended that by granting the FDIC the authority to extend credit to companies in receivership, Title II effectively formalizes a practice of bailing out large financial institutions.[374] Still others have criticized the imposition of ex post assessments on the financial industry to recoup OLF expenditures not recovered from a firm in receivership, arguing that "taxing" prudently operated firms for the benefit of mismanaged firms creates moral hazard and free-rider problems.[375] Finally, some observers have raised constitutional concerns with Title II's (1) 24-hour period for judicial review of the FDIC's decision to place a firm into receivership,[376] (2) limitation of judicial review to only two of the seven factors the Treasury Secretary must consider in making a systemic risk determination,[377] (3) imposition of criminal penalties on persons who

---

[373] *See* Peter J. Wallison, *The Error at the Heart of the Dodd-Frank Act*, Am. Enter. Inst. (Sept. 6, 2011), http://www.aei.org/publication/the-error-at-the-heart-of-the-dodd-frank-act/.

[374] See Lalita Clozel, Will Trump Target FDIC's Dodd-Frank Resolution Powers?, AM. BANKER (Dec. 12, 2016), https://www.americanbanker.com/news/will-trump-target-fdics-dodd-frank-resolution-powers; Failing To End "Too Big To Fail": An Assessment Of The Dodd-Frank Act Four Years Later, Report Prepared by the Republican Staff on the Comm. on Fin. Servs., U.S. House of Representatives at 87-88 (July 2014); Examining How the Dodd-Frank Act Could Result in More Taxpayer-Funded Bailouts, Hearing in H. Comm. on Fin. Servs., 113th Cong. (June 26, 2013) (opening remarks of Chairman Jeb Hensarling) ("Regrettably, Dodd-Frank not only fails to end too-big-to-fail and its attendant taxpayer bailouts; it actually codifies them into law ... Title II, Section 210, notwithstanding its ex post funding language, clearly creates a taxpayer-funded bailout system that the CBO estimates will cost taxpayers over $20 billion.").

[375] Viral V. Acharya, Barry Adler, Matthew Richardson & Nouriel Roubini, Resolution Authority, in *Regulating Wall Street: The Dodd-Frank Act and the New Architecture of Global Finance* 213, 228 (Viral V. Acharya, Thomas Cooley, Matthew Richardson & Ingo Walter eds., 2011); Arthur E. Wilmarth, Jr., *The Dodd-Frank Act: A Flawed and Inadequate Response to the Too-Big-to-Fail Problem*, 89 Or. L. Rev. 951, 1021 (2011).

[376] Merrill & Merrill, supra note 198 at 207-08.

[377] Id. at 208-09.

disclose information about a systemic risk determination or related judicial proceedings,[378] and (4) allowance of compensation claw-backs from executives and directors determined to have been "substantially responsible" for the failure of a firm in receivership.[379]

Defenders of Title II have rejected the argument that the OLA promotes moral hazard, noting that a Title II resolution would result in "the extinction of the firm's equity and the wholesale replacement of its board and management."[380] Others have rejected arguments that Title II puts taxpayers at risk, noting that it requires that the FDIC be reimbursed in full for any OLF expenditures.[381]

In responding to the argument that Title II grants the FDIC excessive discretion, commentators have argued that the level of discretion granted

---

[378] Id. at 230-34; Wallison, supra note 373.

[379] Merrill & Merrill, *supra* note 198 at 238. In the *State Bank of Big Spring* case discussed in note 159 *supra*, certain plaintiffs also challenged the constitutionality of the OLA, arguing that it violated the separation of powers, the Fifth Amendment's Takings Clause, and Article I Section 8's requirement that bankruptcy laws be "uniform." *See* Second Amended Complaint for Declaratory and Injunctive Relief 9-11, State Nat. Bank of Big Spring v. Lew, 958 F. Supp. 127 (D.D.C. 2013). However, the D.C. Circuit affirmed an order dismissing those claims, reasoning that the plaintiffs lacked standing and that their claims were not ripe because the OLA had not been invoked. State Nat. Bank of Big Spring v. Lew, 795 F.3d 48, 56-57 (D.C. Cir. 2015).

Other criticisms of Title II include arguments that (1) the FDIC lacks the expertise necessary to resolve large, complex financial institutions, *see* Wallison *supra* note 373; Failing To End "Too Big To Fail," *supra* note 374 at 64; (2) exempting companies in receivership from taxation amounts to a disguised bailout, Failing To End "Too Big To Fail," *supra* note 374 at 75-76; and (3) by forcing holding company creditors to absorb losses, the FDIC's SPOE strategy undermines market discipline for a firm's operating subsidiaries, *see* Kwon-Yong Jin, *How to Eat an Elephant: Corporate Group Structure of Systemically Important Institutions, Orderly Liquidation Authority, and Single Point of Entry Resolution*, 124 Yale L. J. 1746, 1765 (2015); Joe Adler, *Likely Battle Ahead for FDIC's "Single Point" Resolution Plan*, Am. Banker (Dec. 10, 2013), https://www.americanbanker.com/news/likely-battle-ahead-for-fdicssingle-point-resolution-plan.

[380] Bernanke, *supra* note 231. *See also* Michael Helfer, We Need Chapter 14—And We Need Title II, *in Across the Great Divide: New Perspectives on the Financial Crisis* 335, 339 (Martin Neil Baily & John B. Taylor eds., 2014) (rejecting the argument that Title II promotes moral hazard, and noting that according to a September 2013 paper issued by the Treasury Department, senior unsecured borrowing costs for large bank holding companies had risen more than those of small regional bank holding companies).

[381] Bernanke, *supra* note 231; Lawrence H. Summers, Congress is Considering an Extremely Dangerous Idea Almost Nobody has Heard of, *Wash. Post*. (Jan. 18, 2017), https://www.washingtonpost.com/news/wonk/wp/2017/01/18/congress-is-considering-an-extremely-dangerous-idea-almost-nobody-has-heard-of/?utm_term=.77b8db85dd60; Helfer, *supra* note 380 at 338-39.

by Title II is "fundamentally the same" as that which the FDIC is granted in resolving failed commercial banks.[382] Moreover, in reflecting on crisis management, former Treasury Secretary and President of the New York Fed Timothy Geithner has argued that a certain level of uncertainty regarding "how fast a government will escalate its support" and "how far that support will extend" is beneficial, "leav[ing] investors in and creditors of financial institutions with a healthy sense of fear" that "should lessen the harmful incentives that a strong backstop creates."[383]

In responding to constitutional concerns regarding Title II's limitations on judicial review, one commentator has argued that "it is within Congress's power to set the standard for judicial review," analogizing the deferential standards imposed under Title II to those imposed by the Administrative Procedure Act.[384] This commentator has argued that the 24-hour period for judicial review of a decision to invoke the OLA "is appropriate for the urgency of the issue," and that Title II accordingly provides for due process, if not "as much process as some might like."[385]

Other commentators have focused on the shortcomings of bankruptcy in defending Title II. Some observers have argued that bankruptcy does not offer the speed or opportunity for coordination with foreign financial regulators required to resolve a large institution during a period of financial turmoil.[386] Other defenders of Title II have argued that during times of financial distress, bankruptcy could function effectively for a large financial institution only with "massive government assistance" such as debtor-in-possession financing, effectively allowing the federal government "to call the shots in the bankruptcy," because "that is what [debtor-in-possession] lenders do."[387] According to this view, an effective form of financial institution bankruptcy (in which the federal government could lend to

---

[382] Helfer, *supra* note 380 at 338.

[383] Timothy F. Geithner, Are We Safe Yet?: How to Manage Financial Crises, *Foreign Affairs* (January/February 2017), https://www.foreignaffairs.com/articles/united-states/2016-12-12/are-we-safe-yet.

[384] Levitin, *supra* note 227 at 12; 5 U.S.C. § 706.

[385] Levitin, *supra* note 227 at 12.

[386] Bernanke, *supra* note 231; Lalita Clozel, *Trump Invites Trouble in Targeting FDIC Resolution Powers*, AM. BANKER (Apr. 21, 2017), https://www.americanbanker.com/news/trump-invites-trouble-in-targeting-fdic-resolutionpowers; Helfer, *supra* note 380 at 337.

[387] *See* Levitin, *supra* note 227 at 7-8.

troubled institutions in periods when private financing is likely to be unavailable) would end up replicating many of the features its proponents dislike about Title II.[388]

Proposals to Alter Title II

Proposed Legislation

Legislation proposed in both the House of Representatives and the Senate has focused on amending the Bankruptcy Code to enhance its ability to resolve large financial institutions, either as a replacement for Title II or as a supplement to it.[389]

During the post-crisis debate over financial reform, a bill introduced in the House (H.R. 3310, 111th Cong.) proposed a new Chapter 14 to the Bankruptcy Code to address the resolution of large non-bank financial institutions.[390] In the proposed Chapter 14, the Bankruptcy Code's "safe harbor" provisions for certain derivatives contracts would not have automatically applied.[391] Instead, the bankruptcy court would make a specific determination upon a motion by the debtor whether the debtor should be subject to any or all of the special provisions of the Bankruptcy Code exempting derivatives and other financial contracts from the automatic stay.[392] The bill would also have prohibited a trustee for an institution in Chapter 14 bankruptcy from obtaining credit "if the source of that credit either directly or indirectly is the United States."[393]

---

[388] *Id. See also* Paul L. Lee, The Case Against Repealing Title II of the Dodd-Frank Act, *Columbia L. Sch. Blue Sky Blog* (Dec. 12, 2016), http://clsbluesky. law.columbia.edu/2016/12/12/the-case-against-repealing-title-ii-of-the-doddfrank-act/ (arguing that "the solution to a systemic financial crisis will not be found in Title II or the Bankruptcy Code but in broad-based government liquidity programs to support the financial system.").

[389] See Paul L. Lee, Bankruptcy Alternatives to Title II of the Dodd-Frank Act—Part II, *Banking L. J.* 503 (Nov./Dec. 2015).

[390] See Consumer Protection and Regulatory Enhancement Act, H.R. 3310, 111th Cong. (2009).

[391] Id. § 102(f).

[392] Id. In making this determination, the proposed legislation directed the bankruptcy court to "balance the interests of both debtor and creditors while attempting to preserve the debtor's assets for repayment and reorganization of the debtor's obligations, or to provide for a more orderly liquidation." Id.

[393] Id. § 102(e).

Scholars at the Hoover Institution have also developed proposed amendments to the Bankruptcy Code directed at resolving large financial institutions.[394] In 2010, Professor Thomas Jackson published a proposal to create a new chapter of the Bankruptcy Code in which exclusions for banks, insurance companies, and broker-dealers would not apply.[395] Under the proposal, a financial institution's primary regulator could file an involuntary bankruptcy petition, and a bankruptcy case would be assigned by the Chief Judge of the relevant federal court of appeals to a member of a previously designated panel of special masters.[396] Pursuant to Professor Jackson's proposal, QFCs secured by cash or "cash-like" collateral would enjoy the benefits of the Bankruptcy Code's "safe harbor," but all other QFCs would be subject to the automatic stay and other Bankruptcy Code provisions.[397] The financial institution's regulator would be given special standing to raise motions and the right to file a plan of reorganization.[398] Unlike H.R. 3310 (the bankruptcy bill introduced during debates over financial reform), the institution's regulator would be allowed to provide the bankrupt firm with debtor-in-possession financing subject to the Bankruptcy Code's traditional rules governing the priority of claims.[399] Professor Jackson has released a number of revised versions of his proposal since 2010.[400]

These proposals appear to have served as the basis for a series of legislative proposals to amend the Bankruptcy Code. In April 2017, the House of Representatives passed one of these bills, the Financial Institution Bankruptcy Act of 2017 (FIBA).[401] FIBA creates a new subchapter V of Chapter 11 of the Bankruptcy Code for bank holding

---

[394] See Jackson, supra note 226 at 217.

[395] *Id.* at 229. As discussed, broker-dealers are currently allowed to file for Chapter 7 bankruptcy, but cannot be reorganized under Chapter 11. 11 U.S.C. § 109(b), (d).

[396] Jackson, *supra* note 226 at 227, 231-32.

[397] *Id.* at 232-38.

[398] *Id.* at 238.

[399] *Id.* at 239-41.

[400] *See* Thomas H. Jackson, Building on Bankruptcy: A Revised Chapter 14 Proposal for the Recapitalization, Reorganization, or Liquidation of Large Financial Institutions, in *Making Failure Feasible: How Bankruptcy Reform Can End "Too Big To Fail"* 15 (Kenneth E. Scott, Thomas H. Jackson & John B. Taylor, eds. 2015); Thomas H. Jackson, Bankruptcy Code Chapter 14: A Proposal, in *Bankruptcy Not Bailout: A Special Chapter* 14 (Kenneth E. Scott & John B. Taylor, eds., 2012).

[401] *See* H.R. 1667, 115th Cong. (2017).

companies and financial institutions with over $50 billion in assets.[402] Bankruptcy proceedings under subchapter V would be heard by one of 10 bankruptcy judges designated by the Chief Justice of the Supreme Court.[403] While a case under the new subchapter V could be commenced only by a financial institution itself (and not involuntarily by a regulator), federal regulators could "appear and be heard on any issue in any case or proceeding" under subchapter V.[404] As in the SPOE approach developed by the FDIC for Title II resolutions, a holding company entering subchapter V bankruptcy could transfer certain assets (primarily its equity in subsidiaries and derivatives) to a newly formed bridge company upon the court's determination that the transfer is "necessary to prevent serious adverse effects on financial stability," among other things.[405] The Act also would impose a 48-hour automatic stay on the termination, acceleration, or modification of certain contracts, including QFCs of a financial institution or its affiliates.[406]

The Financial CHOICE Act of 2017, which passed the House in June 2017, also proposes a number of changes to the Bankruptcy Code.[407] The relevant CHOICE Act provisions largely track the reforms in FIBA concerning the creation of a new subchapter V; the appointment of a bankruptcy judge drawn from a panel designated by the Chief Justice of the Supreme Court; the commencement of a bankruptcy case; the transfer of property to a bridge company; and the automatic stay.[408] However, unlike FIBA, the CHOICE Act would repeal Title II.[409]

Other proposals to amend the Bankruptcy Code to deal with large financial institutions have been introduced in the Senate. S. 1840, the Taxpayer Protection and Responsible Resolution Act (introduced in the 114th Congress), differs from FIBA and the CHOICE Act as a formal matter by creating a separate Chapter 14 of the Bankruptcy Code as

---

402 *Id.* § 2.
403 *Id.* § 4.
404 *Id.* § 3.
405 *Id.*
406 *Id.*
407 H.R. 10, 115th Cong. (2017).
408 *Id.* § 122.
409 *Id.* § 111.

opposed to a new subchapter of Chapter 11.[410] However, like FIBA and the CHOICE Act, S. 1840 would have provided that (1) a bankruptcy judge drawn from a panel of 10 judges designated by the Chief Justice would preside over proceedings under the new regime;[411] (2) only a financial institution could commence bankruptcy proceedings, but federal regulators could appear and be heard in a bankruptcy case;[412] (3) the court could approve the transfer of an institution's assets to a bridge company after making certain determinations; and (4) certain contractual rights against a debtor institution would be stayed for 48 hours.[413] Like the CHOICE Act (but unlike FIBA), S. 1840 would have repealed Title II.[414] Moreover, unlike FIBA and the CHOICE Act, S. 1840 would have explicitly prohibited the Federal Reserve from making advances to a financial corporation in bankruptcy or to a bridge company.[415]

The Trump Administration's Views

The Trump Administration's Treasury Department has endorsed efforts to amend the Bankruptcy Code to deal with large financial institutions, and expressed support for reforming (but not repealing) Title II. In February 2018, the Treasury Department issued a report in which it recommended retaining Title II "as an emergency tool for use under only extraordinary circumstances," but proposed a number of reforms to address what it characterized as "serious defects" in its original design.[416] The report "unequivocally" concluded that "bankruptcy should be the resolution method of first resort" for large financial institutions, while recommending "significant reforms to make bankruptcy a more effective option for financial firms."[417]

---

[410] Taxpayer Protection and Responsible Resolution Act, S. 1840 § 2, 114th Cong. (2015).
[411] *Id.* § 4.
[412] *Id.* § 3.
[413] *Id.*
[414] *Id.* § 5.
[415] *Id.* § 6.
[416] OLA Treasury Report, *supra* note 345 at 2.
[417] *Id.*

In recommending changes to Title II, the Treasury Department proposed reforms aimed at (1) limiting the FDIC's discretion in managing a receivership, (2) protecting taxpayers against losses, and (3) strengthening judicial review of the decision to invoke Title II.[418] Specifically, in order to limit the FDIC's discretion, the Treasury Department proposed (1) restricting the FDIC's ability to treat similarly situated creditors differently in a Title II resolution,[419] (2) providing that a bankruptcy court (instead of the FDIC) adjudicate claims against a Title II receivership,[420] (3) clarifying the circumstances in which a financial company is "in default or in danger of default" for purposes of invoking Title II,[421] (3) repealing the tax-exempt status of a bridge company in a Title II receivership,[422] and (4) confirming that the FDIC is committed to the SPOE strategy.[423]

In order to protect taxpayers against losses, the Treasury Department proposed (1) limiting the duration of any advances from the OLF,[424] (2) that loan guarantees be preferred over direct lending to companies in receivership,[425] (3) that the FDIC lend to companies in receivership only on a secured basis,[426] and (4) imposing any industry-wide assessments necessary to recoup OLF funds "as soon as reasonably possible."[427]

In order to strengthen judicial review of the decision to invoke Title II, the Treasury Department recommended allowing a court to review all seven of the Treasury Secretary's required findings (as opposed to only two), and allowing for ex post judicial review after a receiver is appointed, without a statutory time limit for the court to issue a decision.[428]

---

[418] *Id.* at 5-6.
[419] *Id.* at 32-34.
[420] *Id.* at 34-35.
[421] *Id.* at 35-36.
[422] *Id.* at 36.
[423] *Id.* at 36-37.
[424] *Id.* at 37.
[425] *Id.* at 37-38.
[426] *Id.* at 38.
[427] *Id.* at 39.
[428] *Id.* at 40-41.

Appendix. Glossary

Automatic stay	A protection that the Bankruptcy Code provides a debtor against collection activities and many other actions by creditors. This protection does not apply to certain derivative contracts.
Bridge financial company	A company that the FDIC can create pursuant to Title II of Dodd-Frank in order to resolve the failure of a systemically important financial institution ("SIFI"). Under Title II, the FDIC can transfer certain assets and liabilities of a SIFI into a bridge financial company to continue the SIFI's critical businesses on a temporary basis. The bridge financial company would not be saddled with certain debts of the SIFI, and the FDIC would appoint new management to oversee its operations.
Conservatorship	A method by which the FDIC can resolve the failure of a commercial bank, pursuant to which the FDIC or its agent continues to operate the bank in order to preserve the bank's value as a "going concern." Compare with Receivership.
Cross-default rights	Contractual rights (i.e., to terminate a contract, net obligations, or liquidate collateral) triggered by the entry of a party's parent or affiliate into bankruptcy or other resolution proceedings. Compare with Direct default rights.
Derivative contract	A contract (such as a forward, future, option, or swap) whose value depends on the value of some other asset, such as a commodity, interest rate, currency, bond, or stock. Derivatives often provide counterparties with direct default rights and/or cross-default rights, and certain derivatives are exempt from the Bankruptcy Code's automatic stay. These features increase the risks of liquidity "runs" for parties to derivative contracts.
Direct default rights	Contractual rights (i.e., to terminate a contract, net obligations, or liquidate collateral) triggered by a party's entry into bankruptcy or other resolution proceedings. Compare with Cross-default rights.
"Discount window"	A program pursuant to which the Federal Reserve lends to commercial banks in need of liquidity, generally at a penalty rate of interest.
Financial contagion	A process by which a liquidity "run" on one financial institution triggers a broader loss of confidence in the financial system, leading to "runs" on other institutions.
Global systemically important banks ("G-SIBs")	Banks subject to enhanced prudential regulations pursuant to the Federal Reserve's implementation of the Third Basel Accord (Basel III), an international regulatory framework agreed upon by members of the Basel Committee on Banking Supervision. The Federal Reserve requires G-SIBs to maintain minimum levels of total loss-absorbing capacity (TLAC) and has imposed certain requirements for qualified financial contracts ("QFCs") entered into by certain holding companies of G-SIBs.

Liquidity "run"	A process by which large numbers of a financial institution's short-term creditors rush to withdraw their assets from the institution because of concerns about its solvency, forcing the institution to sell its illiquid assets at significantly discounted prices. See also Financial contagion, Maturity transformation.
Maturity transformation	A process by which financial institutions issue short-term debt while investing in longer-term assets, leaving them vulnerable to liquidity "runs."
Money market fund	Funds that generally invest in high-quality, liquid, short-term securities and give their investors the right to withdraw their share of the fund's assets on demand. Unlike commercial banks, money market funds are not required to obtain deposit insurance, and do not have access to the Federal Reserve's "discount window," leaving them vulnerable to liquidity "runs."
Moral hazard	A situation in which a party is protected from risk, creating incentives to engage in excessively risky activities. Arguably, rescuing shareholders or creditors of troubled financial institutions promotes moral hazard.
Orderly Liquidation Authority ("OLA")	A resolution regime established under Title II of Dodd-Frank that is available to resolve the distress or failure of systemically important financial institutions outside of the Bankruptcy Code.
Over-the-counter ("OTC") derivative	A derivative contract that is individually negotiated by parties dealing directly with one another, as opposed to a derivative contract that is traded on an organized exchange.
Qualified financial contracts("QFCs")	Certain derivative contracts subject to (1) stay-and-transfer provisions in Title II resolutions and non-Title II bank resolutions and (2) certain restrictions imposed by rules adopted by the Federal Reserve, FDIC, and OCC in 2017.
Receivership	A method by which the FDIC can resolve the failure of a commercial bank, pursuant to which it liquidates the bank's assets. Compare with Conservatorship.
Repurchase agreement ("repo")	An agreement pursuant to which one party sells securities to another party for cash, while simultaneously agreeing to repurchase the same or similar securities at some time in the future at a premium. Certain "repos" fall within the definitions of qualified financial contracts ("QFCs") in Title II and the Federal Deposit Insurance Act.
Single Point of Entry ("SPOE")	A strategy for implementing the FDIC's Title II authority outlined in a December 2013 notice, pursuant to which the FDIC would be appointed as receiver of only the top-tier U.S. holding company of a troubled financial institution, and the institution's subsidiaries would remain open and continue operations after the FDIC transfers the holding company's assets to a bridge financial company.

Appendix A. (Continued)

Systemically important financial institutions ("SIFIs")	A term used to describe financial institutions whose failure could have serious adverse effects on the financial system. The term is most often used to refer to institutions subject to enhanced prudential regulation under Title I of Dodd-Frank, or institutions for which Dodd-Frank's Title II resolution regime could be invoked. See also Too-big-to-fail ("TBTF") financial institutions.
Too-big-to-fail ("TBTF") financial institutions	A colloquial term used to describe financial institutions whose failure could have serious adverse effects on the financial system.
Total Loss-Absorbing, Capacity ("TLAC")	Certain types of long-term debt and capital. The Federal Reserve requires certain holding companies of global systemically important banks ("G-SIBs") to maintain minimum levels of TLAC in order to enhance their resolvability. This requirement is based on the idea that long-term debt can serve as the source of new capital for a distressed firm because debt-holders' claims on a company's assets can be reduced in a resolution or bankruptcy proceeding.
Tri-Party Repo	A repurchase agreement ("repo") pursuant to which a "clearing bank" intermediates between a repo lender and a repo borrower.

In: Financial Crises and Programs
Editor: Patricia Hall
ISBN: 978-1-53614-159-7

Chapter 5

REGULATING THE U.S. CAMPAIGN ENVIRONMENT: POLITICS AND POLICY*

R. Sam Garrett

INTRODUCTION

Members of Congress run campaigns as candidates and regulate them as policymakers. Recent coverage of Cambridge Analytica voter-targeting using Facebook data is one of the latest examples of the connection between campaign conduct and public policy. Reports suggest that this case involves consumer-privacy questions that are normally beyond campaign regulation, and questions about whether foreign nationals were impermissibly involved in campaign decisionmaking—a topic well within campaign finance regulation. In other recent examples, reports of foreign interference in the 2016 U.S. elections have also raised questions about the prohibition on foreign money in U.S. campaigns and regulation of online political advertising.

---

* This is an edited, reformatted and augmented version of a CRS Insight report, IN10878, dated April 2, 2018.

What is the connection between the U.S. campaign environment, or campaign conduct, and public policy? Are recent concerns about regulating campaigns historically unique? This chapter provides brief discussion that may be relevant as Congress considers legislation or oversight responding to the 2016 election cycle and preparing for 2018. It does not cover the details of individual cases, including the permissibility of specific conduct.

Regulating Campaigns versus Elections

Elections in the United States are highly regulated and primarily a state-level responsibility. Provisions in state law and, to a lesser degree, federal law, address topics such as ballot design, voter eligibility, and election equipment. Except for campaign finance policy, U.S. *campaigns* are subject to relatively little regulation. First Amendment protections, jurisprudence, and American political culture all account for a comparatively deregulated campaign environment. There is mixed evidence about how much campaigns affect electoral outcomes.

Law, Regulation and Campaign Conduct

There is no uniform standard for campaign conduct in the United States. Primarily, federal policy regulates how campaigns and related entities raise and spend money. Most regulation of campaign conduct rests in campaign finance law (the Federal Election Campaign Act, FECA; 52 U.S.C. §§30101-30146) and Federal Election Commission (FEC) rules. These address topics such as

- permissible and prohibited sources of contributions and expenditures (including a broad

- prohibition on fundraising, spending, and certain campaign involvement by foreign nationals);
- contribution limits;
- permissible and prohibited uses of campaign funds;
- public disclosure of contributions and expenditures; and
- disclaimers required for political advertising.

Most of these provisions apply to a limited set of actors known as *political committees*. These are candidate campaign committees, party committees, and political action committees (PACs). In addition, campaign finance policy primarily affects activities that explicitly advocate for election or defeat of political candidates, or, in some cases (*electioneering communications*), certain preelection advertising that mentions candidates but does not explicitly call for election or defeat.

Other areas of law and regulation sometimes affect campaigns, but do not specifically address campaign conduct. For example, state or local property law might govern disputes over campaign assets. In general, however, barring some other provision of federal, state, or local law (such as discrimination based on race; or corporate law), federal campaign finance policy is silent on topics such as

- campaign management, including strategy, theme, and message;
- field activities (e.g., get-out-the-vote (GOTV) efforts);
- voter targeting;
- strategic relationships among political committees and other organizations, provided that they do not violate prohibitions on coordination or result in prohibited in-kind contributions;
- use of political consultants and vendors; and
- commercial transactions, provided that they are at fair-market value

DISCUSSION

Concern about American campaign conduct is not new. Mostly through campaign finance policy, Congress has for decades sought to shape campaign practices through law and regulation. Most campaign conduct, however, is left to the discretion of individual political actors and political professionals. A political consultant code of ethics discourages some practices, such as false attacks on opponents, but adherence is voluntary.

Campaign tactics aside, the campaign environment also has been a steady source of concern in American politics. For example, predicted declines in political parties and party identification among voters have fueled policy debates and scholarly research (with mixed findings) since the 1950s. Shortly thereafter, concern shifted to the rise of "candidate-centered" campaigns, growth in the political consulting industry, and the importance of costly campaign advertising (which some warn is overly negative and others say provides useful contrasts among candidates). Each of those factors, and others, initially was greeted with alarm and later became an established part of American politics, although debates remain.

At least three factors highlighted during the 2016 cycle potentially are noteworthy compared with historical concerns about American campaign conduct. First, fierce competition and changing environments are familiar to American campaigns. However, those campaigns have not traditionally had to wage domestic political battles in an environment that might also be manipulated by a foreign actor.

Second, campaigns have always had to adapt to new technologies. For example, campaigns have long used microtargeting to identify likely voters and produce advertising. Campaigns also successfully use social media to engage new voters and mobilize supporters. On the other hand, social media and microtargeting might demobilize or misinform individual voters, particularly if used by outside actors seeking to disrupt the electoral process rather than domestic political opponents simply offering an alternative, traditional political message.

Third, the potential for foreign interference and cyber intrusions (even from domestic sources) present new challenges for campaign organizations. Most campaigns are short-lived with transient staffs. Longer-term investments in electronic security or other types of organizational continuity are limited by professional experience and budgets. Even with greater awareness of potential security vulnerabilities, many political committees have limited abilities to protect their systems and data. This is especially true for candidate committees, most of which have small professional staffs and depend heavily on volunteers.

Overall, the effect of legislation and oversight designed to safeguard the American political system depends on whether campaigns, elections, or both are covered; and how such efforts balance preserving an open, democratic political system with combatting foreign influence and responding to changing technology. In some cases, these efforts might involve attention to other areas of public policy, and effort from agencies that do not normally affect campaigns and elections.

INDEX

D

E

F

U

V

W